Other Places
Benin
ERIKA KRAUS & FELICIE REID

Published by
OTHER PLACES PUBLISHING

First edition
Published January 2010

Benin
Other Places Travel Guide
Written by: Erika Kraus and Felicie Reid
Cover designed by: Carla Zetina-Yglesias
Cover photograph copyright Ryan Riley
Published by:
Other Places Publishing
www.otherplacespublishing.com

All text, illustrations and artwork copyright
© 2010 Other Places Publishing

ISBN 978-0-9822619-1-0

The Authors

Erika Kraus

Originally from a small town in rural Kansas, Erika graduated college with a degree in Biology and French. After being stumped with finding a suitable outlet for her refined skills, Erika decided to join the Peace Corps, giving her an opportunity to live in a francophone West African nation. Erika was assigned to Benin where she immersed herself in the new surroundings and discovered everything her new home had to offer. Erika currently teaches beginning French and a bit of Biology at Benedictine College. She plans to take advantage of any opportunity she finds—including coauthoring this book.

Felicie Reid

Felicie Reid is a French-born aspiring writer with a degree in Environmental Science. Her passion for nature, travel, and adventure has taken her across much of Europe, the United States, South America, and West Africa. She served for two and a half years with the Peace Corps as an Environmental Action volunteer in Benin, where she had the opportunity to experience firsthand the culture and way of life of this amazing country. Felicie used the knowledge she had gained while living and traveling across Benin to write this book. She plans to continue her adventures around the globe with a second term with the Peace Corps in Morocco.

Acknowledgments

Many people contributed to this book, from Benin and around the globe. The following persons have all played a role in this project and deserve a great deal of thanks from the authors and publisher: Sara Miner, Caitlin Rackish, Jacy Gaige, Margaret Graham, Koudous Adoumbou, Katherine Echeverria, Ly Nguyen, Leonore Hijazi, Kelly Daly, Tom Connelly, Jaren Tichy Schwartz, Ryan Riley, Felix Agossa, Mathurin Akouete, Darly Asse, Jim Rybarski, Clement Reid, Keith and Cathcrine Reid, Anastasia Pahules, Paul Oxborrow, and Carla Zetina-Yglesias.

Quick Reference

The prices in this book are in West African francs (CFA); known in French as the *Communauté Financiere Africaine Francs*.

Exchange rates at time of publication
1 USD = 445.16 CFA
1 Euro = 655.95 CFA
1 GBP = 727.493 CFA

Electricity
Benin accommodates 220V

Business Hours
With the exception of large banks, most businesses close for a two-hour lunch break at midday. Common working hours are 8am-12pm, resuming from 3-6pm.

Time
GMT + 1

Telephone
Country dialing code +229

Important Telephone Numbers
Cotonou Hospital 21.30.01.55
Ambulance 21.30.06.56
State Police 21.31.58.99
Cotonou Security (*Sûreté urbaine de Cotonou*) 21.31.20.11

Dates are for 2010, future religious holidays will be approximate.

National Holidays
New Years Day: January 1
Vodoun Day: January 10
Labor Day: May 1
Independence Day: August 1
Other Celebrated Days
National Tree Day: June 1
Int. Women's Day: March 8
World AIDS Day: December 1
World Malaria Day: April 25

Religious Holidays
All Saints Day: November 1
Christmas: December 25
Easter: April 5
Ascension: May 13
Pentecost (Whit Monday): May 24
Assumption: August 15
Tabaski: November 17
Eid al-Fitr: September 11

Quick Stats

Official name: Republic of Benin/ République du Bénin
Departments (12): Alibori, Atakora, Atlantique, Borgou, Collines, Couffo, Donga, Littoral, Mono, Oueme, Plateau, Zou
Neighboring countries: Burkina Faso, Niger, Nigeria, and Togo
Population: 8.4 million (2008 est)
Capital: Porto-Novo (pop. 295,000)
Political and economic capital: Cotonou (pop. 2 million)
Type of government: Republic under multiparty democratic rule. Elections are held every five years.

Ethnic groups: Fon 39.2%, Adja 15.2%, Yoruba 12.3%, Bariba 9.2%, Peulh 7%, Ottamari 6.1%, Yoa-Lokpa 4%, Dendi 2.5%, other 1.6% (includes Europeans), unspecified 2.9% (2002 census)
Languages: French (official), Fon, Mina, Goun, and Yoruba in the south; Nagot, Bariba, and Dendi in the north

GDP: USD$5.93 billion (2008 est)
GDP per capita: USD$738 (2008 est)
U.N. Human Development Index Value: 0.437, ranked 163rd of 177 nations (2005)
Life expectancy at birth: 55.4 years
Adult Literacy Rate: 34.7%
Percentage of population living on less than $2/day: 73.7%

Average temperature in Cotonou: 25-28°C, 77-82°F

Average Rainfall in Cotonou (inches):

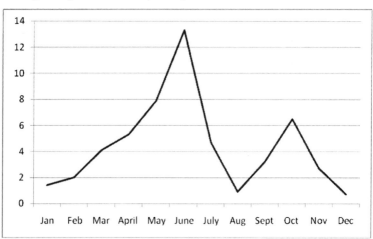

Contents

Introduction

History 16, Politics 22, Economy and Occupations 24, Media 26, Religion 27, Culture 34, Music, Literature, and Art 39, Sports 43, Environment 44

Basics

When to Visit 53, Getting There 54, Transportation in Benin 58, Money and Costs 62, Food and Drink 64, Accommodations 72, Communication 72, Safety and Security 73, Health 75, Helping and Experiencing Local Communities 77

Atlantique & Littoral

Cotonou 80, Ganvié 100, Niaouli 101, Allada 102, Ouidah 103

Ouémé & Plateau

Porto-Novo 111, Avrankou 117, Kétou 118

Mono & Couffou

Grand-Popo 121, Comé 127, Sé 128, Possotomé & Lac Ahémé 128, Lokossa 129, Athiémé 134, Azové 136, Dogbo 137

Zou & Collines

Alibori & Borgou

Atakora & Donga

Maps

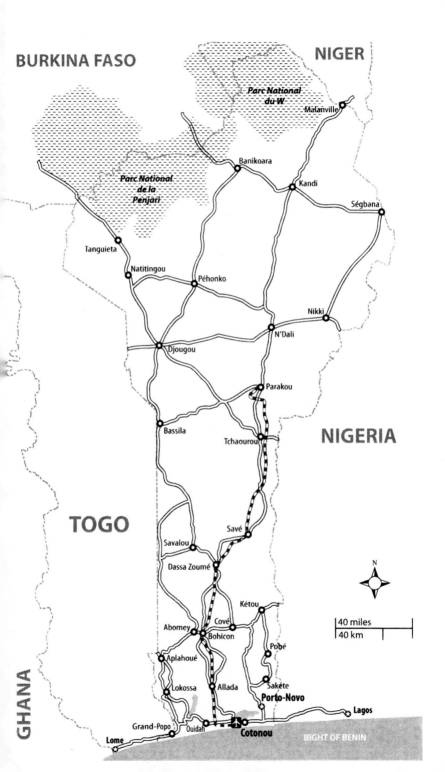

Introduction

From vodoun and slave trade history to sunny beaches and animal safaris, Benin is a land of wonder and mystery. The unique cultural heritage and tumultuous history of Benin began long before the colonization of Africa. This small country on the Gulf of Guinea was the site of one of the most powerful kingdoms in West Africa: the Kingdom of Dahomey. Based in the current city of Abomey, the Dahomey Kingdom emerged in the 15th century and covered a vast territory, expanding through warfare with each successive king. It reached the height of its power with the arrival of the Portuguese, and the subsequent involvement in the highly profitable trans-Atlantic slave trade. Today, the palace ruins of the Dahomey Kingdom can be seen in Abomey, while visits to the European forts and the Slave Route through Ouidah transmit the incredulous realities of that dark era.

Known as the birthplace of vodoun a belief that all objects in nature have a spirit, Benin has a wealth of ceremonies, *fétiches*, and stories awaiting discovery. Islam is also prominent nationwide, as are numerous Christian denominations. Benin is home to dozens of ethnicities, each with its own customs, languages, and folklore; yet amidst this diversity, Benin enjoys social harmony. Accordingly, it was the first West African nation to undergo a peaceful transfer from a dictatorship to a democracy—it continues to develop with a stable government.

Benin offers a brilliant array of attractions, from beautiful beaches and lagoons in the south, to vast savannas, hills, and waterfalls in the north. Visitors plunge into the steaming, turbulent streets of Cotonou to discover the city's thriving markets and nightlife. From there, one can explore the rural settlements along the mighty Mono River to the west, or go hippo-spotting from a dugout canoe on Lake Doukon. Tourists enjoy the tranquil, palm-fringed beaches of Grand Popo, and float through the stilt lagoon community of Ganvié. The picturesque granite hills of the central Collines region are perfect for hikes and panoramic views, after which one can consult with a vodoun soothsayer in a remote village. For wildlife enthusiasts, the north offers animal safaris in the national parks, set in the marvelous plains of the upper Atakora and Alibori regions.

Benin's unique mixture of culture, history, geography, and wildlife attracts thousands of travelers in search of the ultimate West African experience. Above all, the resilient spirit, charm, and vitality of the Beninese people captivate visitors and keep them coming back for more.

HOW TO USE THIS GUIDE

This book is compiled with firsthand, inside-information from locals, giving visitors an upper hand in comprehending the natural and social environments of Benin. Countless individuals contributed to this effort, each added their unique and specialized knowledge. The local food, culture, and history are highlighted for each region, from the economic capital of Cotonou to the small villages along the Niger River. An introduction to some of the local languages, religions, and wildlife also contribute to this trustworthy guide.

Book Icons

Find More... **ON THE WEB** — Provides links to more information on the internet

INSIGHT — Unique insight into the culture and people

👍 — Author recommended accommodation or eatery

Map Icons

🏠 Accommodations
✈ Airport
S Bank/ATM
Y Bar/Nightclub
🚌 Bus/Taxi Station (Gare)
⬛ Camping
✪ Capital
✝ Church
◉ City/Village
⊞ Clinic
H Hospital
⬤ Landmark
☪ Mosque
℞ Pharmacy
⬛ Point of Interest
✉ Post Office
🍴 Restaurant/Buvette/Eatery
🚆 Train Station
.... Highway/road
▪▪▪▪ Railroad

ALIBORI
ATAKORA
BORGOU
DONGA
COLLINES
ZOU
COUFFO
PLATEAU
MONO
OUEME
ATLANTIQUE
LITTORAL

Benin is divided into 12 departments and this book covers two departments in each chapter. The cultural nuances and unique characteristics found throughout Benin are insightfully explained, in a way only a local would know.

GLOSSARY

Anasara (anna-sah-ra): The northeastern translation for 'white person.' Heard mostly in Parakou, Kandi, Malanville, and Karimama.

Batouré (bah-too-ray): The northwestern translation for 'white person.' Common in Djougou and Natitingou.

Buvette (boo-vette): Typically an open-air bar that sells beer, soft drinks, and bottled water.

Doucement (doo-suh-mahn): Beninese-French word used for a variety of expressions, including 'watch out,' 'be careful,' and 'excuse me.'

Fétiche (fay-teesh): A site of vodoun worship. Often with a small statue and the remains of previous sacrifices.

Féticheur (fay-tee-shure): The religious person responsible for a certain *fétiche* or sacred area.

Gendarme (jawn-darm): Local military stationed throughout the country at certain communal capitals and large cities. They are usually seen at *gendarmeries,* or local military posts, at check points along roads, and at border crossings.

Maison des Jeunes (may-zon day juhn): Youth Center, located in every major town and commonly used for any sort of public gathering, political meeting, concert, or cultural demonstration.

Maquis (mah-kee): Casual, open-air restaurant, often coupled with a *buvette* or bar, serving local cuisine by the plate from large cauldrons and coolers.

Marché (mar-shay): Market.

Oyinboh (oh-yee-boh): The Yoruba and Idaatcha word for 'white person.' Mostly heard in the east-central regions.

Pagne (pah-nyah): A piece of fabric two meters long, typically used as a simple wrap or tailored into traditional outfits. A *pagne* is also used as a towel, a baby-strap, a head cushion for heavy loads, a blanket, and to provide shade from the sun.

Paillote (pah-y-ott): Thatch-roofed structure in the form of an awning, resembling a gazebo and used as a shaded place to rest, dine, or hold meetings.

Pirogue (peer-ohg): Dugout canoe commonly made from Samba, Iroko, or other local trees.

Tantie (tahn-tee): Literally translated to 'auntie' and used generally as a term for a young woman. Also used when referring to a beer-maid or food vendor.

Yovo: The Fon word for 'white person.' This term can be extended to anyone who is not black, including Beninese people with lighter skin tones and albinos.

Zemidjan (zem-ee-djan): A motorcycle-taxi. The motorcycles are quite small, similar to a scooter. *Zemidjan* drivers are unionized and wear colored shirts with a registration number on the back. The shirt colors vary with each city, but most are yellow, green, purple, or blue.

Zemidjan ride on a rural stretch of road

The *Yovo* Song

As a tourist, be prepared to hear many repeated renditions of the *Yovo* song (especially from children) almost anywhere you go:

Yovo, yovo,	*Yovo, yovo,*
Bonsoir,	Good evening,
Ça va bien?	Are you well?
Merci!	Thank you!

History

EARLY HISTORY

La République du Bénin, or the Republic of Benin, has been formerly known as the French colony of Dahomey, the People's Republic of Dahomey, and the Republic of Dahomey.

The two ethnicities that now dominate southern Benin, the Adja and Fon, originated from Tado in Togo. According to Beninese lore, the Fon are descendants of a mystic couple: A Tado princess named Aligbonon and a spirit in the body of a panther.

Their son, Agassou, founded the Fon. Agassou left Tado for political reasons in the 16th century and settled to form the Kingdom of Allada, based 40 kilometers north of present-day Cotonou. In the first half of the 17th century, two additional kingdoms were formed: the Kingdom of Dahomey based in Abomey to the north, and the Kingdom of Hogbonou southeast and near the coast. The reason for this split is uncertain, though it was most likely due to a disagreement amongst the heirs to the Kingdom of Allada. The Dahomey Kingdom became the dominant power in the region and extended its territory through impressive military warfare. During King Agadja's reign from 1708 to 1740, Dahomey expanded to the coastal town of Ouidah. Though Agadja initially opposed the sale of prisoners of war, his desire to expand his territory triumphed and Dahomey flourished because of direct involvement in the growing slave trade during the 18th and 19th centuries.

An Oral History

Throughout Africa, history generally passes from one generation to the next via oral traditions. Written records are rare, and traditional history varies according to the tribes involved and their religious beliefs. However, written accounts of West African oral tradition compiled by 16th, 17th, and 18th century European explorers contribute to a generally accepted version of the regions' early history.

The name Amazons comes from the Dahomey female warriors' similarity to the semi-mythical Amazons of Ancient Greece.

One key to Dahomey's military success was the kingdom's possession of an elite militia of women warriors known as Mino, or 'Our Mothers' in Fon. Most of whom were recruited from the king's hundreds of wives, called Ahosi, and were originally trained as elephant hunters, as well as the king's personal body guards. The Mino gradually grew to represent one third of the Dahomey army and their renowned strength and courage later earned them the popularized name 'Amazons' from the

French legionnaires whom they fought. The European observers in the 19th century dubbed the Kingdom of Dahomey as 'Black Sparta' in recognition of this military might.

EUROPEAN ADVANCE

Up until 1598, the Portuguese were the sole European force with a strong foothold in West Africa. Having already established trading posts north of Senegal, the Portuguese traders built a fort at El Mina on the Gold Coast (present day Ghana) in 1482. By the 1520s, the Portuguese had trading posts throughout West Africa, including at Hogbonou, later renamed Porto-Novo, as the area became an important part of the growing slave commerce. These posts, though physically small and contained, extended cultural, political, and economic influences further inland due to the importance of their trade.

Beginning in the late 17th century, other European nations began to show interest in West Africa as a source of human labor to build new colonies in the Americas. By 1843, the French had settled in Ouidah and, over the next twenty years, would continue to extend their occupation throughout the territory. In an effort to fend off the Dahomeans to the northwest and the British based in Lagos to the east, the King of Hogbonou joined forces with the French in the mid-1800s. Soon thereafter, King Glélé of Dahomey authorized the French to settle in Cotonou. King Behanzin, the successor of Glélé, later sought to regain control of the region but was defeated and sent into exile. In 1894 the Dahomey Kingdom was fully colonized by France and officially absorbed into the federation of French West Africa.

EUROPEAN EXPANSION IN WEST AFRICA

Primarily France, Britain, and Portugal 'discovered' West Africa. The Spaniards, Danes, Swedes, Belgians, and even the Brandenburgers sought their share of the continent (yet these countries were not sizeable enough to compete with the first three). The French and British colonized the majority of the Guinean region between Senegal and Nigeria, dividing the coast into the Grain, Ivory, Gold, and Slave Coasts. The Portuguese retained parts of Cameroon and the territories farther south. Angola in particular was a remarkably profitable Portuguese slave state. Between 1617, when a group of settlers formed the Benguela community in present-day Angola and the end of the slave trade in the late 1800s, Angola suffered human loss greater than any other African nation involved in the slave trade. Angola was referred to as the 'Black Mother' of many slaves on foreign lands.

THE SLAVE TRADE

West African kingdoms had been practicing slavery before Europeans made their way to the region in the 15th century. In this practice, people became slaves by birth or by indebtedness. Though these persons had no lawful rights in society, they were treated well and typically became members of the family. The owners rarely sold their slaves, and usually only did so in a case of severe misconduct. A slave could even become free entirely due to good character. Former slaves could thus become heads of households and respected leaders in the community.

When the Portuguese first arrived in West Africa, they introduced foreign concepts of slavery to these established, organized kingdoms. They captured slaves and sold them in Europe, where they were still considered a rare luxury. As Europeans began to settle the newly discovered Americas in the 16th century, a Spanish priest named Bartholome de las Casas proposed the use of West Africans as an alternative source of labor to the native American populations, which were nearly decimated from extreme physical labor and diseases brought by colonists. In 1510, a ship filled with the first lot of fifty West Africans set sail. The hardiness and great strength of the West Africans saved the native American populations from slavery, but sparked one of the most historically significant international trade markets.

The Portuguese traders discovered early on that raids were an ineffective means to gather human cargo as the proficient West African military forces were capable of quickly overwhelming the small European forces. Peaceful deals with African kings became a much more efficient means of fulfilling the market demand for slaves. The Portuguese brought fabricated items such as textiles, firearms, gunpowder, knives, ironworks, beads and trinkets, and alcohol to trade with local tribes for prisoners from territorial wars. These goods, especially the ammunition and firearms, propelled the expansion of the dominant kingdoms such as the Dahomey and the Oyo, an ethnic group from present-day Nigeria.

The ideal slave was a healthy 12- to 35-year old male. No matter how many men of this demographic were available, the demand never ceased. To attain the required numbers, European traders accepted children, older and/or less-fit men, and women up to age 25, beyond which childbearing greatly lessened their value. In Benin, a male slave in good form and strength could be exchanged for as many as 21 cannons. Both attractive female slaves and child slaves would be traded for 15 cannons.

Once in America, slaves were purchased at double the price for which they were bought in West Africa. As the demand for slaves grew through the centuries, so did their price. Within the 18th century alone, the price for a prime slave in America increased from about $60 to $100. Despite the obvious monetary profit, traders endured much economic loss due to the risk of their trade. Many ships were lost at sea, and men commonly fell ill and died during the voyage from poor nutrition, inhumane living conditions, and foreign diseases.

As other nations became involved in the West African markets, competition also began to affect the profitability of the slave trade. The Dutch soon overtook the Portuguese with better management skills, and were in turn overcome by the French. Ultimately, however, the British controlled the majority of the trade from the 16th to 18th centuries. During the early 1900s, the British began setting restrictions on the slave trade and gradually pushed it to abolition. With other European countries joining the British point of view, the last Portuguese slave ship departed from the coast of Benin in 1885.

The Slave Trade in Numbers

	Slaves from Africa	Arrived in Europe	...in the Americas
Up to 1500	---	33,500	---
1501-1600	330,000	116,400	125,000
1601-1700	1,560,000	25,100	1,280,000
1701-1810	7,520,000	---	6,265,000
After 1810	1,950,000	---	1,628,000
Total	11,360,000	175,000	9,298,000

*From J.D. Fage's The History of West Africa

IMPACT OF THE SLAVE TRADE

The loss of so many young males left the population of West Africa at a zero growth rate. Once the slave trade ended, the growth rate in West Africa quickly became one of the highest on the continent. Today, the region is the most densely populated in Africa.

In Benin, the slave trade had a significant effect on the geography, customs, and development of the Dahomey Kingdom. Even though it traditionally expanded its kingdom by force, the demand for slaves encouraged more battles, forcing victim communities to take extreme measures to avoid annihilation. The Idaatcha peoples, for example, of the Collines département sought shelter from the Fon warriors in the hills around Dassa and established communities therein. The stilt villages of Ganvié (see pg 100) were formed in a desperate attempt to flee the Dahomeans. The severe decrease in population hindered the natural development of the communities in ways which will forever be unknown. As stated in *The History of West Africa* by J.D. Fage, experts have estimated that roughly 12,500 humans were exported from the Beninese coastal ports per year. This makes up an approximate 14% of the total number of slaves shipped from Africa annually during the 1780s.

Most of the slave ships departing Ouidah and Porto-Novo were destined for Brazil, though many went to the Caribbean or to the colonies in the Americas. After emancipation, many slaves returned to settle in Ouidah and Porto-Novo. These two towns were greatly influenced by the Afro-Brazilian culture brought back with the diaspora, such as in the architecture and food. New crops from the Americas were introduced and cultivated, including new species of corn, tomato, tobacco, and peanuts. The returned descendants also played a large role in developing the export of palm oil to Europe.

COLONIAL ERA

When the ruler of Porto-Novo signed a trade and friendship agreement with the French, the first brick was laid for a path to colonization. Dahomey became an official colony of France in June of 1894 and the French installed a centralized government parallel to the one already established in Senegal. The highest ranking French official in Dahomey took orders from the governor based in Senegal, who in turn reported to the appropriate minister

Find More...
ON THE WEB

Organizations today study genealogy and link people of African descent to their genetic roots in Africa. For more information, visit www.africanancestry.com

in Paris. Laws and decrees descended in this order for all of French West Africa, a system that aimed to homogenize the great variety of cultures suppressed under the new colonist regime. Only the French could hold governmental positions in each region; the position of village chief was the highest authority a native Dahomean could occupy. The French assumed the colonized population would eventually assimilate to the French culture, and thus become citizens of France. Once this assimilation had been accomplished, the now French Dahomeans could hold higher positions of authority to uphold colonial laws. Yet because the French region of West Africa was so vast, there were insufficient French officials to hold all the governmental positions created. The few colonists in control were obliged to install natives as authorities until a Frenchman could be nominated. Furthermore, the people of Dahomey and other colonized countries were not easily persuaded to leave their ancient customs. In 1937, out of an estimated total of 15 million people colonized, as few as 80,500 West Africans under French colonial rule were French citizens. Only 2,500 of the 80,500 had become French citizens through cultural assimilation. The remaining were located in the earliest-formed colonies where French citizenship was granted at birth. This system of rule was very unstable with growing resistance and uprisings in the 1900s, peaking after the Second World War.

RECENT HISTORY

Dahomey achieved independence from France on 1 August 1960. Hubert Maga, born in Parakou, was the first president (see pg 167 for more information on Maga). In 1975 the newly independent country took the name *République Populaire du Bénin*, the Popular Republic of Benin. The name 'Benin' comes from the ancient and powerful Benin kingdom located in present-day Nigeria.

A succession of military governments ruled Benin until Mathieu Kérékou came to power in 1974, establishing a Marxist-Leninist government. European interest in overseas territories waned over the decades and proved treacherous to the development of Benin. The only political party in France with sustained support for the new republic was the Communist Party, which explains in part why Benin first adopted this form of government.

In 1989, President Kérékou abandoned communism due to pressure from the population and from international investors. Kérékou stepped down from power in 1991 after the country's first free elections instated the former Prime Minister Nicéphore Soglo as the new President for a five-year term. This marked the first peaceful transfer of power from a dictatorship to a democracy on the continent of Africa. Kérékou returned as president via elections in the following two terms after Soglo. In March 2006 the current president, Thomas Yayi Boni, replaced Kérékou. A former president of the West African Development Bank, Yayi Boni has initiated a proactive fight against corruption in Benin while promoting economic growth across the country.

Witch Hunts and Politics INSIGHT

In the 1970s, President Mathieu Kérékou led a movement to replace local political leaders across the country with individuals loyal to him. Because many of the old leaders were vodoun priests, Kérékou launched a campaign to uproot sorcerers and witches and punish evil-doers. Initially, this campaign only brought accusations against certain political leaders, but it ultimately shifted to a campaign that targeted mostly women and the elderly, who are commonly associated with being vodoun sorcerers. This modern day witch hunt used torture to extract confessions, and caused severe family and communal feuds. In the end, Kérékou succeeded in his campaign and many local leaders were replaced by government loyalists.

Politics

The current government is a democracy comprised of four parts: the Chief of State elected for a five-year term, a cabinet and council of ministers appointed by the Chief of State, and a National Assembly of 83 seats elected by popular vote for a four-year term. Benin is divided into 12 provinces called *départements*, each headed by a *préfet* and divided into communes. There are 77 communes, each governed by a mayor. The communes are divided into *arrondissements*, or districts, led by a chief. Within the districts, the population elects a council of governing members representing each town and village. The council then appoints the mayor, delegate, and deputy positions.

During governmental elections, every political party has an official symbol. Candidates for government councils must be affiliated with a recognized political party.

If the candidate is an independent, he or she must still be formally recognized within the voting region. All candidates are only allowed to campaign during a designat-designated ten-day period. During this time, they work to associate their name with the representative political symbol, by which the literate and illiterate voting population will recognize the candidates on the ballots. As part of the campaigns, candidates visit local groups and hold animated rallies where they thank the attending population for their support with 'gifts.'

Similarly, non-government elections, such as those held within clubs and small organizations, are conducted according to the needs of the illiterate population. In this voting system, each candidate chooses an object to represent his or her candidacy. The voters then place a leaf or a pebble in a calabash bowl next to the object of the chosen candidate. The pebbles are tallied for each candidate, thus determining the victor.

By law, all political party posters must be removed and campaigning must cease 24 hours before the vote. Nevertheless, many candidates make last minute visits to 'friends' and surreptitiously give 'gifts' to supporters. On election day, official and circumstantially apolitical moderators supervise the voting, which are held at any public place within the voting region. This can be a concrete building, a *paillote*, or even a table beneath a tree in a common area. The moderators ink the thumb of the voters, who then cast their vote by leaving a thumbprint on the symbol associated with the candidate (which serves as proof of having voted). The ballots are counted publicly at the end of the voting period.

A voter is free to vote for one party on the communal council and a different party on the village council, but the idea is to remain loyal to the same political party and 'vote the list,' as the Beninese say, from top to bottom. If a single party wins the majority of the vote, it takes all the positions on the council. If there is no majority, a multi-party government is created between the parties. For presidential elections, if no party wins 51% of the first vote, the top two political parties with the highest percentage continue to a second vote, wherein a clear majority determines the president.

Village meeting

Economy and Occupations

The livelihood for the majority of the population is subsistence agriculture. Corn predominates in the south, where it is sometimes harvested twice a year due to two rainy seasons. Other significant crops include cassava, yams, soybeans (and other types of beans), peanuts, and pineapples. In the north, millet is the main subsistence crop.

The most economically important product is cotton, which generates about 40% of Benin's GDP and about 80% of the country's total export revenue. Cotton is widely cultivated in the north and in some areas of the south.

Other exports are palm oil (and its derivative products), cashews, shea butter, livestock, and seafood. The extraction of Benin's natural resources like phosphates, chromium, rutile (titanium dioxide), and iron ore are typically underdeveloped, though marble, limestone, and petroleum are exploited commercially.

EARLY ECONOMY

Even before the arrival of Europeans, West Africans produced and traded salt, fish, soap, cloth, leather, and metals such as iron and copper. Coastal communities, such as present-day Ouidah, harvested important quantities of sea salt. The salt was strained from blocks of mud collected between tides. Fishermen along the coast and significant waterways used smoked fish as trade items throughout the region, and soap was formed from boiled palm oil and ashes. Europe developed a high demand for this soap, so much so that by the 17th century Portugal banned its importation to protect the trade of Portuguese soap makers. Cloth and rope were made from animal skins and plant products, and before 1000 CE, the Yoruba people of present-day Benin and Nigeria were adept at spinning, weaving, and dying wool and cotton. The Yoruba were also noted for their blacksmithing abilities, as gold and iron were available for harvesting without much effort. Copper was alloyed with zinc to form brass, or tin to form bronze. The Fulani and Hausa in the North developed the trade of leather goods including harnesses, shields, bags, and sandals. Cowrie shells were used as currency, but markets usually practiced a trade system wherein, for example, a certain quantity of tomatoes would be worth a negotiated quantity of fish.

Today, typical subsistence income depends on crop harvests, fishing, hunting, and the sale of surplus crops or other derivative products such as *sodabi* (distilled palm wine) or prepared food. The entire family participates in farming, with each member fulfilling their respective roles: men and women do the field preparation labor together, and the women and children plant seeds. Everybody helps with the harvest. Men usually have a second occupation such as fishing, hunting, or working in a mechanic, tailor, or other kind of shop. The women, too, often work in small businesses as a seamstress, hair stylist, or as a market vendor.

The traditional system of inheritance excludes daughters from land bequests, but recent laws have made this exclusion illegal, and thus increasingly less common.

Successful business men and women are capable of generating enough income and do not rely on farming. Higher tiers of society include those who have a government position, school administrators, *gendarmes*, and post office employees.

Tourism is a growing sector of the economy, particularly through the wildlife parks in the north and the cultural hot spots of Ouidah, Abomey, and Porto-Novo. Smaller communities are beginning to gain from tourism through the work of non-governmental organizations and tour guide businesses. Examples of community development initiatives are the Lake Doukon hippopotamus tours (see pg 130) near Lokossa, and the CPN eco-lodge in Camaté-Shakaloké (see pg 156).

Media

The government operated radio and television station ORTB (*Organisation Radio-Television Bénin*), is broadcasted nationwide in French, English, and 18 local languages, and it reaches even the most remote locations. The ORTB station shows the daily news and press review, cooking shows, music videos, political discussions, obituaries, and a few popular Brazilian soap operas. A second television station is the commercial channel LC2, which mostly shows West African music videos and the daily news. In communities with a more constant source of electricity and higher income level, satellite television is becoming more popular, bringing a wider selection of international channels such as France 24 and TV5.

Televisions are not as common as radios. Not only are they more expensive, many communities remain without a constant source of electricity.

Radio is the most accessible and reliable source of news and entertainment because most radios are easily powered by batteries. Aside from playing Beninese songs, foreign tunes, and hosting various talk shows, the radio stations are used by local organizations to disseminate information. For example, the Family Planning

Popular Radio Stations

Southern Benin	Frequency
Radio France International (RFI 1 Afrique), French	90.0 FM
Radio Planete, Cotonou	95.7 FM
Radio Immaculée Concepcion, Cotonou, Religious, Catholic	101.0 FM
BBC World Service Africa	101.7 FM
Africa 1, Porto-Novo	102.6 FM
Radio Maranatha, Cotonou	103.1 FM
Golfe FM Magic Radio, Cotonou	105.7 FM
Atlantic FM , Cotonou (Operated by ORTB)	92.2 FM
CAPP FM, Cotonou	99.6 FM
Northern Benin	
RFI 1 Afrique, Parakou, French	106.1 FM
Fraternite FM, Parakou	96.5 FM
Radio Regionale de Parakou, ORTB regional station	5025 kHz

League could discuss the importance of gender equality, or the local health center's workers advocate the importance of hygiene and waste management in the community. One station, broadcasted from the enormous Italian-run Catholic Church in Allada, is entirely devoted to sermons, hymns, and religious talk shows. The biggest commercial radio station is Golfe FM, broadcasting the BBC World Service and Radio France Internationale (RFI) throughout the south of Benin.

There are two daily newspapers, *La Nation* and *Le Matinal*, and several other weekly or monthly papers such as *Le Point, L'Araignee, Le Progès, La Citadelle, Les Echos du Jour, Le Republicain,* and *Gazette du Golfe.* All newspaper publications are printed in Cotonou and Parakou. Delivery of printed news to outlying villages and towns is typically delayed, if it ever arrives at all. In Cotonou, papers can be purchased at the Etoile Rouge intersection and behind the hospital, toward Cadjehoun. Parisian newspapers and magazines are available at the French Cultural Center, the *Librairie Notre Dame* at the red and white cathedral, or *Sonaec,* the book store across from the Ganxi market on Avenue Clozel. For neighborhood descriptions of Cotonou, see pg 84.

Religion

Beninese are very religious. Places of business are often named in proclamation of the owner's faith: 'God is Great Seamstress' or 'Jesus' Blood Cafeteria.' Christian churches are found in every town and most villages. Islamic mosques are more frequent in large, diverse communities and especially in the northern part of the country. Yet amongst this religious diversity, the most respected and intrinsic religion of Benin is vodoun. The official census states that 50% of the population is animist or vodoun, but many Beninese agree that these traditional beliefs are still held by 100% of the population, no matter which other religions have been adopted.

Many forms of religion exist in Benin, and often the Beninese may relate to religion on several different levels. One person may claim to be a devout Catholic, but have a vodoun amulet hung over their door for protection from evil spirits. A Beninese who does not outwardly embrace vodoun often has an instinctual fear or superstition pertaining to the religion. Beninese breathe the air of vodoun and are imbued with the religion of their ancestors.

Polygamy

Polygamy predates Islam in Benin. It is practiced by most ethnic groups, regardless of religion. Traditionally, a man's wealth is determined by the number of wives and children he has. Many West African Muslims regard polygamy as a religious obligation, as well as a male status symbol. Men often start out wanting to be monogamous, but change their minds as they grow older; increased prosperity lends to the capacity to support multiple wives. A man may also have one or more unofficial wives or mistresses in the same town or in a different village. Since not all women agree with their husbands taking on a new wife, the co-spouses often live in separate homes. There is often tension between women in a polygamous marriage, particularly in urban households. Some rural women, however, welcome other wives as additional workers in the fields or around the house as families can become very large.

VODOUN

Benin is the proclaimed birthplace of vodoun. It was transported to the Americas via the slave trade, where it evolved into the often misconstrued pop culture image of voodoo or black magic. Beninese vodoun is based on the animistic belief that all objects in nature—animate or inanimate—have a spirit and the world is made up of four essential, driving elements: fire, air, earth, and water. Earth is considered to be the most powerful as it has the ability to encompass the three other elements.

In the Fon language, vodoun is called *vaudou*; vodoun priests are called *hounon* or *vaudounon*; practitioners are called *voudounsi* or *hounsi*; and the word *houn* is used to reference anything that concerns vodoun. In Nagot, a branch of Yoruba, the religion is called *orisha*.

Vodoun can be split into three general practices: talisman vodoun, which is the practice of placing a spirit inside an object; the vodoun of venerated ancestors, honoring those who were respected and wise in their lifetime; and thirdly the deity-vodoun, wherein believers worship gods and spirits such as Mahu-Lissa, Hevioso, Ayidohwedo, Dan, and Sakpata (see *Voundon Gods* pg 30).

Vodoun is openly practiced and discussed. Communities throughout the country have many fetishes or statuettes of local vodoun spirits. These statuettes are often associated with a sacred forest, where important medicinal herbs and trees can be found. The forests have strict rules, to which any non-member of the particular cult involved must adhere. Fetishes in each community are cared for by a *voudounon* and the *voudounsi*. During ceremonies, voudounsi can be recognized as groups of men and women clad in white *pagnes*, chanting and dancing through the village. In the markets, the vodoun section can be overwhelming with its strong smells and sometimes shocking sights. Full of dead animals, wooden figurines, and some unrecognizable objects to the untrained eye, this is the place where adepts shop for protective amulets and rings. If a visitor displays genuine curiosity about the subject, the voudounsi are willing to explain and even demonstrate their practice and faith. Some vodoun practices can be extreme, and even dark, but in general the religion is simply another way to worship a higher power.

Even though sacred forests are venerated and protected by traditional beliefs, they are not immune to deforestation and have slowly begun to diminish in the quest for more farmland.

Ancestral-venerating vodoun is fairly obvious throughout the country via talismans in the markets and families routinely hosting ceremonies in memory of their lost relatives. The deity vodoun is not so visible. The sacred forest in Ouidah (see the *Sacred Forest of Kpassè* on pg 106) displays an impressive array of voudoun gods, and the Abomey Museum (see pg 145) portrays a sense of these gods' strength, but the depth of this aspect of the religion is not readily conceivable to outsiders.

Diviners, also called *Ifa* priests or *babalawos*, are considered neutral spokespersons for spiritual forces. They act as mediums to convey the meanings of past events or interpret messages from the gods and ancestors. By interpreting physical signs, a diviner usually works with an assortment of items such as seeds, shells, bones, and some manufactured items, like iron, that are important in daily life and are associated with deities. During a consultation, diviners will use these items in a series of interactions with the subject in order to read messages from the spirits. More involved consultations may result in animal sacrifices, especially when a subject is advised they must appease the gods to fulfill a wish or resolve a problem.

Vodoun Gods

Much of the following information is based on Marc Monsia's *Religions Indigènes et Savoir Endogène au Benin.*

Mahu-Lissa is comprised of both a male and female form, and is considered the Supreme Being, the Creator, in an expression of Positive and Negative. Mahu, the female form, represents the Negative and the 'magnetic fluid.' Lissa is the male form and represents the Positive and the 'electric fluid.' Lissa is further identified with the color white and the number one. Mahu is identified with the number two. Since 1+2=3, three is considered the number that expresses life. The Mahu-Lissa symbol is a calabash bowl.

The god **Hevioso** represents the element of Fire and its principals: Power, Will, Strength, and Justice. This deity is associated with thunder or lightning and is depicted holding a thunder axe. Hevioso's primary color is flamboyant red.

Dan Ayidohwedo is symbolized with a rainbow uniting the sun and water. This god represents the relationship between Fire and Water and acts as an intermediary between them. The name Dan represents the element of water, and *hwé* is the word for sun, representing Fire. The principals of this deity are Wisdom, Happiness, and Prosperity. It is said that Dan Ayidohwedo presides over all movement in the universe.

The gods Dan and Ayidohwedo also act independently of one another. Ayidohwedo is the god of Air, symbolizing the relationships between the material and immaterial, the sky and the earth, and the body and soul. Dan is the god of Water and Love. In the Fon language, *dan* means serpent. Tradition explains that Dan originated from the ocean; the movement of a serpent is uninterrupted, and in this way relates to the movement of water across the earth, both leaving behind a similar trace.

Sakpata, or Ayivoudou, is the most respected god as he represents the most important element: Earth. In Fon, *ayi* is pronounced two different ways: the level-tone pronunciation means earth, and in a lowered-tone pronunciation it is the word for conscience. His symbol is a human with a sphere-tipped tail. The sphere represents the globe and the manifestation of all of the elements together. He can sense the electromagnetic forces throughout all actions. Sakpata is also worshipped as the God of Smallpox, and he is the protector against diseases.

Legba, the messenger god, is a liaison between man and the spirits. Legba statuettes are found throughout the country. The most common and visible ones usually resemble shapeless eyes,

Vodoun Gods

a hole with bits of bones representing the mouth, and a large phallus at its base. These legbas are meant to serve as an altar where one can solicit a spirit's help, particularly in tasks such as protecting a place or sending a message to another vodoun being. Many villages, homes, and markets will have their own protective legba statuette at the entrance. The less visible legbas are those found in a secret place of worship or a spirit's physical home. They are usually managed by a vodoun priest and only aproachable by initiated cult members.

Ogoun is one of the principle deities of the Yoruba form of vodoun, called Orisha. He is the god of war and iron. Representations of Ogoun can be found throughout the country, and as far as Brazil and the Caribbean. Ogoun altars usually consist of iron rods protruding from the ground.

Voudoun and Politics

INSIGHT

Vodoun divination is meant to be practiced on a purely familial or community level, yet Beninese politics have also gotten involved especially during electoral campaigns when village *babalawos* receive many visits from political candidates seeking support from the spiritual forces.

Women participating in a voudon ceremony

OTHER RELIGIONS

Islam

Religions Represented

Christian 42.8%
    Catholic 27.1%,
    Celestial 5%,
    Methodist 3.2%,
    Protestant 2.2%,
    other 5.3%
Muslim 24.4%
Vodoun 17.3%
other 15.5%

Trade routes across the Sahara desert brought Islam from the northern nations of Egypt and Libya to the ancient West African Songhaï Empire, a state based in present-day Niger and Burkina Faso. The Songhaï, in addition to traveling Hausa merchants from the same region, contributed to the spread of Islam in the major cities of Parakou, Djougou, and indirectly Cotonou and Porto-Novo. Islam was practiced in the big trade towns by higher society, and was therefore regarded as a sophisticated religion. Outside of the city walls, little knowledge of Islam existed. Some kings attempted to convert their populations, but significant changes did not occur until further trade and transport brought more Islam to the country. Most converts to this religion did so because of the high level of intellect associated with Islam, including studies of governance, poetry, natural sciences, and world geography.

Today, most sizeable towns in Benin have a mosque, typically at least one per commune. The neighborhood housing the mosque is named *zongo*, where one can hear the call to prayer five times a day. In Cotonou, the entire *zongo* neighborhood pauses for prayer, as followers roll out their prayer mats. Cleanliness is a routine part of prayer and many Muslim cafeterias (and other roadside stands) have plastic tea kettles used to pour water for washing the face, hands, and feet before every prayer. Muslim truck drivers carry their mats beneath their trucks, and use the truck's shade to nap, pray, eat, and drink tea.

Tabaski (more commonly referred to as Eid al-Adha) is a Muslim holiday also known as the 'Feast of Sacrifice' that takes place around December, about one month after Ramadan. According to the Qur'an, Allah asked Abraham to sacrifice his only son. Though Abraham was deeply troubled by Allah's request, he agreed to perform the sacrifice to prove his faith. However, just before Abraham carried out the sacrifice, Allah asked him to offer a sheep instead. In remembrance of Abraham's offering, Muslim families sacrifice a sheep (usually a ram) on the morning of Tabaski. On the days leading to Tabaski, truckloads of sheep are transported from the north to be sold at the giant sheep market on the beach road between Cotonou and Porto-Novo. One sheep costs CFA100,000-120,000, approximately US$200-250. Since many Muslim families cannot afford this, they will split the costs between several families. On the eve of Tabaski, *zongo* neighborhoods are elaborately decorated while large, white rams await the morning sacrifice.

The ram is divided into three parts: one part to be consumed the day of the ceremony, one part to be offered to neighbors and friends, and one part for the family, or the household. The rest of the day is spent in prayer and celebration. Everyone wears matching colorful outfits, pays visits to family and friends, and gives gifts to the children.

Christianity

Though present in Ethiopia and Egypt from 100 to 400 CE, Christianity wasn't introduced into Sub-Saharan Africa until European settlers established themselves in the region around the 15th century. Christians in the earliest settlements rarely attempted to convert remote communities, focusing instead on serving the European population. Christianity therefore remained centered around coastal areas until the 19th century. Toward the end of the slave trade and the beginning of the colonization of West Africa, some missionaries attempted to win over Beninese rulers and used them to spread their faith. After the slave trade, European Christian groups felt a need to aid the African populations previously construed as a mere source of labor. By 1850, Catholic and Protestant missions had entered the territory and established churches, primary schools, and hospitals. Conversion to Christianity, however, was not considered glorious during these early missionary times. Local communities often ostracized a person who chose the European church, while the new convert had to completely abandon their traditional belief system in order to gain acceptance from the missionaries. However, because of the respect the West Africans had for literacy, the churches gained ground through schools and hospitals. In fact, Dahomey was nicknamed the 'Latin Quarter' of Africa during the Colonial era due to the large number of schools.

Catholicism is a prominent religion in Benin, with impressive cathedrals and churches throughout the country. There are also many Protestant churches, including Methodist, Bethel, Biblical, and others. The many

The oldest Catholic Church in Benin is in Ouidah, built directly across the street from the vodoun Python Temple (see pg 106).

places of worship come in all shapes and forms, some consisting simply of a series of wooden benches under a makeshift awning.

Find More...
ON THE WEB
www.celestialchurch.com

One unique religion in Benin is Celestial Christianity, a mixture of traditional animistic and Christian practices. A carpenter from Porto-Novo named Samuel Oshoffa founded the Celestial Church of Christ in 1947 with the desire to create a form of worship free from foreign priests and greedy local féticheurs. Every Sunday the Celests attend very long services wearing white robes with no shoes.

Find More...
ON THE WEB
www.eckankar.org

Another Christian denomination practiced in Benin is Eckankar, a religious movement founded in 1965 by American Paul Twitchell. This religion preaches spiritual practice that enables practitioners to experience what they call 'The Light and Sound of God.' The Eckankar church is based in Minnesota.

Culture

Prominent Ethnic Groups

Betammaribé
Bariba
Somba
Dendi
Tchabè
Idaatcha
Fon
Nagot
Adja
Gun
Mina

DIVERSITY

A multitude of ethnicities and cultures form the vibrant Beninese population. South and central Benin are comprised of those with historical ties to native West African populations, while those in the north are related to the savannah populations of Niger and Burkina Faso.

Primary ethnic groups settled certain regions of the country, then evolved and branched out over time. One major group, the Yoruba, migrated from Nigeria in the 12th century and eventually developed into other ethnicities and languages including Nagot, Tchabè and Idaatcha. Today, the descendants of the Yoruba peoples are found mainly in Porto-Novo and the departments of Ouémé, Plateau, and Collines. The Dendi, who live in north-central Benin, came from Mali in the 16th century. The Bariba are a Muslim group from northern Nigeria and are found in the Borgou and Alibori departments. The Betammaribé, or Ottomari, and Somba live in the Atakora and Donga regions. The Mono and Couffo are mostly populated by Mina and Adja, who came from Togo. The Fon, the most ubiquitous ethnicity in Benin, are concentrated around Abomey, the capital of the former Kingdom of Dahomey. Other southern Benin ethnicities include the Gun and Yoruba.

Other African nationals including Nigerians, Togolese, and Malians, reside within larger Beninese cities. As in many West Africa nations, Chinese, Lebanese and other Middle-easterners have become important tradesmen in Cotonou.

With so many different ethnic groups, there are at least 55 languages spoken throughout the country. French is the official language of Benin and plays an important role in unifying the population for work, social exchanges, and formal education. Fon is the most common native language, especially in the south. Some of the local languages have recently been introduced into the public school system. *See the Language Charts on pg 200 for helpful phrases in the local languages.*

GREETINGS
Greetings hold great importance in Beninese culture, and they are essential in portraying consideration for others in every day interactions. A conversation always begins by asking about the other person's well-being; if the other woke up well that morning; if they are in good health; how are the children and co-inhabitants of the home; or how work is going. The typical greeting in most southern languages translates into something like this:

> 'Did you wake up well?'
> 'Yes (I woke up well).'
> 'Thank you for yesterday.'
> 'Thank you.'

If the two greeters know each other well but haven't seen each other in several days, the greeting would be adapted to say, 'Thank you for three days ago.' This adaptation is also used between strangers who have never met, and is basically a polite gesture. Seemingly obvious questions are frequently asked, such as 'Have you done a little?' Or, 'Are you here?' The typical response is a simple 'Yes.' These questions demonstrate the Beninese capacity of recognizing one's fellows and acknowledging their work and presence.

Proper Etiquette

Upon arriving at someone's home, Beninese generally clap their hands and say, 'ko ko ko' to announce their presence. They will then wait to be let into the home. If one asks, 'Who's there?' the response will most likely be, 'me!' and one must deduct from the voice whether or not they know the visitor.

Another important aspect of the Beninese greeting is the handshake. People who are more familiar with one another will add a snap of the fingers to their handshake. To display heightened respect for someone—such as when greeting an elder, a king, or a member of the local government—individuals grasp their right elbow with the left hand while offering the right hand in greeting (be sure to bend your knees in a slight bow). Similarly, children greet their elders by crossing their arms, holding their elbows, and giving a slight curtsy while they say hello.

In a large crowd, where shaking each person's hand would take too long (even by Beninese standards), it is accepted to clasp both hands above the head and acknowledge everyone in the room with a shake of the clasped hands.

A shot of *sodabi* is a popular welcome gesture. If one prefers not to drink, a polite *non merci* will work—though sometimes the offer must be accepted to avoid offending the host. It is also perfectly normal to offer the drink to the ancestors by saying *pour les ancêtres*, and pouring the *sodabi* on the ground. (Caution: do not pour the sodabi on the ground without saying 'pour les ancêtres!' That would be considered impolite and rude.)

Another sign of respect is the use of titles in addressing friends and others. For example, teachers or local government officials are called by their professional title, such as *profésseur* (instructor) or *délégué* (delegate). An *arrondissement* chief who is also a father and a former teacher could be called 'Chef' by the local population, 'Papa' by his children, or '*Maitre*' (*chicha* in some local tongues) by his students. Even within the immediate family, the husband and wife will refer to each other by title as a sign of mutual respect. When a woman has a child, the community automatically addresses her as 'Mother of (child's name).' The same goes for the father. This title, using the name of the first born, remains even after the births of subsequent children, only to be changed if the first child dies. In the Fon language, for example, a woman who has a son named Jacques will henceforth be called Jacques-non, or Jacque's mother. Jacque's father will be re-named Jacques-ton.

Due to this customary use of titles, most Beninese prefer to address tourists by a title. The most common title is *yovo*, but *monsieur*, *madame*, or *mademoiselle*, are also used. The use of *mademoiselle* can be construed differently when proffered from different people. Sometimes it is used to address a young woman, and at other times it is meant to question a young woman if she is married or not. If preferred, one must insist on being called by one's proper name; it is highly advised, however, to add a title such as *tata* or *grande soeur*, (meaning aunt and older sister), or *tonton* or *grand frère*, (meaning uncle and older brother). The titles coincide with the respect of one's elders which is unhesitatingly practiced in this culture.

Young, single women, especially *yovo*, are likely to be targeted as prospective wives. Though marital propositions can be tiresome and an obvious hassle, keep in mind that such a proposition—even for a *yovo*—may not be intended to be taken literally, and can be interpreted as a compliment. In Benin, women serve an important role as wife and mother and are raised to desire such titles.

Turn an undesired marriage request into a good-natured joke, or simply respond with a white lie.

DRESS

Dress and appearance are very important among Beninese. No matter what the income level, individuals take great care to be clean and well-kept. This is expected of any foreigner, especially since the majority of the population assumes that all tourists have a lot of money and should dress accordingly. Though it is not necessary to dress like a million francs every day, it is important to be clean and presentable. Men should wear clean t-shirts or loose button-down shirts and long pants. Shorts and plastic flip-flops are worn only for outdoor work or by young boys. Women in Benin dress with conservative elegance. Generally, any skin above the knee should not be visible, as the upper legs, belly, and lower back are considered sexually taunting. Shoulders and cleavage should also be respectably covered; long skirts or loose trousers and short-sleeved shirts are appropriate. Wom-

Keep in mind that the weather is usually very hot and humid. Light, loose-fitting clothing is ideal.

en travelers in more Muslim areas and the north are advised to wear particularly conservative clothing out of respect for the local customs.

Beninese appreciate foreigners making an effort to dress in Beninese style. Colorful fabric, sold in every market at affordable prices, can be taken to a tailor to be made into stylish and comfortable outfits. Fabric is sold in long sheets, measured in two-meter lengths called **pagnes**, and range in price from CFA1,000-4,000. A traditional outfit takes two to three pagnes and costs CFA1,000-5,000 depending on the complexity of the pattern.

The locally tailored outfits are easy to wear, dry quickly, and are usually well designed for the terrain. If unprepared and not impressed with the local garb, one can find second-hand t-shirts and other *yovo* style clothes at the local markets.

COMFORTS

If at a *buvette*, restaurant, or at someone's house, the question 'Where are the restrooms?' will quite often be responded to with the crude but necessary question of '*pour pisser*?' or, 'to pee?' Different accommodations are provided for different needs. Those who need to urinate will simply be sent to a designated shower stall or a patch of ground. A man can easily find a corner where he can take care of business. A woman though, if not adept at the *pagne*-spread squat (which is a highly valuable skill in which a woman wearing a pagne manages to relieve herself in a half-squat without showing any part of her body or wetting her clothes), can ask to find a more sheltered place to urinate. There is usually a community pit latrine for defecation, which is often a dark and wretched place, to be avoided if possible. Toilet paper is customarily replaced by the more accessible newspaper, magazine pages, or school notebook paper. It is best to always carry personal toilet paper, like small packages of Kleenex, as the former options are a bit rough to get used to.

Feminine hygiene can be complicated in more remote areas. It is best to use O.B. brand tampons to reduce waste. Do not even attempt to flush tampons as the plumbing systems are incapable of handling such refuse. Tampons should be dropped down a latrine, though if that is not available, take care to burn the trash or use one of the abundant black plastic bags. Feminine napkins should be similarly disposed of. Simply ask for soap and water when all is said and done.

Supermarkets in Cotonou, like LeaderPrice and Mayfair, sell feminine napkins and tampons. This is the only city where these items are certain to be sold, though they could also be found elsewhere.

Laundry is done by hand, and one can easily find someone willing to wash a load of clothes. A suggested payment for this service is a minimum of CFA500 per load. Undergarments are considered intimate and should be washed privately in either a sink or a basin. Hang these private items to dry in a place hidden from public eye.

Music, Literature, and Art

MUSIC

Benin has a rich cultural arts history, with ancient oral traditions in both music and storytelling. The country is home to a vibrant and inventive music scene, combining native folk music with rhythms from Ghana, Congo, Latin America, France, and th U.S. Some of the most influential post-colonial musicians include Ignacio Blazio Osho, Gnonas Pedro, G.G.Vickey, Les Volcans de la Capitale, and Picoby Band d'Abomey.

Gnonas Pedro (1943-2005) was part of the famous salsa band Africando All Stars. Orginally formed in 1990 and known as Africando, the group fused New York-based musicians and West African vocalists. Because salsa-style music has been very popular in Central and West Africa since the 1940s, the group formed to unite the African rhythms with those of the American continents. The songs are sung in Wolof (the native language of Senegal), Spanish, or a mix of both. Gnonas Pedro's last recording is the title track *Ketukuba* (2006), though he died before the album was released.

Orchestre Polyrythmo' was a popular band in the 1970s in Benin. Though the group hasn't produced new material in a while and the members are in their 60s, the music still sounds good.

Angélique Kidjo is a world renowned Beninese artist, especially popular in Europe. Mesmerized as a child by a Jimi Hendrix album cover, Angelique Kidjo followed African music to the United States, Brazil, and the Caribbean. As a teenager she began recording and toured West Africa. Shifting politics prevented her from becoming an independent artist in Benin, so in 1983 she moved to Paris and studied music. Kidjo started out as a backup singer for local bands, but by 1985 she had become the lead singer for Three Pili Pili, a Euro-African jazz/rock band. By the end of the decade, she was one of the most popular live performers in Paris. She has three Grammy award winning albums: Oremi, Black Ivory Soul, and Oyaya. Her most recent work is entitled *Djin Djin*—the title refers to the sound of a bell awakening a new day in Africa—which is also a Grammy award winning work. The percussionists in Djin Djin, Crespin Kplitiki and Benoit Avihoue, are members of the Gangbe Brass Band. Their Beninese roots, along with Kidjo's, influence the music. Angélique Kidjo is fluent and sings in four languages: Fon, French, Yoruba, and English.

There are many other popular Beninese artists, including Petit Miguelito and John Arcadius. Ivorian and Nigerian music is popular in Benin as well.

The Gangbe Brass Band was formed in 1994 by eight native Beninese musicians wanting to combine Western jazz and big-band music with native rhythms. Gangbe means 'the sound of metal' in Fon. Their music is both traditional and contemporary: the French colonists imported brass instruments and taught the Beninese to play European-style military and dance hall music. The unique combination of instruments and rhythms bridge the past and present. The group sings in the native tongue of its members, namely Fon, about society, political injustices, and women's suffering. Gangbe has released three albums: Gangbe (1998), Togbe (2001), and Whendo (2004).

LITERATURE

Jean Pliya is an important Beninese author. His books *L'Arbre Fétiche* and *La Secrétaire Particulière* depict Beninese culture and are widely read in the region. Pliya has transcribed the Fon's oral tradition into French and has even dabbled in playwriting. Due to his popularity, Jean Pliya has held various government positions and was vice-chancellor of the University of Benin.

L'Esclave is set in a village in southwest Dahomey and satirizes the Dahomean elite during the colonial period.

Felix Couchoro wrote the first Beninese novel, *L'Esclave* in 1929, which is also considered the first African novel. He was born in Ouidah in 1900, and moved to Togo in 1939 where he lived the majority of the rest of his life.

Couchoro worked as a teacher, businessman, journalist, and newspaper editor. He published his works in serial form in the local Togo-Press newspaper, gaining local and international acclaim. After *L'Esclave*, his next works were published in the 1950s and 1960s. Couchoro later adapted his French grammar to a more local style, incorporating Ewe and Fon expressions and proverbs.

ART

In the 15th century, when Europe was 'discovering' West Africa, local art was taken to Europe where it grew in popularity. This art mostly entailed masks and figurines made of wood, gold, bronze, clay, and ivory. The most widely credited West African craftsmen were those of the Ifè and Benin kingdoms in present-day Nigeria. They implemented a method called 'lost wax' to create bronze figurines of humans and animals. This ancient method is still used today and involves sculpted wax that is melted inside a clay mold, where the space created from the displaced wax is filled with molten metal.

European artists such as Pablo Picasso and Henri Matisse were so inspired by West African art that they began the cubist movement in the same style.

Due to its extraction from the continent, much of the original, ancient Beninese art is today housed in international museums, including the Louvre and the Musée de l'Homme in Paris. Most art found in Beninese museums are replicas. That said, the Abomey and Porto-Novo museums have some impressive displays of original artwork.

Contemporary Beninese art ranges from hand crafted *batiks*, sculptures, and patchwork tapestries called *toiles appliqués* to modern artwork found in churches, public parks, and personal artist studios. There are significant contemporary artist communities in Cotonou and Porto-Novo. Artists in the town of Dassa-Zoumé also promote the development of Beninese culture and the collaboration of contemporary artists by hosting international symposiums and festivals.

Some prominent contemporary artists in Benin are Ludovic Fadaïro, Virgil Nassara, Gerard Quenum, Tchif, Dominique Zinkpé, and more.

Felix Agossa was born in Parakou. His artistic career began during his high school days when, in 1987, he created his first cement sculpture, *L'Eleve Inconnu*, in the dusty Parakou school yard as a tribute to Benin's students. It still stands today, braving the elements and inspiring younger generations.

Immediately recognized as a promising artist, Agossa was invited to Liege, Belgium for a nine-month study in an animation studio. By 1993, the young artist had become well-known in the West African art scene. Jovial, easy going, and full of integrity, Agossa became a highly solicited sculptor and author-illustrator throughout West and Central Africa, from Senegal to the Congo. In 2000, he set off once again for more exhibits and artist residencies in Europe, taking Marseilles, Bordeaux, Brussels, and Berlin by storm.

Art by Felix Agossa

Shortly upon his return from Europe, the Beninese clergy took notice of Agossa's remarkable work and called upon him to decorate many of Benin's churches and cathedrals. Thus began a new dimension for Felix Agossa: spiritual art. This new form of art has brought him a certain inner peace and serenity; he continues to explore the realm of spiritual art, combining the various religions that have shaped his life and continent: vodoun, Christianity, and Islam. His paintings contain an extraordinary strength, full of indigenous and personal emblems and symbols that can be applied to all forms of personal and spiritual journeys.

Agossa's work depicts the everyday expressions and shapes of the people he so duly observes. Like many African artists, Agossa makes brilliant use of local materials in order to create rare authenticity in his work, true to his African origins.

Richard Korblah was born in Ivory Coast in 1978 and raised in the south of Benin. He has been showing his work in Cotonou since 1998, all the while traveling to Europe for numerous artist residences. This young artist often works shirtless, a bandana tied around his neck and a Neem stick in his mouth (often used to clean teeth). He likes to sleep among his unfinished canvases, and doesn't grasp their full significance until he has completed them and can take a step back. His strong spirituality subconsciously expresses itself through his brushstrokes, as his paintings regularly contain a representation of the cross. Korblah becomes so consumed with his work, as if under a spell, that he often falls ill upon completing a piece.

In one series of paintings, Richard uses a combination of photographs, paint, and fabric to create distorted images depicting the sufferings and jubilations of life expressed in the traditional scourging ceremonies practiced by the *Peuhl* (Fulani) people of West Africa. These mixed-media compositions, with the use of bold streaks, embody the brutality and power of these gripping ceremonies. A medley of earth tones, blood-red and blue hues, represents the harsh, yet colorful, lifestyles of the *Peuhl*, as if these young men use their bodies as stretched canvases, while the strokes of the whips draw their blood to paint the expression of their integral virtue. Korblah's work aims to transmit the strength, power, and understanding of the complex, austere, yet magnificent world in which we live.

More information on Beninese contemporary art can be found at the following websites:
www.okuta.cfun.fr
www.metmuseum.org/explore/oracle/figures49.html

 Find More...
ON THE WEB

Sports

With local offices in each département, the *Ministère de la Jeunesse, du Sport, et des Loisirs* (the Ministry of Youth, Sports, and Recreation), oversees all organized sports in Benin. In Cotonou, this ministry works with the Olympic Committee—an autonomous group made up of the leaders from various national sports organizations—on sports such as soccer (football), basketball, handball, volleyball, tennis, table tennis, tae kwon do, and many others. Teams on the local level are officially recognized through sanctioned leagues and clubs. The lowest division is the '18 and under,' or youth division. Consecutively more competitive divisions are the district, third, second, and first divisions. Though teams of each level are found throughout the country, the most competitive first division teams are in the large urban areas, especially Cotonou and Porto-Novo.

Outside the cities, where there are fewer funds for equipment, the most popular sport is soccer which requires less equipment to play. Basketball, handball, and volleyball follow in popularity, varying regionally according to the youth preference. Another handicap in rural areas is the lack of qualified coaches. Most often the secondary school physical education teacher is the coach of any given sport, whether or not he is skilled in that sport. These teachers are trained for general physical education and not competitive sports.

Secondary schools participate in a nationwide tournament at the end of each school year, organized by the département's ministry of sports and the physical education teachers. The schools strive to send as many men's and women's teams as possible each year.

The Squirrels

Les Ecureils, the Squirrels, is the name of the national soccer team. There have been a few debates on the ferocity of a squirrel, yet the name remains, arguing that squirrels don't tumble. In 2008, the team made history by advancing to the final round of the Africa Cup of Nations (CAN). The stadium in Cotonou, *the Stade de l'Amitié*, hosts the team and also contains the track and field and swim arenas.

The Environment: Geography, Flora and Fauna

Benin is a relatively flat country, characterized by plateaus and valleys in the south, rolling hills toward central Benin and the northeast, and a mountain range in the northwestern Atakora region. The highest point is Mount Sokbaro (658 meters) in the Atakora range.

Located between the Tropic of Cancer and the Equator, Benin is part of the **Dahomey Gap**, also known as the Intertropical Convergence Zone (ITCZ). The Dahomey Gap is created by cold sea currents flowing close to the coastline. It is an oscillating low pressure zone which creates the wet and dry season patterns. High pressure winds blow toward the Dahomey Gap from two directions: the tropical winds from the Atlantic blow northeast from April to October, and the dry winds from the Sahara, also known as the **Harmattan**, descend southeast from November to March. The Gap runs along the coast of Benin, Togo, and part of Ghana. In this region the savanna reaches farther south, nearly touching the coast. The land to the east and west of the Gap is characterized by the Guinea Forest zone, which was originally densely wooded but deforestation has created a 'derived savanna' consisting of cultivated fields, farmbush, secondary-growth forests, and savanna grasses.

Benin is mainly covered by savanna, though strips of Guinea Forest prolong laterally through the south. The majority of these forests have been harvested, though some relicts remain along rivers and in isolated patches. Two such examples are the Lama Forest in central Benin and the forest of Niaouli, just north of Cotonou. Both forests are considered sacred.

During the dry season, the Harmattan spreads a veil of dust over the country. The vegetation becomes dry and brown, and water becomes scarce. In this period, many farmers burn their fields in an effort to rejuvenate the soils and to clear the weeds in preparation for the next planting season. Hunters use the slash and burn technique during the dry months to hunt wildlife.

The climate varies greatly from the semi-arid north to the humid, tropical south. The southern climate, due to its proximity to the coast, is more easily affected by the ocean currents. The south has two dry seasons; a long dry season from December to March, and a brief one during the month of August. The two rainy seasons are from March to July and then September to November. Torrential downpours on the parched, sandy soils often result in floods, especially in Cotonou and the surrounding lagoon villages.

ENVIRONMENTAL CONCERNS

Management of trash and wastewater is a problem in Benin. In the past, all of the household waste was organic and decomposed naturally; the scrap and debris could simply be thrown into piles outside the home and be used later to fill low spots. However, stagnant water provides a habitat for breeding mosquitoes, and thus the malarial parasite. Today, the introduction of modernized items into daily life has resulted in non-biodegradable waste, such as tin cans, plastic bags, and batteries. The cities are too crowded and poorly planned to compensate with a more efficient and environmentally sound waste management system. In these dense populations, household waste is discarded in nearby fields, burned, or buried within the household courtyard. Refuse collection services exist in larger towns, but do not reach all the neighborhoods, nor is there priority for keeping the city clean. There are no public trash cans; piles develop along the sidewalks, transforming gutters and open-air canalizations into veritable public dumps. Trash located near concessions, schools, wells, and community clinics emit stinking odors, attracting many insects and rodents that cause health issues for the population. More than 80% of industrial and household waste in Cotonou does not reach the municipal dumps.

Clash of Livelihoods

INSIGHT

In the north where cattle herding is more common, the existence of transhumance, that is the seasonal movement of people with their livestock, causes serious friction between farmers and herders. Over-cultivation by local farmers and the nomadic pastoralism of the Fulani resulting in trampled crop fields is a source of significant environmental degradation.

Floods are a serious concern throughout the country. Cotonou is especially succeptible to this problem as the city sits on an over-crowded and narrow strip of land between the ocean and several lagoon lakes. The Mono River typically has five-year periodic floods that stretch from the dam at Nangbeto, Togo, to Grand Popo. The Mono River floods in increments: the first couple waves empty quickly back into the river bed, but the third wave often creates eddies and ponds throughout the vast flood plain, destroying fields, homes along the river banks, and village docking points. Roads are completely blocked for up to a week before the water recedes to its banks and the land begins its slow drying process. This most recently occurred in September 2009.

FAUNA

Beware: do not bother the ants! Ants are commonly seen in the countryside filing across paths or thick grass and brush. These ants definitely bite. Take care to step over their busy line; if by mishap a foot intrudes upon the ant file, be prepared to drop clothing and slap like crazy! They will even invade homes in search of moisture. Boil-

Beware of scorpions in the dry season or up north, as well.

ing water, fire, or other extreme measures are necessary to diverge their path.

Reptiles

Lizards in Benin are quite harmless and even help deplete the cockroach population. Large agama lizards, popularly called *margouillat* in French, are gregarious. The males come in an array of flashy green, blue, red, and yellow hues and can be seen perched on rocks and walls, bobbing up and down as they survey their surroundings. Female agama lizards are smaller and more slender, with bright green dots on their heads.

Geckos are frequent in homes and subsist from moths and insects as they dart across walls and ceilings. The chameleon is not common, but can be found in the bush and for sale in local markets. This lizard has a mean bite, so be aware before handling one.

The reptile deserving the most concern is the snake. Pythons are common yet not venomous. They are venerated in the vodoun religion, so they enjoy some form of protection but are not immune to hunting. Other snakes, including spitting cobras, boa constrictors, boomslangs, and green and black mambas are dangerous and usually killed outright.

Crocodiles can be found in rivers distant from human populations. Sea turtles come seasonally to the beaches, especially around Grand Popo (see pg 126).

Mammals

Most of the original mammal species of Benin have been hunted out of the countryside, though they still live in very remote, unpopulated areas. Small mammals, like the bush rat (agouti), small deer, and monkeys, are heavily hunted. In the protected territories of the wildlife parks, species such as the elephant, hippopotamus, warthog, harnessed bushbuck, western kob, western hartebeeast, oribi and western bush duiker attain populations of several thousand. The most numerous species are the African buffalo and the western roan, with numbers exceeding ten thousand. The territory also supports smaller populations of the sing-sing waterbush, nagor reedbuck, and the korrigum, a West African species of topi.

In the feline family, there are an estimated 750 lions and a number of leopards, servals, caracals, African wild cats, and possibly even one to two dozen cheetahs, one of the last surviving populations in West Africa. Other predators include jackals, hyenas, the African civet, genets, otters, badgers, and several species of mongoose.

Hippopotamuses are somewhat common in the parks of the north, the Ouémé River near Dassa, and around the Mono River near Lokossa. There are an estimated 2,000 hippopotamuses throughout the combined West African nations of Ivory Coast, Ghana, Togo, Benin, and Burkina Faso.

The West African Manatee

The West African Manatee is an elusive creature in both myth and reality. Though previously thought extinct in the region, some evidence shows that the species is still present in several West African nations. In 2000, for example, Ivory Coast claimed a population of up to 800 manatees. These mammals are herbivores that inhabit estuaries with mangroves or freshwater with overhanging vegetation. Of all manatee species, the West African Manatee is the most threatened. Though legally protected worldwide, manatee populations continue to decline due to hunting and incidental trapping in fish nets, turbines, and control gates in dams.

Mistaken Identity

In coastal West African communities, the goddess Mami Wata is a mermaid deity who represents irresistible beauty and wealth. There are legends of people following Mami Wata to a deep and watery death. It is believed that the female manatee, which has a somewhat scaly body with lungs and mammaries to nurse her young, could easily resemble a woman on the surface of the water and thus be at the source of these spiritual beliefs.

BIRDS

A great variety of birds are abundant in the wildlife parks, the Niaouli forest, and most rural areas throughout the country.

Small birds

The common garden bulbul lives up to its name in that it is very common, much like the American robin. This species of bulbul has a dark head and drab brown body. It measures roughly the length of a hand and is most often seen on the ground, or in low bushes and trees.

Village weavers are colloquially called *oiseaux gendarmes*, or 'army birds.' They are oriole-sized with a black head and a yellow-orange body. They measure about seven to eight inches tall and live in colonies. A colony of village weavers will invade a tree, where they weave nests and make incessant, obnoxious noise. The weavers will inhabit this tree until it either falls down or, if in a village, the villagers cut the tree down or smoke the birds out.

Pin-tailed whydahs, when in breeding season, make wonderful cat toys: the males grow long tail feathers, perhaps two feet long at most. Out of breeding season, one can identify a pin-tailed whydah by its distinct orange beak, black and white spotted coloring, and its small size, about three to four inches tall. These birds are most often seen while feeding on the ground.

Red bishops, also known as black-winged bishops, are fairly common birds and easily spotted in the tall grass on which they float. They have a red mane, a black body, and measure about five inches tall.

The Senegal firefinch, or red-billed firefinch, is so named from the male's bright red coloring. This bird is four to five inches tall, and is most commonly seen feeding on the ground.

Endangered and Vulnerable Species in Benin

Wildlife populations in the parks have declined over the past 25 years, resulting in the giraffe and the African wild dog now reportedly extinct in the region. On the other hand, the roan, elephant, hippo, and buffalo numbers seem to have increased.

Endangered
> Red-bellied Monkey (Cercopithecus erythrogaster)
> Wild Dog (Lycaon pictus)

Vulnerable
> African Elephant (Loxodonta africana)
> African Golden Cat (Profelis aurata)
> Cheetah (Acinonyx jubatus)
> Fox's Shrew (Crocidura foxi)
> Ja Slit-faced Bat (Nycteris major)
> Lion (Panthera leo)
> Red-fronted Gazelle (Gazella rufifrons)
> Spotted-necked Otter (Lutra maculicollis)
> West African Manatee (Trichechus senegalensis)
> White-thighed Black-and-white Colobus (Colobus vellerosus)

Medium-sized birds

Senegal kingfishers are often perched high, not necessarily near water. About eight inches tall, their bright blue color, orange beak, and terrific screech make these birds easy to identify.

The **white-throated bee-eaters** are beautiful green birds often seen perched on electrical wires, usually in groups. Their white throat is quite visible in contrast to the black stripes on their face and throat. Their flight is graceful, with the couple of pin-tail feathers trailing neatly.

The **common fiscal shrike** is also seen on electrical wires, though not in groups. The shrike has black and white coloring, and a helmet shaped head with a stout black beak. This bird is about seven inches tall.

African black crakes and **African jacanas** are sure to be seen in freshwater ponds and marshes. The crake is about ten inches tall, and has an amusing clown colored body with long, bright orange legs, a yellow beak, and red ringed eyes. Jacanas are also known as lily trotters, as they use their large feet and long legs to walk on lilies. The jacanas have longer legs and more graceful coloring than the crake, with a soft blue colored forehead, a white throat, and a brown body. Both of these water birds are trapped by locals for consumption.

The **helmeted guinea fowl** roams wild throughout the north of Benin and is commonly raised for consumption. The **double-spurred francolin** and the **stone partridge** are also part of the local diet and have a pleasant, sweet meat.

Large birds

Western grey plantain eaters are found in the crown of mid-sized trees, thrashing about for plantains or other fruit. They are large and grey with a yellow beak, and almost two feet tall including the tail feathers.

The **Senegal coucal** has a noticeably clumsy gait, aerial or terrestrial. The call sounds like big fat drops of water: *blop blop blop blop blop*. It measures about a foot long, and is very dark colored with a black head, brown body, and red eyes. It is most often low to the ground in brush.

Black kites are notorious pullet-killers; Beninese paint their baby chickens in neon colors to fool these constantly-circling predators. Black kites have a tell-tale screech, yellow beak, forked tail, and dark brown body.

The **piping hornbill** is a forest-dwelling bird, usually seen flying between stands of trees, calling nasally. Their undulating flight is an identifiable characteristic, along with their black and white coloring and horned bill.

FLORA

The vegetation in Benin varies greatly from the north to the south, due to the diversity in soils, climate, and human activities. Coastal communities—notably Cotonou, Ouidah, Grand Popo, and around Lake Ahémé—have many lagoons and mangroves. Farther north, the vegetation visibly reflects the low average rainfall as it becomes less dense and more scrub-like.

Southern and Central Regions

Indigenous vegetation in this region has practically disappeared, replaced by a mosaic of cultivated fields and fallow farmland. Plantations of coconut palms, mangroves, teak trees, and oil or raffia palms dot the flood zones of the south. The oil palm is used in many ways for Beninese daily life: the leaves are used to construct huts and cabins, or they are stripped to the central vein and used as poles for maneuvering *pirogues*. The sap is harvested as palm wine and distilled into the infamous *sodabi*. Red oil is extracted from the palm nuts and used for cooking. As one moves away from the coast, various tree plantations exist in addition to the oil palm, such as mango and cashew nut trees. The **flamboyant tree**, common in the south, has lovely red flowers, making it one of the most beautiful trees in West Africa.

Northern Region

The most common trees in the north are the néré, shea tree, boabab, ronier palm and kapok tree. The **kapok** can grow very tall, with white flowers and spines all over its trunk. It is often regarded as sacred. **Ronier palms** are mostly seen throughout the far North, especially in Park Pendjari. Its leaves are used to make hats and bracelets worn by Bariba tribes and nomadic Fulanis. Ronier shoots are a tasty, earthy snack, often eaten with chunks of coconut. The **kola tree** produces the kola nut, which contains alkaloids and is widely chewed across the Sahel due to its stimulating virtues similar to those of caffeine. The kola nut also serves as a traditional gift in ceremonies and rituals. The **cailcedrat** is used for making furniture.

The Basics

When to Visit

Each season has its pros and cons for visiting the country. During the wet season, which is May to October, the temperatures are generally a bit cooler and the scenery is lush, even in the north. However, during this time the mosquitoes are out in full force, and the south is quite humid. It does not rain every day, but when it does, it can be impressively heavy, resulting in damaging flash floods which have increased in the past couple years. Dirt roads wash out and become impassable. The national parks in the north remain open, but wildlife is more dispersed and difficult to see in the overgrowth. From July to August, there is a lull in the rainy season in the south, and visitors enjoy the green, cooler climate of this period. During the first part of the dry season, from November to January, the humidity lessens, and the dry heat begins to settle across the country. The air is clear and the nights are breezy. In January/February, the dry Harmattan wind (see pg 45) from the Sahara covers the north with dust and makes its way to the southern half of the country. Typically, temperatures are much cooler during this time. It is also a good time to go hiking, especially in the hills around Dassa, as the vegetation has dried or has been burnt by hunters, trails are more accessible. In March and April, before the rainy season begins and after the Harmattan has stopped, the heat intensifies and becomes nearly unbearable in the North. At the same time, this is the optimal period for viewing wildlife in the parks because many animals gather at the few remaining watering holes.

The country's annual rainfall is about 1,100 mm, and the average temperature is 27°C (82°F).

The drier months cause dirt roads to become dusty; those traveling on zemidjans will quickly be covered in red dirt.

Getting There

VISA REQUIREMENTS
Beninese Visa Requirements:
- Two photographs
- International certificate of yellow fever vaccination
- Passport valid for at least six months

Plus, one of the following:
- Copy of a flight itinerary
- Supporting document from an employer or travel agency
- Letter from a bank indicating sufficient funds for the trip

Typical tourist visas are multiple-entry, 90 day visas valid for 36 months. In the United States and Europe, the minimum turnaround time when applying by post is 10 days, or 48 hours if applying in person at an embassy.

Transit visas, valid for 48-hours, are available at all Beninese border posts for CFA10,000. These can then be extended at the Direction Immigration in Cotonou, on Avenue du Pape Jean Paul II, or in Natitingou. These offices only take care of visa extensions, and there is no official body that issues tourist visas in Benin.

Another option is to get the *Visa Touristique Entente*, which is valid for two months and allows multiple entries to Benin, Ivory Coast, Niger, Burkina Faso, and Togo. This visa costs CFA25,000, and requires two photos. Allow two days at the respective embassies in Cotonou (all embassies are located in Cotonou). Europeans can obtain the *Visa Touristique Entente* at the Benin Embassy in Paris for €40.

AIR
Overseas
AirFrance and Delta are the most commonly used airlines for travel from the U.S. and Europe. Ticket cost averages around US$2,000 from the U.S. Air Maroc also flies from New York City to Cotonou via Casablanca, but the layover in Casablanca is lengthy (a minimum of 12 hours). There is a direct flight from New York to Accra, Ghana, from where one can travel by land through Ghana and Togo with the appropriate visas. STC travel, which has an office in Cotonou, has buses traveling to/from Accra and Cotonou. There is no direct flight from the UK to Benin but Air France flies from London (via Paris) to Cotonou.

Visa Costs and Procedures by Country

United States

Embassy of Benin in the U.S. *Tel: +1-202-232-6656; Fax: +1.202.265.1996; 2124 Kalorama Road, NW, Washinton, DC 20008; Consular Section: Tel/Fax: +1.202.232.2611*

From the United States, the cost for U.S. citizens is US$100. For non-U.S. citizens, the following prices apply:

> For a stay of up to 30 days:
>> One entry: $40
>> Multiple entries: $45
> For a stay of 31 to 90 days:
>> One entry: $45
>> Multiple entries: $50

basics

Canada

Embassy of Benin in Canada *Tel: +1.613.233.44.29; Fax +1.613.23389.52; 58, Avenue Glebe, Ottawa (Ontario) K1S 2C3; ambaben@benin.ca or ambaben2@surf.ca*

From Canada, 90 day visas cost CA$85 for single entry, and CA$105 for multiple entries.

European Union *The regional embassy is in Paris*

Ambassade du Benin (France) Tel: *+33 (1)145.009882 / +33 (1) 42.223191; Fax: +33.145.18202; 87 Avenue Victor Hugo 742116 Paris*

Single visas cost:
> 1-7 days: €20
> 8-30 days: €35
> 31-90 days: €50
Multi-entry, 90 days €50

United Kindgom

Honorary Consulate of Benin in the UK *Tel: +44 (0) 20 8830 8612; Fax: +44 (0) 20 7435 0665; l.landau@btinternet.com; Millennium House, Humber Road, London, NW2 6DW*

From the UK, visas are available with the Honorary Consulate in London. However, only single entry visas are issued at the following rates:
> 15 days: £45
> 30 days: £55
> 90 days: £65

Air – Regional

The Cotonou airport receives a number of regional flights. Destinations include: Douala, Tripoli, Libreville, Ouagadougou, Paris, Abidjan, Lagos, Niamey, Accra, Bamako, Bangui, Brazzaville, Conakry, Dakar, Kinshasa, Malabo, Nairobi, Johannesburg, Casablanca, and N'Djamena.

AirFrance and Royal AirMaroc have regular flights to the capitals of surrounding nations: Togo, Ghana, Burkina Faso, and Niger. Afriqiyah Airways is a Lybian airline with frequent flights between Cotonou, Lagos, and Tripoli. Toumai Air Tchad connects Lomé, Douala, Brazzaville, Bangui, and N'Djamena. Other main companies are Air Senegal International, Air Burkina, Air Mauritanie, Air Ivoire, Air Gabon.

Regional Airline Offices in Cotonou:

Cameroon Airlines *Tel: 21.31.52.17/30.09.08 www.cameroon-airlines.com*

Afriqiyah Airways *Tel: 21.31.76.51/21.31.49.02; www.afriqiyah.aero; (ELDA International) Avenue Steinmetz, 06BP891*

Air Senegal Internationale *Tel: 21.30.18.15/21.30.17.61/21.30.12.98*
Air Senegal is represented by CBM Voyages Travel Agency.

Air Burkina *Tel: 21.31.37.06 www.air-burkina.com*

Air Gabon *Tel: 21.31.20.67/31.21.87*

Air Ivoire *Tel: 21.31.86.14/15; www.airivoire.com*

Toumai Air Tchad *www.toumaiair.com; webmaster@toumaiair.com*

Air Mauritanie *Tel: 21.31.49.02 www.airmauritanie.mr/airframeset.htm*
This company is represented by CBM Voyage Travel Agency.

Royal Air Maroc *Tel: 21.30.86.04; anazih@yahoo.fr; Route de l'Aéroport*

Air France *www.airfrance.com; Route de l'Aéroport*

Travel Agencies

CBM Voyages Hôtel du Port CMB Voyages represents some of the African airlines in Cotonou, such as Air Senegal Internationale and Air Mauritanie. They share an office with Group ELDA touring agency, which offers tours of the southern hotspots in Benin: Ouidah, Porto-Novo, Grand Popo, Ganvié, and Cotonou. *Tel: 21.31.08.42 / 21.31.08.50; 06BP891; www.groupelda.com/voyage; cbm@groupelda.com or cbmcoo@intnet.bj*

Satguru Travel & Tours Service Satguru offers great service on international flights, particularly around Africa.They have offices all over the world, including Senegal, Cameroon, Burkina Faso, Ghana, Ivory Coast, with its headquarters in Dubai. They work with all the airlines around Africa and are efficient at obtaining the cheapest flights in a timely manner. Booking tickets through Satguru takes away the hassle of searching for different airline offices around Cotonou. *Tel: 21.31.35.43; satgurutravelscotonou@yahoo.com; Next to Continental Bank in Dantokpa*

LAND

Buses travel regularly to regional capitals and other prominent cities.

Togo

The STIF bus between Lomé and Cotonou takes about three hours and costs CFA3,000.

Taxis from the *gare* in Jonquet depart regularly for Lomé. The trip also lasts three hours and costs CFA3,000. One can split the ride and stop at the Hilla-Condji border crossing, then take another taxi to Lomé. There are other border crossings farther north, such as by the Beninese towns of Athiémé, Aplahoué, Bassila, and near Boukoumbé. The scenery in the north is beautiful, but the roads are rough and dusty.

Embassy of Togo Visas do not take long to obtain. Bring passport photos, CFA15,000, and complete the application. With luck, the consular will be in his office and can sign it at the same time. *Across the street from St. Michel's Cathedral*

Ghana and Ivory Coast

Intercity STC buses to and from Accra and Abidjan depart at noon on Monday, Wednesday, and Friday from the station near the Halls des Arts and Maman Bénin Restaurant. A taxi from Cotonou to the Benin-Togo border costs about CFA2,000, from there another taxi will continue to Lomé. Taxi-motorcycles from Lomé to the Ghana border only cost CFA100.

Embassy of Ghana The Ghanaian visa process can take up to three days and requires four photos. Destination details are also required, such as a hotel address or phone number. A six-month visa is CFA60,000, and a one month, one time entry visa is CFA15,000. Drop off the visa application before 2pm and pick it up the following day after 2pm. If the application is dropped off after 2pm, it will take an extra day *Tel: 21.30.07.46; Avenue du Pape Jean-Paul II, close to Haie Vive and near the AirFrance and AirMaroc offices; Open Mon-Thurs, 9am-4pm*

Niger

SNTV runs buses three times a week to Niamey. The station in Cotonou is at the Cadjehoun intersection. The trip takes 15 to 20 hours, the buses are usually completely full, and it costs CFA20,000. Southbound buses depart from Niamey at 4am, and northbound buses usually depart Cotonou around midnight.

A *zemidjan* from Malanville to cross the border into Gaya, Niger costs CFA1,000, and a bush taxi ride costs CFA500. A taxi ride from Gaya to Niamey lasts five hours and costs CFA4,500. If lucky, one can also get a seat on one of the Cotonou-Niamey buses.

Embassy of Niger One month visas cost CFA22,500. Two photos are required and the processing time is two days. *Tel: 21.31.56.71 Behind the Ganxi market, near the Hôtel de Plage; Open Mon-Fri, 9am-5pm*

Burkina Faso

TVC busline has a Sunday bus from Ouagadougou to Cotonou for CFA20,000, which takes 18 hours. The same bus continues to Lagos for a total of CFA30,500.

Taxis depart at least once a day from Natitingou to the Burkina Faso border crossing at Porga. It is a 100 kilometer ride that lasts two hours and should cost about CFA2,000. Porga market day, Monday, is the best day to find a ride.

Consulate of Burkina Faso *Tel: 21.31.25.73; Fax: 21.31.01.49; Lot 1159 Haie Vive*

Nigeria

Taxis to Lagos frequently depart from the Dantokpa *gare*. The cost is CFA3,000 and takes three hours. There are currently no coaches between Cotonou and Lagos. Visas to Nigeria can be difficult to obtain. Tourist visas are more easily issued to Beninese nationals. Foreigners must first get a transit visa and then extend it once in Nigeria. The transit visa cost is CFA68,500, requiring two photos and several days to issue.

Embassy of Nigeria *Tel: 21.30.15.03 / 21.30.11.42 / 21.30.44.87; Fax: 21.30.11.13; Boulevard de France, near the Benin Marina; Open Mon-Thurs, 9am-5pm*

 Find More... *For information on embassies in Benin, visit:*
ON THE WEB   www.embassiesabroad.com/embassies-in/Benin

Transportation in Benin

Bush taxis are the most common mode of transport for long distances. The vehicles are usually recycled Peugots shipped from Europe, after they have been deemed unfit for the road. Each town has a taxi station or *gare*, positioned according to destination, where taxi assistants direct passengers to the appropriate vehicles. Fare negotiation is very important, and must be settled before getting in the car. A standard taxi takes a minimum of six adults; four in the back seat, two in the front passenger seat. More ambitious *chauffeurs*, or drivers, squeeze slender individuals in to the left of them by the driver's window or straddling the stick shift. Restrictions are mildly enforced by *routiers* (*policiers* or *gendarmes*), or traffic controllers along the paved roads. *Chauffeurs* usually do not leave until their car is nearly full, so patience and flexibility is key. If with luggage, be sure to keep an eye on it once it has been placed in the trunk or on the roof—luggage gets moved around throughout the journey as passengers come and go. The fare is almost always paid once passengers have arrived at their desti-destination, though sometimes *chauffeurs* will demand part or all of the fare en route in order to pay for gas. Be cautious as some drivers may stop halfway to the desti-nation and transfer their passengers to another vehicle. Renegotiate the price with the new *chauffeur* before setting off.

City Taxis, recognizable by their distinct green and yellow colors, are only found in Cotonou. Since 2007, these taxis have been restricted to carry a maximum of four passengers per taxi: one in front and three in the back seat. Taxis are common on the main roads, and an efficient way to travel to and from distant locales or to transport luggage. Prices are usually lower than *zemid-jans*, but they take more time due to frequent stops as they pick up and drop off passengers around the city.

Buses are a convenient way to travel cross-country and to neighboring countries. As opposed to bush taxis, in which break downs, delays, and detours are more frequent, bus lines respect set schedules, are better organized, and more secure. Furthermore, the rates are usually set, which eliminates the hassle of negotiating with the driver, and each passenger gets a separate seat.

There are no city buses and apart from a Confort Line's bus that goes to Ouidah, all intra-country bus

Bush taxi

routes go north-south from Cotonou to Karimama or Natitingou. These buses only stop in select towns along the way. Cotonou-Karimama buses stop in Abomey-Calavi, Bohicon, Dassa, Parakou, and Karimama. Cotonou-Natitingou buses stop in Abomey-Calavi, Bohicon, Dassa, Djougou, Natitingou, and some go all the way to Tanguieta. Reservations for any bus company are only imperative around the important holidays (New Years, Christmas, etc), but if one bus breaks down, other buses fill up quickly, so it's never a bad idea to reserve in advance.

At most scheduled stops, a swarm of vendors wait at the stations, offering a variety of snacks such as sweet soy crackers, fried corn biscuits, partially peeled oranges, pineapple, spicy bits of grilled pork, rice and bean dishes, cold sodas and bags of tap water. It is important not to stray far from the bus, as the drivers will not wait for stragglers when it is time to continue on the road.

Zemidjans, also known as *kekenos* or motorcycle-taxis, are often compared to ants because they can be found everywhere in the country and tend to swarm any prospective client. *Zemidjan* means 'get me there fast' in Fon. Young men often resort to work as *zemidjan* drivers because it is a quick way to make money while they learn a trade or save to go to school. They typically earn between CFA1,000-3,000 a day. Many *kekenos* roam the city streets; it is important to choose one with a motorcycle that seems to be intact and with a confident yet conscientious driver—don't worry, they are easy to spot. To signal a *zemidjan*, send a slight nod in their direction or give a palm-down finger wave. The Fon word for 'come here' is wa, and in these situations is used liberally (example: fingers flapping, repeating 'wa!'). Before mounting the motorcycle, negotiate the price and be sure the driver knows the destination.

Be careful to mount from the left side of the motorcycle to avoid a nasty burn from the hot muffler on the right side.

Train

There is one railway in Benin that goes from Cotonou to Parakou, with stops in Bohicon, Dassa, and Savè. It generally runs once a day to three times a week. The train station in Cotonou is located one block from Avenue Clozel by the Ganxi neighborhood. One can purchase tickets there and get a recent schedule. The train is temporarily out of service, but is due to be up and running by 2010. The rates are as follows (1st class/2nd class):

Cotonou-Bohicon CFA1,400/1,100
Cotonou-Dassa CFA2,950/2,150
Cotonou-Savè CFA3,700/2,700
Cotonou-Parakou CFA5,600/4,000

Car Rental/Hire

Local car rental is available and the price generally in-cludes the driver's fee, food, and lodging. Prices can vary greatly depending on the type of vehicle, its overall con-dition, and the current price of gas. Renting a bush taxi costs around CFA20,000 per day, plus gas. A jeep or SUV costs around CFA60,000 per day plus gas. The following travel agencies in Cotonou will coordinate car-hire and various tours of Benin and neighboring countries:

Agence Africaine de Tourisme *Tel: 21.31.54.14; www.aatvoyages.com*

Pacific Tourisme *Tel: 21.30.36.99; pacific_voyates@yahoo.fr*

Concorde Voyages *Tel: 21.31.34.13*

Evènemenciel *Tel: 21.31.19.36, info@evenemenciel.com*

For those wanting to travel more independently, there are several international car rental agencies that have offices in Cotonou:

Avis *Tel: 21.38.33.40 / 97.97.70.80; www.avis.com; At the Coto-nou Airport; Open Mon-Fri 8am-12:30pm and 3pm-6:30pm*

Europcar Benin *Tel airport location: 21.31.85.27, downtown of-fice: 21.31.76.35; www.location-voiture.europcar.com; Carré 09 Guinkomey, Avenue Steinmetz 06 BP 10; Open 24 hours*

Hertz *Tel: 21.30.19.24; www.hertz.com; Akpakpa, Complexe 2S1; Open Mon-Fri 8am-12:30pm and 3pm-6:30pm, Sat 8am-1pm, closed on Sundays. There is currently no office at the airport.*

Gas stations are found throughout large cities and along the paved roads in crossroad towns. Pirated gas siphoned off the Nigerian pipelines and smuggled into the country is also sold at roadside stands, displayed in rows of recycled glass bottles.

Typical Price of Gas
Diesel: CFA375/liter
Petrol: CFA350/liter
Prices often fluctuate

Roadside gas service in Benin

Money and Costs

All travelers cheques should be exchanged in Cotonou, as the banks in other large cities such as Bohicon and Parakou are not consistent with their exchange procedures.

Benin shares the same currency as other francophone West African nations, the Franc CFA. The most common bills are CFA 1,000, 2,000, 5,000, and 10,000. In smaller villages and areas beyond commercial centers, change for bills, sometimes even a CFA2,000 bill, can be very difficult to come by. The coin breakdown is: 25, 50, 100, 250, and 500 franc pieces, along with the rare 1, 5, and 10 Franc pieces. Always keep at least CFA1,000 in small change and several small bills to be able to pay a *zemidjan* ride to the bank or place of business where bigger bills can be broken down.

In Cotonou there are several banks and foreign exchange offices around the Ganxi market. The larger banks include Bank of Africa, Société Générale Bancaire Beninoise (SGBB), and Ecobank. Each bank has an ATM where money can be withdrawn in CFA. A quicker bill exchange can be done on the black market: Nigerian money vendors in Jonquet or Zongo sit on their wooden benches under parasols and beckon any foreigner walking by with promises of cheap rates. Take care exchanging money on the street and be sure to know the most current official exchange rate before negotiating. Be sure to count the money before leaving. It is wise to only exchange from U.S. dollars to Francs, and not the other way around; false bills can cause issues once back home.

There are ATMs at the major banks in Cotonou, mostly in the Ganxi neighborhood. Western Union services are accessible in all major towns around the country. Currency exchanges differ from bill to bill. Not all exchange bureaus will accept twenty-dollar bills. Large bills, especially the one hundred-dollar bill, have the best rates. New bills are the best, but if that is not possible ensure that the bills are of the newest print design with minimal wrinkles. Exchange bureaus will reject money if they think it is too wrinkled. British pounds are generally not accepted, so it is wise to travel with Euros or U.S. dollars.

Negotiation is an important component of marketplace purchases and is nearly always expected. A simple bargaining tactic is to avoid acting too interested in an item. Pretend to walk away after hearing a high price and when offering a price, know that it is normal to ask for less than half of the beginning price. Areas with high tourist traffic will prove to be the most difficult in which to negotiate, but it is important to play the bartering game, which can be an intense but enjoyable process. Food sold by the plate at street stands, on the other hand, are generally standard and not really negotiable.

Budget

The amount travelers should budget when visiting Benin obviously depends on the itinerary and the level of comfort preferred. Daily expenses in Cotonou and other cities will be higher if you choose to stay in high-end hotels and eat at Western restaurants. In rural areas, the choices are more limited and less expensive. In small villages, apart from lodging, it is difficult to spend more than CFA2,000 a day. Budget travelers should calculate an average of CFA7,000 per night for lodging, plus CFA3,000-5,000 for food. Getting around in cities by *zemidjan* can cost an additional couple thousand CFA per day. Remaining costs would be for bus and bush taxi travel, museum fees, and souvenir shopping. Consider as well the prices for safaris in the national parks, which can quickly increase the budget.

Tipping

Tipping is generally not expected in hotels, *buvettes*, or restaurants. At the same time, it is not uncommon for people to round up a tab at a *buvette*, for example, and give the server a couple hundred CFA extra. As a traveling *yovo*, one may experience a variety of situations regarding tipping. Beninese are more than willing to help and will do what they can to assist someone who is lost or in need of information. Some may refuse or even seem offended if offered payment for giving directions. Others will take it with gratitude, and a few will ask for a small fee or offer to be hired as a guide.

Food and Drink

Food is a commonly offered gift in Benin. It is also considered impolite to eat in front of someone without offering to share. Don't feel obliged to accept every invitation of *venez manger!* (meaning 'come eat with me!'). It is courteous to simply respond with *bon appétit*. However, if offered a meal in gratitude or in greeting, recognize the importance of sharing a meal. It is an honor to welcome visitors this way.

If possible, avoid giving money with the left hand, which is also considered inappropriate.

In Benin, people often eat with their right hand rather than use silverware. To eat with the left hand is considered inappropriate, though the use of silverware is always polite. A bowl or pitcher of water and soap with which to wash hands is readily available in any casual dining establishment. Avoid using the left hand to give someone food or to shake hands in greeting.

Beninese cuisine is comprised of traditional West African and Brazilian flavors brought from descendants of slaves returning to their ancestral land. Food varies from region to region, largely dependent on the climate and soil composition. Corn, cassava, rice, yams, millet, and sorghum are the staple foodstuffs throughout the country. Fish, game meat, pork, beef, and goat meat are highly valued protein sources. Sauces commonly include tomatoes, onions, chili peppers, various vegetable oils, leafy greens, and spices such as garlic, ginger, and black pepper. Okra sauce, called sauce gombo, is characteristically slimy and usually quite spicy. Some leaves are used to make slimy sauce, while others, such as the gboma leaf, are used to make a sauce that resembles spinach.

The Maggi cube, a chicken or shrimp flavored bouillon, is used ubiquitously to add flavor. Starches—such as corn, potato, cassava, or yam—are commonly served with a small side of raw or fried ground hot peppers.

POPULAR DISHES

Corn based

Pâte - Corn flour, mixed with water, boiled, and stirred until thick and fairly firm. Found in every household at least once a day, this dough-like staple is also sold from small plastic containers and are thus molded, similar to polenta or cream of wheat. Servings of *pâte* cost CFA25 per bowl in villages, and up to CFA100 in the city. *Pâte* can be found nearly everywhere at any time of day, accompanied by a sauce and a form of protein, like boiled eggs or fish. A variation is *pâte rouge*, which has the added ingredients of chicken stock, onions, hot peppers,

A common meal is beans and gari, drizzled with peanut or palm oil, paprika powder, and sometimes dja sauce.

Pâte Recipe

Ingredients

1^1/$_2$ cups corn meal homogenized with 1^1/$_2$ cups water
1^1/$_2$ cups additional corn meal
2 cups water

After thoroughly mixing the corn meal and water, heat the two cups of water until just before boiling. Add the homogenized corn meal/water to the heated water, without decreasing heat. Stir. When boiling, add additional corn meal and beat with wooden spoon over heat. Reduce heat slightly and let the mixture thicken for 3-5 minutes. Remove from heat and pour into serving dish.

Sauce

4 tbs oil
2 large onions
3 cloves garlic
black pepper to taste
14 oz. crushed tomatoes (or, in Benin, 'many' crushed tomatoes)
2-3 chili peppers, or to taste
1 tbs chicken or beef bouillon, or vegetable or meat stock.

Sauté all ingredients, except the bouillon, in hot oil for about five minutes or until the onions are soft. Add the liquid and let simmer for about 20 minutes, or until the ingredients are well mixed. Add other spices, green leaves, and/or meat and fish as desired.

basics

tomatoes, and/or red palm oil. Known in Fon as *amiwo*, this form of *pâte* is traditionally served during festivities or ceremonies when chickens are prepared and the stock can be used in the preparation.

Akassa - Fermented white *pâte* with a more gelatinous consistency and a slightly acidic taste. In villages, *akassa* is wrapped in the leaf of a teak tree or cassava leaves and sold with *dja*, a widely used spicy sauce of ground onions, tomatoes, hot peppers, and other spices fried in oil. Another popular akassa accompaniment is fried fish with a boiled tomato and onion sauce called *moyo*.

Bouillie - Sweetened corn flour porridge often served with peanuts or fried peanut butter snacks called klouie-klouie. Sometimes bouillie is made of soy flour, for a more nutritional breakfast.

Com - Another variation of *pâte* but this version is even more fermented than *akassa*, and has a stronger flavor. It is usually served with smoked hot peppers and fried fish. This is a popular dish in the Mono region.

Cassava Based

Africa is the biggest producer of cassava, a starchy tuber that is the third largest source of carbohydrates for human consumption in the world. It is filling and has a significant amount of calcium and vitamin C, but it is poor in protein and other nutrients. It is a common staple in the Beninese diet in many different forms.

Gari is made from peeled and grated cassava tubers, which are then pressed, allowed to ferment for a few days, dried, and sifted to resemble course flour. It is often simply mixed with water, sugar, peanuts, a little lemon juice, and sometimes evaporated milk. This is a common snack, though the Beninese warn that if eaten too often it will cause ulcers. It expands significantly upon contact with water, thus once in the stomach it quickly induces a sensation of being full. Gari production is a simple way to preserve cassava, which renders it readily available and inexpensive. Because it is also easy to prepare, gari has been dubbed the 'poor man's food.' Gari flour is also used to make a form of *pâte* called *eba*.

Gari for sale

Tapioca pudding is made from a derivative of cassava resembling pearl-like grains which turn translucent when boiled. *Attiéké* is an Ivorian cassava dish that resembles couscous, served with hot peppers and onions or moyo sauce with fried fish.

Cassava tubers are also eaten fried or boiled like potatoes, or pounded into a thick mash called foufou, with a consistency resembling elastic mashed potatoes. The leaves of the cassava plant are used to prepare sauces rich in minerals and protein.

Yam Based

The West African yam is a large white tuber, similar to the cassava.

Igname pilé is a dish of pounded yams traditionally served with peanut or palm nut sauce and an accompaniment of meat, fish, or fried wagasi. This dish is served throughout the country, but the Collines département and much of the north is known for having the best *igname pilé*. Since the yams are boiled and pounded to order, the dish takes time to prepare. It must be consumed immediately or the consistency of the yams will become hard and less palatable. The pounding of the yams is a must-see: three to four strong workers pounding in synchronized strokes into one giant mortar.

The sap from the yam tuber is a skin irritant.

Ignames frites, or fried yams, are a popular substitute for French fried potatoes.

Pâte noir, or black *pâte*, also known as *telibo*, is made of dried, ground yam tubers that are sifted into fine flour, and then stirred into boiling water to form a dark gray dough. The yams are dried and preserved to make black *pâte* between yam harvests. It is not considered a refined meal and has a similar association as *eba*.

Rice

Rice is served in many dishes, most often cooked plain and served with a sauce. A variation is the notorious **West African jollof rice**, or *riz au gras* (grease rice). This dish consists of rice, tomatoes, tomato paste, onion, salt, palm oil, spices (such as nutmeg, ginger, black pepper or cumin) and chili pepper, all cooked in one pot. Some cooks also add vegetables and meats.

SNACK FOODS

Western food such as Fries, steak, salad, pizza, and pasta can be found in upscale hotels and restaurants of larger towns throughout the country. American, Middle Eastern, and Asian meals are available, but mostly limited to Cotonou.

Snack foods are prevalent in Beninese cuisine. **Beignets**, or doughnuts, are sold throughout the day in almost any location. In the afternoons and evenings bean *beignets* are served with ground chili pepper sauce. There is a fried, spicy, corn flour *beignet* called **avoomi**, which means 'dog poop' in Fon. These are made by rolling corn flour dough into teaspoon-sized balls, pressing five of them together in a line (tapering the ends) and then deep frying them. It's a delicious, crunchy snack, and fun to talk about!

Dokons are sweet, fried balls of wheat flour most popular in the morning with bouillie. **Gateaux** are a crunchy form of dokon, like fried cookies. **Klouie-klouie** are crispy and crunchy snacks made with corn or peanut butter that vary in shape and form according to region. In Couffo they resemble dry rings of fried peanut butter. In Djougou and much of the north, they are made with the added ingredients of ginger or hot pepper and sugar.

Other filling snacks, ideal for lunch or before dinner time, are deep fried breadfruit slices, plantains, sweet potatoes, cassava, or yams. All of these snacks taste best and are safest to eat when hot. Little bags of roasted peanuts, boiled corn and peanuts, and sweet cookie-like snacks such as soy biscuits and coconut milk cookies are sold at taxi stops and market stalls. There are endless varieties of fried staples to be discovered, sweet, salty, or spicy.

Chick peas and beans for sale

Bread is popular in Benin, and most towns have a bakery that produces fresh, crusty baguettes daily. Vendors bike or drive through the town and countryside to sell fresh bread, yelling '*Pain chaud!*' or 'Warm bread!' Varieties of sweet breads, or *brioche,* are sold at street stands and in the market. The sweet breads are great gifts for Beninese neighbors and popular with the children. In more remote villages where there are no bakeries or bread vendors, bread is a luxury.

Cafeterias in Benin typically consist of a bar with stools where one can buy instant coffee or tea saturated with sweetened condensed milk. Also available are fresh baguette bread, omelet sandwiches, spaghetti, and yogurt or curdled milk. Cafeterias are commonly managed by Muslims from the north of Benin and other countries including Guinea and Burkina Faso. They generally do not sell alcohol, and are open early in the morning and late at night.

FRUITS AND VEGGIES

There are many fruits available according to the season and climate. Fresh tomatoes, chili peppers, onions, and other typical vegetable ingredients are mainly available during the rainy season. **Mango** and **avocado** season is from mid-March to June. Wild mangos are small and the flesh is stringy, though the flavor is wonderful. Grafted mangos, which are larger and have a smoother texture, are much more popular. **Papaya** season is usually from November to January. Southern départements have an abundance of **bananas**, **plantains**, **pineapples**, and **oranges** sold in the markets and alongside the roads. These fruits are mostly available throughout the year. Less common fruits include **guavas**, **watermelons**, and **breadfruit**. Guava and breadfruit depend on the trees, though watermelon depends on the harvest and water availability in the region.

Inside a Beninese Kitchen

A typical Beninese kitchen burns wood or other vegetation for fuel. Charcoal is made locally and sold, and can also be used in the kitchen fire. Propane gas and stoves exist but are much less common, and mostly unheard of in small villages. Traditional cooking stoves, called *foyer* in French, are most often made of worked earth, though less efficient versions consist simply of three or more stones that support the *marmite*, or cooking pot. The kitchen is kept apart from the rest of the home because of the heat and smoke. Other necessary elements to a basic Beninese cuisine, or kitchen, is the stone grinding block, a flat slab on which tomatoes, garlic, onions, peppers, and spices are crushed and liquefied. Once *pâte* and accompanying sauces have been prepared in marmites, they are kept warm in plastic coolers before the meal is partitioned and distributed to family members. The patriarch receives the largest share, meat included, on his own plate. The elderly and the children then each receive a portion befitting their age and needs. The mother, or the woman responsible for cooking, eats her share after everyone has been served. If eating with a guest, the host often shares the same plate as a sign of friendship.

DRINKS

La Beninoise is the national **beer** and the cheapest. It is brewed in Cotonou and Parakou. Other common beers are Castel, Flag, and imports such as Heineken, Tuborg, Star, and Guiness. Though not every brand is available everywhere, these are the basic prices nationwide for beer, which come in small/large bottles.

Bottles are recycled and must be returned if the drinks are taken from a *buvette*.

Beninoise: CFA250/500
Castel, Flag: CFA325/700
Star and other Nigerian beers: CFA700
Imported European beers: CFA700/1,200

Palm wine is harvested directly from the felled palm tree. This milky white liquid is sweet and tangy and best when refrigerated. A glass costs about CFA100 at a *buvette* and is usually served cold, or for the more daring, direct-ly from the felled tree.

Sodabi is distilled palm wine, or moonshine. This is the most renouned national drink, though its quality and potency vary greatly. Prices range from CFA600-1200 per liter.

Tchoukoutou, also known as *shakparo*, is a tradi-tionally brewed beer. Village women use sorghum, the second most important cereal grain in Africa, to make this beer. The drink is brown and cloudy in appearance, thirst-quenching, earthy, tart, and slightly acidic. The women allow the beer to ferment naturally in familial calabashes or clay pots. Tchoukoutou is sold at the mar-ket throughout the country, but especially in the north. Stalls are reserved especially for the consumption of this popular drink. Men and women alike sit along a cement wall and Tchoukoutou vendors serve their product in calabash bowls (one serving costs CFA50-100). In larger towns, one might find 'bottled' tchoukoutou in clear plastic bottles with a breathing hole in the cap to release the gases dispersed in the fermentation phase that con-tinues after bottling.

Non-alcoholic drinks are served at all bars and *bu-vettes* and include Coca-Cola, Sprite, Fanta, and various flavors of Fizzi or Youki drinks: Grapefruit, Fruit Cock-tail, Tonic, and Moka. In the south and along the Togo border, another popular sweet drink is Lion Killer, which resembles Sprite but with a slight orange flavor. Stan-dard prices are CFA250/400 for a small/large.

FanMilk is a brand of ice cream, yogurt, and fruit juice snack packaged in Ghana and sold throughout Be-nin, Togo, Niger, and Ghana. Refrigerated trucks bring shipments to the FanMilk shops where men on bicycles fill their attached coolers with the frozen desserts, and then pedal throughout the town selling these refreshing treats. Flavors include FanChoco, FanYogo, FanIce, and Tampico. Prices range from CFA50 to 200.

Women and children at the market often have coo-lers of cold water and iced drinks. Frozen hibiscus juice, lemon water, sweet Lipton tea, and tap water are sold for CFA25-100 in clear little plastic bags. They may be quite refreshing and tasty, but aren't recommended for those with sensitive stomachs.

basics

Accommodations

Cotonou offers a broad range of accommodations, from backpacker hostels to multi-national luxury hotels. The majority of hotels across the country fall into three categories: Budget (CFA4,000-9,000), mid-range (CFA10,000-20,000), and upscale (CFA20,000-40,000). Budget hotels usually offer a private shower and toilet in the room, or have a shared toilet. In rural locations, modern plumbing is often replaced with communal pit latrines and bucket showers. Many hotels do not provide mosquito nets, but instead have a fan in the room which helps deter the mosquitoes. Not all establishments have screened windows, so it is essential to travel with mosquito repellent and incense coils (available in roadside kiosks). Mid-range hotels usually have private baths, air-conditioning and in-room televisions. Due to frequent water cuts and power outages inherent throughout the country, most hotels have a bucket of water for back-up in the bathrooms. If the bucket is not full upon arrival, be sure to fill it and keep it filled in case the water is cut when it comes time to shower or use the toilet. Some upscale hotels, especially in Cotonou, have their own water reserves and generators, so they usually remain immune to outages.

It's a good idea to carry a mosquito net if planning to stay in more budget accommodations.

Only the top end hotels in Cotonou such as Novotel, Marina, and Hotel du Port accept major credit cards and Euros, the rest will only accept CFA francs. Room keys are commonly left at the reception desk upon leaving the building. If guests prefer to keep the key in their possession, it should be discussed with the receptionist.

Camping is not altogether common in Benin, but there are facilities in tourist hot-spots such as Grand Popo and around the wildlife parks in the north. Camping typically costs CFA2,000-5,000 per person. Permission is necessary to camp on hotel properties in other towns for a similar rate. (See hotel descriptions by region.)

Communication

Internet cafés are common throughout the country, especially in large cities. Cotonou and Porto-Novo are filled

with cafés; Lokossa, Bohicon, Abomey, Parakou, and Natitingou have a few as well. Towns like Azové, Dassa,
Savalou, Djougou, Tanguieta, Kandi, and Malanville
should have at least one, but service can be inconsistent.

Cellular phones are worth purchasing for longer
stays. Phones and SIM cards are inexpensive and can
easily be filled with credit and resold at the end of a trip.
There are mobile phone stores in all major towns. Nokia
phones are the most affordable and start at about
CFA30,000. A SIM card usually costs about the same, but
promotions are frequent, and one can find them as cheap
as CFA10,000.

There are multiple cellular companies with many
towers in or near all major towns, but service can be
unreliable and is ever-changing. Some remote villages
have coverage, while many still do not. The current pre-
vailing companies are: Areeba MTN, Telecel MOOV, Bell
Benin, Global Com, and Librecom. Phone credit cards are
sold in kiosks, boutiques, cellular phone booths, and
from roaming merchants at busy intersections throughout the country, even in the smallest villages. They are
sold in increments of CFA100, 200, 500, 2,000, 5,000,
and 10,000. The cheapest means of quick communication is by text message. Incoming calls are free, and
often one will 'beep' the other to instigate a return call.

Safety and Security

Benin is a generally safe country to travel, but
as in any foreign country, visitors should observe basic precautions. DO NOT travel after
dark unless it is an emergency, especially on
remote highways and dirt roads. There have
been a number of road block robberies at night

> The Beninese are very
> hospitable and open to
> foreigners. Harassment
> is not common.

in recent years, especially in the north. The National Police periodical-
ly conduct vehicle checks at provisional roadblocks in an effort to
improve road safety and reduce the increasing number of carjackings.
When stopped at such a roadblock, drivers must have all of the vehicle's documentation available to present to the authorities. If
traveling in a taxi, the police and local military may request foreigners
to present identification or passport.

If you are the victim of a crime while in Benin, it is important to
contact both the local police and your nearest embassy or consulate
where the staff can assist in the legal process. Your country's repre-

sentation will also assist in finding medical care and help contact family members or friends. The investigation and prosecution of the crime is solely the responsibility of local authorities, but embassy officers can explain the local criminal justice process and find an attorney if needed. The loss or theft of a passport should also be reported immediately to the local police and the nearest appropriate embassy or consulate.

Foreign travelers who commit a crime are subject to Beninese laws and regulations, and may not be given the protections available to individuals under their home country laws. Penalties for breaking the law can be more severe and may result in being expelled, arrested, or imprisoned. Penalties for possession, use, or trafficking in illegal drugs in Benin are severe, and convicted offenders can expect long jail sentences and heavy fines.

Emergency Call Numbers in Cotonou

Cotonou Hospital (C.N.H.U.) *Tel: 21.30.01.55*

Ambulance *Tel: 21.30.06.56*

State Police *Tel: 21.31.58.99*

Cotonou Security Sûreté urbaine de Cotonou *Tel: 21.31.20.11*

Embassy of the United States of America *Tel: 21.30.06.50 / 21.30.03.84, www.cotonou.usembassy.gov, Near Camp Guézo military camp and across the street from the French Embassy, Open Mon-Thurs 8am-12:30pm and 1:30pm-5pm, Friday 8am-1:30pm*

Embassy of the United Kingdom *Tel: 21.30.32.65, Mobile: 95.85.38.73, 08 BP 0352; At the British School of Cotonou in Haie Vive.*

Embassy of France *Tel: 21.30.02.25 / 21.30.02.26; www.ambafrance-bj.org; ambafrance.cotonou@diplomatie.gouv.fr; Avenue du Pape Jean Paul II BP 966; Open Mon-Fri 8am-12:30pm and 3pm-6pm*

Embassy of Germany *Tel: 21.31.29.67 / 21.31.29.68; info@cotonou.diplo.de,7 Avenue Jean Paul II, BP 504*

The Embassy of Canada *www.dfait-maeci.gc.ca/abidjan*
The Government of Canada has no resident representation in Benin. Services are offered through the Canadian Embassy in Abidjan, Cote d'Ivoire.

Swimming Off the Coast

Swimming in the coastal waters of Benin is dangerous due to its violent rip currents. There are no lifeguards or established emergency services on the beaches, and drowning occurs frequently among local fishermen. Swimming should perhaps be kept to the safety of hotel swimming pools.

Health

Malaria is prevalent year round throughout the country, and is a serious risk to travelers. The highest risk period is the rainy season, from April to November. Malarial prophylaxis is highly recommended and visitors should consult their doctor regarding which type is appropriate. Common prophylaxes include Larium, Doxycycline, and Malarone.

The Anopholes mosquito, which carries the malaria parasite, typically comes out late at night, between 11pm-5am, so be sure to sleep beneath a mosquito net. In case none are available, be sure to travel with mosquito coils. This effective bug-repellent incense is sold for around CFA800 at nearly any kiosk. When out at night, wear long pants, sleeves, socks, and covered shoes, or at least bring insect repellent, as the mosquitoes are aggressive and will penetrate thin clothing.

To avoid parasites and waterborne diseases in food and water, drink only bottled water or travel with purifying tablets as bottled water is not always available outside the cities. Street vendors offer sealed plastic bags of water, but these are filled from the tap water and should be avoided. If staying for a longer period of time, it is possible to grow accustomed to the tap water by mixing tap water with bottled, though many villages only have access to well water, pumps, or irrigation ponds. Avoid consuming raw foods, including vegetables, lettuce, and fruits that cannot be peeled, which can transmit gastro-intestinal illnesses such as food poisoning and typhoid fever.

Vaccinations

Mandatory vaccination: Yellow Fever
Recommended vaccinations: Tetanus, Polio, Meningitis, Typhoid Fever, Hepatitis A, Hepatitis B, Rabies, Diphteria.

MEDICAL FACILITIES IN COTONOU

Medical facilities in Benin are limited and not all medicines are available. Travelers should bring their own supplies of prescription drugs and preventive medicines. Not all medicines and prescription drugs available in Benin are USFDA-approved. That being said, pharmacies, hospitals, and private clinics are located in most major towns. Consultations and lab tests are not at all expensive and commonly required medication and antibiotics are widely accessible. Doctors speak French very well, but few speak English. In case of emergencies, go to the nearest hospital. Otherwise, it is best to seek treatment in Cotonou.

Clinics

Polyclinique Les Cocotiers, Dr. Assani. *Tel: 21.30.14.31 / 21.30.14.20; BP 1227; Cadjehoun intersection across from Cadjehoun post office*

Clinique d'Akpakpa *Tel: 21.33.14.37 / 21.33.06.40; PK 2 on the road to Porto-Novo, on the right.*
The clinic is generally used for x-rays. Dr. Agboton speaks English.

Clinique Mahouna *Cadjehoun neighborhood not far from UNICEF*
It is primarily an obstetrician's office (Dr. Hekpazo) but the rooms are rented for other cases and doctors from other specialties consult there. Also has a laboratory.

Doctors

The following doctors can be consulted in their offices. Some will make house-calls:

Dr. Dominique Atchade *Tel: 21.30.10.70; Speaks English. His office is located at the National University Hospital (CNHU).*

Dr. Anne Brunet Apithy *Tel: 21.31.35.26; Speaks English. Office located in "La Residence" neighborhood.*

Dr. A.M. Caudron-Tidjani *Tel: 21.31.56.34; In the SCOA-Gbeto neighborhood.*

Dr. Anne Hekpazo, OB/GYN *Tel: 21.30.14.35; Located at Clinic Mahouna*

Fruit vendor slicing pineapples

Helping and Experiencing Local Communities

One great way to contribute to a community is through educational support. The majority of students drop out of school in the equivalent of 5th or 6th grade because of the inability to afford the basic fees, uniforms, and books (only primary education is free in Benin). These costs can total US$100-$150 per year, a significant amount for a country with such low per capita annual income.

Education is highly valued in Benin and schools are very receptive to foreigners. Find a local school teacher and arrange to observe classes and interact with the students. Notebooks, pens, and pencils make fantastic gifts and are best donated via the school staff, who can organize an official distribution. Partnerships with foreign schools are common, especially with France. A visitor could easily establish correspondence partnerships with secondary English classes, or raise funds to sponsor students.

There are many Benin-based nongovernmental associations who welcome volunteers, including orphanages and environmental and health education groups. Many are listed below.

BENINESE DEVELOPMENT ORGANIZATIONS

Local and Regional

Association FEFA *www.assofefa.africa-web.org*
FEFA is a Cotonou-based NGO that engages in humanitarian and development activities such as woman and youth development in literacy, micro-finance, and trade skills. They are also involved in sanitation and health dispensary projects, for which FEFA hosts foreigners in the health field seeking to learn and train in Benin.

Nature Tropicale *www.ntong-benin.ifrance.com*
Established in 1995, Nature Tropicale is an environmental NGO that promotes natural resource management and the appreciation of nature through environmental education in local populations. This organization works mostly with youth groups, and encourages young leaders to participate in educating their communities on the importance of conservation. Nature Tropicale works nationwide, with their main office in the Akpakpa neighborhood of Cotonou.

ESE-Benin *www.esebenin.africa-web.org*
ESE (Education, Santé [Health], Environnement), is a Cotonou based NGO fighting poverty at a local level. They place special focus on working with youth and women, promoting literacy and aiding the population in reducing malnutrition and illnesses.

Bethesda Benin *www.bethesdabenin.org*
Bethesda is based in Cotonou and works in partnership with German Evangelical Development Services. It is divided into three departments: Health, Environment, and Microfinance. Since its establishment in the 1990s, Bethesda has initiated

significant projects in each of these domains; they constructed the Besthesda Hospital in Cotonou, led recycling workshops, and waste management projects.

International

Benin Education Fund (BEF) *www.benineducationfund.org*
Established in 1998, the BEF is a U.S. based not-for-profit that provides scholarships and educational support to students in the Atakora département. Over the last decade, more than 450 students have been able to stay in school because of their program. BEF is primarily funded by donations from individuals in the U.S. and Canada, with material support such as school supplies and office space donated from individuals and organizations in Benin. For $300 a year, one can sponsor a high school student. This donation includes public school tuition and fees, supplies, uniforms, books, tutoring when needed, and housing assistance for those who must leave their villages to attend high school.

Peace Corps Partnership Fund *www.peacecorps.gov*
The Peace Corps website offers opportunities to read about projects initiated by current Peace Corps Volunteers around the globe. Specific projects are posted and potential donors may sift through the list until one beckons their interest. Or, alternatively, donations may be made to a general fund for special areas of focus such as business development, agriculture, or education.

Kiva *www.kiva.org*
Kiva's mission is to connect people through lending for the sake of alleviating poverty. It is the world's first person-to-person micro-lending website, empowering individuals to lend directly to unique entrepreneurs around the globe. Starting at US$25, one can contribute to a loan for an individual in Benin and then receive updates on the evolution and progress of the individual's projects.

Hands Around The World *www.hatw.org.uk*
Hands Around the World is a UK-registered charitable trust which seeks to help vulnerable children around the world, encouraging enthusiastic and well-prepared short-term volunteers to offer practical help, skill-sharing, support and friendship.

Online Volunteering Service *www.onlinevolunteering.org*
The Online Volunteering service is one of the United Nations Volunteers (UNV) program's corporate tools to mobilize volunteers for development. It connects volunteers with organizations working for sustainable human development:

The Hunger Project *www.thp.org*
The Hunger Project is a global, non-profit, strategic organization committed to the sustainable end of world hunger. It has been working in Benin since 1997 and is currently empowering over 31,000 partners in 11 epicenter communities to end their own hunger and poverty

Atlantique & Littoral

The Atlantique *département* is divided into the communes of Abomey-Calavi, Allada, Kpomassè, Ouidah, So-Ava, Toffo, Tori-Bossito, and Zè. In 1999, the Littoral *département* was split off from the Atlantique and now encompasses only the city of Cotonou.

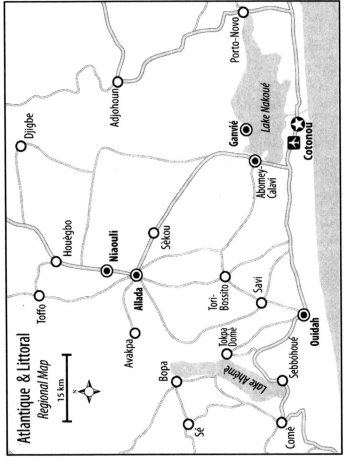

Atlantique & Littoral
Regional Map

15 km

Cotonou

Cotonou, meaning 'the mouth of the river of death' in Fon, was originally a small fishing village based at the mouth of the Ouémé River within the powerful kingdom of Dahomey. The French first arrived here in 1851 and established a trading post in agreement with King Guézo of Dahomey. The king later granted the French control of Cotonou, where the French navy could be based to defend the people of Dahomey from the British in nearby Lagos. Through the decades, Cotonou grew to be the economic capital and the largest city in the country. Today, it houses two-thirds of the nation's industries, the headquarters of the nation's largest banks and Benin's Autonomous Port, an important trade hub with neighboring countries and Europe. Cotonou continues to grow at an alarming rate and has over 1 million residents (by far the largest population of Beninese cities). The city is cut in two by a lagoon canal, dug by the French in 1855, which connects Lake Nokoué and the Atlantic Ocean. Two bridges span the water; the *Ancien Pont*, or Old Bridge, and the *Nouveau Pont*, or New Bridge. Even though Porto-Novo is the official capital of Benin, most government buildings and all embassies are in Cotonou.

> The pollution from the lack of waste management and the huge number of cars and motorcycles combine with the heat to create a humid, grimy atmosphere.

GETTING THERE AND AWAY

Bus/Taxi

Buses heading north, such as Benin-Routes (*Tel: 97.07.18.89 / 93.14.76.22*) and Confort Lines (*Tel: 21.32.58.15*), depart each morning at 7am sharp from the Etoile Rouge round point in Cotonou. Others take off from Carrefour St. Michel or *Gare de Jonquet* (see neighborhood descriptions on pg 84). Be sure to arrive at least 20 minutes in advance to get a seat for closer destinations such as Bohicon and Dassa. There is a set fare for each bus line depending on the destination, with higher fares for the air-conditioned buses. There may be an additional fee of CFA500-1,000 to store luggage underneath the bus if it exceeds one or two bags per person.

For information on travel to bordering countries from Cotonou, see *Getting There – Land* (pg 57)

Airport Information

The international airport (*Tel: 21.30.10.01 / 21.30.13.78*), baptized 'Cardinal Bernardin Gantin' in 2008, is located at the far west end of town. The airport has a small terminal where arriving travelers pass the proof of vaccination and visa checkpoint, and then continue to the baggage collection. Porters in uniform swarm the baggage claim, offering their services for a small fee. There is a money exchange bureau in the main building, and several top class hotels such as Hotel du Lac, Croix du Sud, Le Chevalier, and Novotel (see accommodations on page 97) provide complimentary shuttle service to and from the airport. Taxis are at the doors and the normal rate to the city is CFA2,500-5,000. *Zemidjan*s are not allowed to be stationed there, but a group of them wait just beyond the parking lot. A *zemidjan* ride is CFA200-500 (new arrivals should be prepared to bargain to avoid being over-charged by ambitious *zem* drivers).

Bernardin Gantin

Bernardin Gantin is hailed as one of the most successful Beninese people. Born in Toffo in 1922, Gantin joined the seminary at age 14, and achieved priesthood in 1951. He then went to Rome to study theology and was named archbishop of Cotonou by Pope John XXIII in January 1960. For over a decade he worked from his home country to promote the founding of religious schools and support catechism in the diocese. In 1971, Gantin was called back to Rome where he participated in the Second Vatican Council and was made a cardinal in 1977 by Pope Paul VI. He worked for 30 years with the Roman Curia in a variety of positions and was the first black African cardinal to hold such high appointments within the Vatican City. Cardinal Bernardin Gantin retired and returned to Benin in 2002, where he continued to work with the Catholic Church until he died in 2008.

atlantique & littoral

Traffic in Cotonou

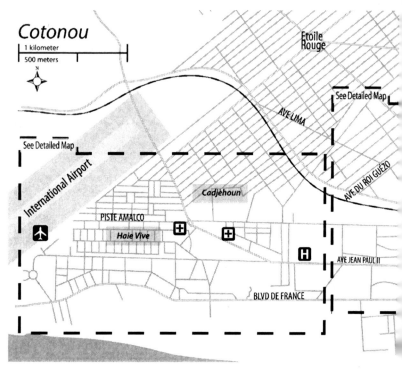

GETTING AROUND

The four-lane highways leading into the city are very congested throughout the day. Traffic here is stereotypical of a 'third world' country: a two-lane road is squeezed to hold at least three vehicles across, while small motorcycles weave in and out of the bumper-to-bumper traffic. Many intersections are roundabouts, and these, combined with the local driving style, give the impression of utter chaos. *Zemidjan*s in Cotonou have yellow shirts and can be seen on every corner, at any time. They make some narrow escapes and it is important for passengers to hold on to the seat of the motorcycle and not the driver. Luggage can be stored in front, balanced across the handlebars or between the driver's knees. The ride can be harrowing—don't be afraid to ask him to slow down. It is important to relax, because it's much easier to ride a motorcycle in oppressive traffic with a calm passenger, than with a stiff and anxious one. Some major intersections are: *Etoile Rouge*, or Red Star, in memory of the communist era, St. Michel, found by the church of this name, *Le Stade d'Amitié*, the national stadium, and *Carrefour Godomé*, which is the junction between the highways heading north and west. These intersections are common land marks and many taxis park along the road. Most *zemidjan* rides within the central, commercial part of Cotonou should cost

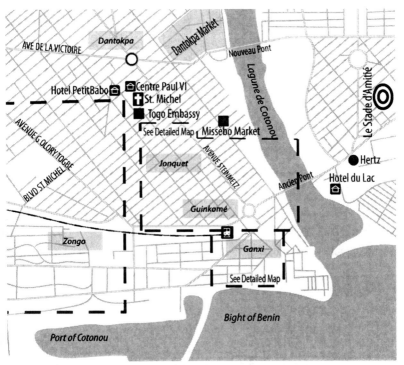

between CFA100-200. There is no intracity bus system in Cotonou, but there are shared city taxis on the main roads that cost CFA200-700 to get around town. Otherwise, neighborhoods such as Ganxi, Haie Vive, Jonquet, Guinkonmé, Dantokpa, and Cadjehoun are worth exploring at leisure on foot.

STAYING SAFE

Crime issues in Cotonou are similar to any big city around the globe. The beaches have a high risk of muggings for foreigners at any time, day or night. Women should be careful out in clubs and bars alone at night. Avoid traveling on foot after nightfall, especially alone, and do not take dark side streets. Be particularly cautious of your valuables in congested areas such as Missèbo and Dantokpa markets. Riding *zemidjan*s at night can be dangerous. Some motorcycle drivers may approach foreigners and claim to be *zemidjan*s when they really aren't so be sure to insist on seeing the yellow shirt with the registration number before getting on. Foreigners have fallen victim to violent organized muggings by teams of fake *zems*.

Police/Security

Cotonou Security -Sûreté urbaine de Cotonou *Tel: 21.31.20.11*

Hospital

Centre National Hospitalier et Universitaire (C.N.H.U) *State-run; Tel: 21.30.01.55/Ambulance Tel: 21.30.06.56; Cadjehoun, near the French Cultural Center and across from the Presidential Palace*

Clinics

These two clinics are privately run and have the best reputation, especially among expatriates:

Polyclinique les Cocotiers *Private; Tel: 21.30.14.20; Haie Vive*

Clinique Mahouna *Private; Tel: 21.30.14.35; Cadjehoun; Near Carrefour Cadjehoun, off the paved road.*

Pharmacies

Pharmacie Cocotiers *Near Haie Vive*

Pharmacie Jonquet *In the center of Jonquet*

Pharmacie Camp Guezo *Close to the U.S. embassy and Bangkok Terrace Restaurant*

Pharmacie Notre Dame: *Avenue Clozel in Ganxi*

NEIGHBORHOODS

Haie Vive and Cadjehoun Neighborhoods

Located close to the airport, these upper-class neighborhoods are where many expatriates reside. The paved road running down the center of the Haie Vive neighborhood, called Piste Amalco, stems from *Carrefour Cadjehoun,* a round-point distinguished by its green-painted water tower advertising the Moov mobile phone company. This particular area boasts high-end European restaurants, grocery stores, and internet cafés. Palatial villas and walled concessions decorated with bougainvilleas have security guards, rendering the neighborhoods peaceful and chic in contrast to the rest of the city. A group of Touareg vendors set up shop next to the New Livingstones restaurant, with a brilliant display of fine silver jewelry and stone carvings. Pricier handicrafts and souvenir shops can be found along Piste Amalco, such as Farafina and Bric a Brac.

Jonquet and Guinkomé

These two neighborhoods border each other and house many small hotels, pleasant and reasonably priced restaurants, bars, and dance clubs. The main strip in Jonquet is lively day and night, lined with kiosks, food stands including tasty rotisserie chicken, and Nigerian money vendors. The Jonquet taxi *gare* has vehicles destined for the Mono-Couffo region. There is both a large mosque and a Catholic church near one another on Avenue Proche. Ganxi market is within easy walking distance of Guinkomé.

Ganxi Neighborhood

Ganxi, pronounced *ganhee*, is a commercial neighborhood situated by the beach. It has a smaller covered market that specializes in fresh produce, seafood, and meat. Voluptuous *marché mamans* beckon shoppers with a wealth of tropical fruits and vegetables—even hard to find squash and eggplant. Around the perimeter of the market, other vendors offer handicraft souvenirs, CDs, and Nigerian bootleg DVDs. Beyond the market, there are Lebanese-run grocery stores with imported goods from Europe, book and stationary stores, and a great variety of restaurants (see pg 91). Much of Cotonou's working class comes to eat lunch in the cafeterias towards the beach. Ganxi neighborhood also has a number of banks with ATMs and money exchange bureaus.

atlantique & littoral

Dantokpa taxi gare

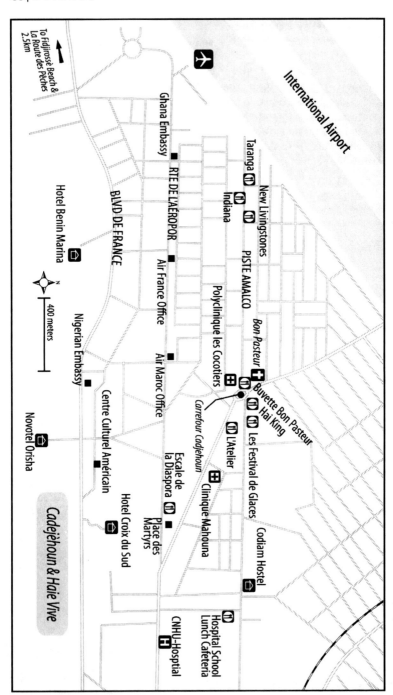

International Airport

To Fidjrossè Beach &
La Route des Pêches
2.5km

Ghana Embassy

RTE DE L'AEROPOR

BLVD DE FRANCE

Hotel Benin Marina

N

400 meters

Nigerian Embassy

Centre Culturel Américain

Novotel Orisha

Taranga

Indiana

New Livingstones

PISTE AMALCO

Polyclinique les Cocotiers

Air France Office

Air Maroc Office

Bon Pasteur

Buvette Bon Pasteur

Hai King

Carrefour Codjehoun

Escale de
la Diaspora

L'Atelier

Les Festival de Glaces

Clinique Mahouna

Codiam Hostel

Hotel Croix du Sud

Place des
Martyrs

CNHU-Hospital

Hospital School
Lunch Cafeteria

Cadjèhoun & Haie Vive

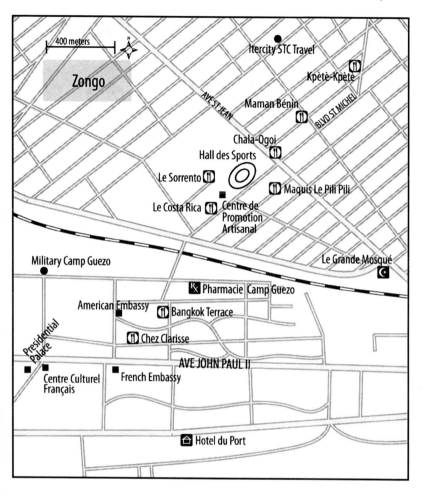

Itercity STC Travel
Kpètè-Kpète
Zongo
400 meters
N
AVE ST JEAN
BLVD ST MICHEL
Maman Bénin
Chala-Ogoi
Hall des Sports
Le Sorrento
Maquis Le Pili Pili
Le Costa Rica
Centre de Promotion Artisanal
Military Camp Guezo
Le Grande Mosqué
Pharmacie Camp Guezo
American Embassy
Bangkok Terrace
Chez Clarisse
Presidential Palace
AVE JOHN PAUL II
Centre Culturel Français
French Embassy
Hotel du Port

La Gerbe D'Or
Bank of Africa
La Verdure
O'Grill
Marché Ganxi
AVE CLOZEL
La Brochette d'Or
Post Office
EcoBank
La Fondation Zinsou
Nigerian Embassy
Ganxi Maquis
Hotel de la Plage
Ganxi
100 Meters

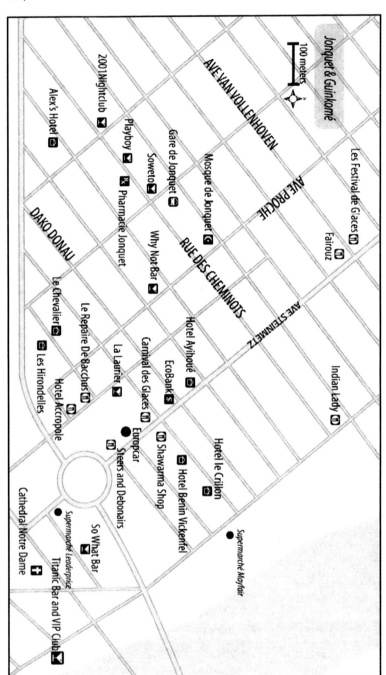

Jonquet & Guinkomé

100 meters

AVE VAN VOLLENHOVEN

AVE PROCHE

RUE DES CHEMINOTS

AVE STEMMETZ

DAKO DONAU

Les Festival de Glaces 🏨
Fairouz

Indian Lady 🏨

2001 Nightclub

Alex's Hotel 🏨

Playboy

Gare de Jonquet

Soweto

Mosque de Jonquet

Pharmacie Jonquet

Why Not Bar

Hotel Ayihoué 🏨

EcoBank $

Carnival des Glaces 🏨

La Laurier

Le Chevalier 🏨

Le Repaire De Bacchus 🏨

Les Hirondelles

Hotel Accropole 🏨

Europcar
Steers and Debonairs 🏨

Shawarma Shop

Hotel Benin Vickenfel 🏨

Hotel le Crillon 🏨

Supermarché Mayfair

Supermarché Leaderprice
So What Bar

Cathedral Notre Dame ✚

Titanic Bar and VIP Club

SIGHTS AND ACTIVITIES

Dantokpa Market

Walk through the 40-hectare maze of Cotonou's commercial hub. *Dantokpa,* meaning 'snake out of the water' in Fon, is Benin's largest market. It is reported to have a commercial turnover of one billion CFA per day. Here, just about anything is available: fresh produce, packaged imported foods from Asia, traditional and Western clothing, jewelry, electronics, and, of course, ceremonial vodoun items. Endless rows of merchant stands crammed with peddlers and shoppers spread along the lagoon. A simple walk through this market will leave visitors exhausted, yet satiated with the unforgettable memories of the sights, smells, and sounds of a thriving Beninese market.

> **'Real' Prices for Popular Handicrafts**
>
> Small clay necklace:
>   CFA1,500
> Glass bead necklace:
>   CFA3,500
> Ebony keychain:
>   CFA500
> Indigo dyed fabric: (1 *pagne):*
>   CFA4,000
> Small patchwork tapestry:
>   CFA4,000
> Fulani leather sandals:
>   CFA1,500
> Batiks:
>   CFA2,000 (small)
>   CFA10,000 (large)

atlantique & littoral

Missèbo Market

Located near Dantokpa, this giant second-hand clothing market is a whirlwind of aggressive vendors and a great place to find amazing deals. If one has the patience, brand name clothing and shoes can be found at great bargains. Missèbo is also home to many boutiques run by Indians and Middle Easterners selling textiles, miscellaneous household items, and groceries in bulk. There is a wide range of Beninese fabric of all shades, designs, colors and patterns throughout this market.

Cathedral of Notre Dame des Apotres

This eye-catching red and white striped church is commonly known as the *Cathédrale de Cotonou.* It houses a book store that sells books by West African authors, as well as text books. The cathedral is the seat of the Roman Catholic Archdiocese of Cotonou. Bernardin Gantin was the Cardinal of this church from 1960 to 1971, followed by Marcel Honorat Leon Agboton. *Ganxi neighborhood, near the Ancien Pont*

Centre de Promotion Artisanal (CPA)

Handicraft Promotion Center

Located on Blvd Saint Michel, this typical African souvenir shopping center is a village of bungalows laden with ebony sculptures, vases, glass and silver jewelry, Batik drapes, colorful hand-woven fabrics, masks, bronze pieces, and much more. Artisans can be seen at work in the common courtyards behind the bungalows. The CPA is a popular tourist destination, where visitors spend their last day in Benin shopping for gifts before flying home. Vendors are very ambitious and competitive, stopping at nothing to lure shoppers into their Ali Baba-type caves. Prices tend to be quite high, but there are many beautiful crafts and hours worth of exploring.

Centre Culturel Français (CCF)
French Cultural Center
The French Cultural Center is a common meeting place for the French ex-patriats and Beninese artists. The French library includes Parisian magazines and newspapers from the day before. The entrance gallery always has art exhibits, and the center organizes numerous cultural performances in the outdoor theater such as plays, concerts, and dance galas. Contact the center for information on upcoming events. *Tel: 21.30.08.56/21.30.74.79; ccf.cotonou@serv.eit.bj; Avenue Jean Paul II, near the French embassy; 01BP416; Open Tues-Sat, 8am-6pm, plus scheduled events*

Centre Culturel Américain
American Cultural Center
Despite heightened security since 2001, the cultural center has a library and other resources available. The center is often a testing site for collegiate and English language tests. It also offers English classes, internet access, movie nights, and an American education counseling office. *Tel: 21.30.06.50; Fax: 21.30.66.82; Off Avenue de France; Open Mon-Thurs 8am-12:30pm and 1:30pm-5pm, Friday 8am-1:30pm*

La Fondation Zinsou
Started by the Zinsou family in 2005, this private foundation is dedicated to the promotion of traditional and contemporary African art. It displays photography and paintings by prominent Beninese artists such as Romuald Hazoumé, Tchiff, and Bamouss. A principal objective of the museum is to bring the public to appreciate the artistic culture of Benin. With continual exhibits from local art collectors, a shuttle to bring children to the museum, a children's art program called *Les Petits Pinceaux,* and a 'Free Wednesdays' program at the Museum of Abomey, the Fondation Zinsou is making headway. The most recent exposition is 'Benin 2059,' a multimedia artistic installation envisioning Benin in 50 years time. *Tel: 21.32.38.51 / 21.32.27.19; www.fondationzinsou.org; Ganxi neighborhood, behind Ecobank; Open 10am-7pm, closed on Tuesday*

Fidjirossè Beach & La Route des Pêches
The Fishing Road
La Route des Pêches, or The Fishing Road, is a sand road that follows the coast from Fidjirossè Beach all the way to Ouidah, about 30 kilometers west of Cotonou. The road is lined with coconut palms and beachside, makeshift cabins that are available to rent for a picnic. On Sunday afternoons the beach is packed with working class Beninese and expatriates alike, enjoying a picnic and showing off their gleaming

A secluded stretch of Fidjirossé Beach

atlantique & littoral

motorcycles and cars. There are several *buvettes*, restaurants, and a growing number of hotels at Fidjirossè. Some even have sea-water swimming pools.

Abomey-Calavi

This northern suburb of Cotonou is along the road leading to Parakou. The main campus of Benin's National University, founded in 1970, is located here. There are over 16,000 students enrolled at Abomey-Calavi's University, of which at least 3,500 are women. The university has 19 departmental schools and six campuses. The second largest campus is in Parakou. A taxi ride to Abomey-Calavi from the city-center of Cotonou is CFA500-600.

The tourism office for the stilt village of Ganivé (see pg 100) is also located in Abomey-Calavi. Since many tourists head straight for Ganvié via Lake Nokoué upon arrival in Abomey-Calavi, a curious visitor might well be the only *yovo* in town.

EATING AND DRINKING

There are many places to eat in Cotonou and discoveries are made everyday. The international population in Benin stimulates tasty and varied multicultural dining. Lebanese restaurants are common, as are Western-style spots serving pizza, hamburgers, pastas, and ice cream. There are a few Indian, Chinese, and other Asian-style restaurants throughout the city. African cuisine, from Beninese to Senegalese and beyond, can be found on most city blocks and there are now two

South African fast-food chains, Steers and Debonairs, on Avenue Steinmetz. Prices vary depending on the accommodations of the restaurant, such as air conditioning and table service.

High-End

L'Atelier L'Atelier is a French-owned, classy restaurant that serves very high-end African cuisine with French influence. Lunch and dinner are served daily, with jazz every Friday night. The restaurant also serves as an art gallery with exhibition space open to Beninese artists. *Tel: 21.30.17.04; Carrefour Cadjéhoun, beside the SONACOP gas station; Meals CFA20,000; Open daily, 12pm-10pm*

Le Sorrento One of the more expensive restaurants in Cotonou, Le Sorrento specializes in Italian cuisine. It is certainly a sophisticated place to dine and offers great pizza and pasta dishes. *Tel: 21.30.37.79; Blvd St Michel, behind Hall des Arts; CFA5,500-15,000; Open daily, 12pm-10pm*

New Livingstones New Livingstones restaurant serves western and Western cuisine including oven baked pizzas and burgers and is very popular with expatriates. The style is similar to a modern pub, with beer on tap, dart boards and big screen TVs. *Tel: 21.30.27.58; Haie-Vive, along Piste Amalco; CFA7,000-15,000; Open daily, 11am-12pm*

Le Costa Rica This popular expatriate hang-out serves Western cuisine such as pasta and pizzas under a thatched roof. Draft beer is also available. The French-owned establishment is decorated with paintings of Asterix and Obelix, Viking characters from a French cartoon. It has a fun atmosphere, with a central location. *Tel: 21.30.20.09; Blvd St Michel, at the Centre de la Promotion Artisanal (CPA); From CFA5,000; Open daily, 11am-10pm*

Bangkok Terrasse There is an air-conditioned dining room plus a terrace and fountain. The exotic Asian-style atmosphere combined with good Thai food makes a great meal. *Tel: 21.30.37.86; Near Pharmacie Guézo; CFA6,000-12,000; Open Thurs-Tues, 12pm-10pm, closed Wednesdays*

Medium

Hai King Serving Chinese cuisine, the upper balcony dining room overlooks the Cadjehoun intersection. Karaoke is also available! *Tel: 21.30.60.08; Corner of Carrefour Cadjehoun; CFA5,000-10,000; Open daily, 11am-11pm*

Taranga Lebanese cuisine including delicious hummus and falafel, not to mention great pizzas. Also has an exceptional quality high-speed internet café. *Haie Vive, near Livingstone's at the end of Piste Amalco; CFA3,000- 10,000; Open daily, 11am-11pm*

Indiana Indiana serves authentic and tasty Indian cuisine with a buffet (CFA6,000) on Sundays starting at 7pm. The dining room is adorned with knick-knacks and fabrics; though the decorations are hotter than the food (the spiciest curries aren't that spicy). *Haie-Vive, Piste Amalco, CFA4,000-10,000, Open daily, 12pm-10pm*

Le Repaire De Bacchus Western-style bar and restaurant with beer on tap, a relatively long list of cocktails, and happy hour every day from 6-7pm. Live jazz every Thursday, and West African sounds such as Ivorian rumba on Friday and Saturday. Bacchus resembles an Irish pub with its booths and low lighting. *Off the south end of Avenue Proche, Guinkomé; CFA3,000-10,000; Open daily, 11am-12am*

Le Laurier This small restaurant has a pleasant upper-level, open-air dining room with good service and draft beer. The evening breezes create an easy and relaxing atmosphere for dinner, which could be a light salad or a full African or European style meal. *Guinkomé, behind Bacchus; CFA2,000-5,000; Open daily, 12pm-12am*

 Fairouz Enjoy excellent hummus served with fresh tomatoes, mint leaves, and pickles, along with other Middle-Eastern cuisine. There is an outdoor patio, but because of the busy street it is much more pleasant to eat inside with air conditioning. *On the far left-hand corner facing away from the Missèbo market intersection; CFA2,000-7,000; Open daily, 11am-10pm*

Hotel Accropole This spot has a pretty good ice cream and bakery selection, real coffee, a clean, air-conditioned dining room, and welcoming service. Though it doesn't quite have the same value as La Gerbe d'Or, Hotel Accropole is located away from the speedy clamor of Avenue Clozel. *Southern end of Avenue Proche, Guinkomé; Open daily, 8am-11pm*

Maquis Le Pili Pili This higher-end African restaurant is quite popular among Beninese and expatriates alike. There is an extensive and varied menu; the roasted chicken is particularly delicious. *Tel: 21.31.29.32; Off the paved road near Blvd St Michel, northwest of the town center; CFA3,000-6,000; Open Mon-Sat, 12pm-12am*

Maman Bénin Similar to *Maquis* Pili Pili, Maman Benin is locally popular and serves delicious Beninese cuisine including beef, chicken, and fish dishes. There is a second, more up-market dining room on the second floor, with a more expensive menu. *Off the paved road near Blvd St Michel, northwest of the town center; CFA3,000-6,000; Open Mon-Sat, 9am-12am*

La Verdure This Belgian owned bar/restaurant serves only French cuisine and seafood dishes. The bar is lively with pool tables and pinball machines. A pleasant courtyard of tall buttress trees makes for a relaxed dining atmosphere. *Tel: 21.31.31.75; Near Ganxi market, off Ave Clozel; CFA3,000-7,000; Open daily, 12pm-1am*

 La Gerbe D'Or The ground floor is a bakery and grocery store, selling fresh baguette bread, croissants, and exquisite pastries such as eclairs, rum babas, fruit tarts, and custard from around CFA500. Upstairs, a restaurant lounge is perfect for a hearty breakfast or lunch. *Ave Clozel, across from Ganxi Market; CFA2,000-7,000; Open daily, 8am-8pm*

Chez Clarisse This restaurant specializes in high-end French, Beninese, and West African cuisine. The ventilated dining room is comfortable and tastefully decorated, with professional and attentive servers. This is a great place for fresh grilled fish with rice and moyo sauce, or escargots with garlic and herbs for lunch or dinner. *Tel: 21.30.60.14; Behind the U.S. embassy; CFA10,000; Open daily, 11am-10pm*

 Les Festival de Glaces This popular bakery, pizzeria, and ice cream parlor is becoming a national chain (a third restaurant is under construction in Cotonou). The meal portions are a bit small, but there is a delicious variety of gelato-style ice cream flavors. The air-conditioned dining room is blissfully cool, a pleasant place to escape the sticky, hot, and polluted air of the city. Taking ice cream oustide to eat reduces its price; there are tables available at the front door. *Two locations: Avenue Steinmetz past Missebo market and at Carrefour Cadjehoun; CFA5,000-10,000; Open daily, 8am-10pm*

La Brochette d'Or This simple sandwich shop also sells Lebanese schwarmas and hotdogs. There is a big screen TV in the corner, and an outdoor patio at the entrance offering a comfortable place to dine. *Ganxi neighborhood, across the street from La Gerbe d'Or on Avenue Clozel; CFA1,500-4,000; Open daily, 10am-10pm*

O'Grill O'Grill serves European cuisine including fresh salads and quality steak, with a full bar and beer on tap. The dining room is decorated with a series of wicker dividers, creating private tables and lounge areas. *Ganxi neighborhood, across the street from the market and next door to FujiFilm Photography; From CFA3,000; Open daily, 11am-11pm*

Steers and Debonairs These two South African fast food chains offer beef, chicken, or vegetarian burger combos with fries. Debonairs specializes in pizza, which can be ordered to deliver. This is the place to go for a change of taste and style if the Beninese meals are too hard to digest. *Ave Steinmetz, not far from the Cathedral Notre Dame; CFA3,000; Open daily, 11am-9pm*

Carnival des Glaces This Indian-managed restaurant and ice-cream parlor was established to resemble the wildly popular Festival des Glaces. The ice cream isn't exactly what one hopes, but the burgers and fries coupled with a relaxed ambience provide for a good meal. *Ave Steinmetz, Guinkomé; From CFA3,000; Open daily, 9am-10pm*

Café Cauris Coquillages Café Cauris Coquillages is popular with the expat community, with its sea-water swimming pool and a restaurant that serves delicious fresh fish. There are five basic and comfortable guest rooms for rent. *Tel: 90.90.04.72; Fidjirossè Beach, along the fishing road toward Ouidah.*

Helvetia Local and Swiss cuisine is served here under a thatched roof. Helvetia is notable for its life-size chess board and horseback riding adventures. Located by the beach, lounging mattresses and parasols are available. *Tel: 95.95.79.66; Last restaurant on the Fishing Road toward Ouidah.*

Budget

Chala-Ogoi This open-air *buvette* has stand-up service, with a great selection of tasty Beninese cuisine such as *igname pilé, pâte*, pied de boeuf, fried chicken and fish, and salads. *Ave St Jean, across from the Hall des Sports and near Boulevard St Michel; CFA1,000-3,000; Open daily, 10am-11pm*

Restaurant L'Amitié L'Amitié is a rustic Senegalese restaurant that serves delicious poulet yassa and other dishes from Senegal. The staff is quite small, and the food may take some time to come out, but it is fresh and tasty. Because it is a Muslim establishment, no alcoholic beverages are sold, but one can purchase beer across the street and drink in the restaurant. *Jonquet, along the brick road leading to Blvd St Michel; From CFA1,000; Open daily, 12pm-10pm, closed on Muslim holidays*

Kpètè-Kpètè This large outdoor dining and beer-drinking area is surrounded by food vendors offering grilled meats, fish, fried plantains, and salads. The atmosphere is lively - it is a great place to enjoy the evening breeze and experience local nightlife. *Off Blvd St Michel, around the southwest corner of l'Eglise St Michel and close to Petit Babo Hotel; CFA500-2,000; Open daily, 12pm-12am*

 Escale de la Diaspora Sandwiches, burgers, and spaghetti are served from a bright yellow mini-bus located at the edge of a large public square, under the shade of Néré trees and parasols. The tables are on a raised concrete platform, away from the noise of the traffic. Soft drinks, beer, and select liquors are available. *Place des Martyrs, along the Route de L'Aéropor; CFA1,000-2,000; Open daily, 12pm-12am*

Children eating breakfast in Cotonou

Shawarma Shop This Lebanese butcher-restaurant has been dubbed 'Secret Shawarma' by Benin's Peace Corps Volunteers due to its 'hidden' location just off Avenue Steinmetz. Savory, laden with garlic, and quite filling, the shawarmas are made to order with choices of vegetarian, sausage, beef or chicken. Accompaniments of fries, salad, and hummus cost CFA500. The air-conditioned dining room is quite small and cramped, and often busy at lunch and dinner. Many locals come in to watch the Middle Eastern music videos on TV. Delivery is also available. *Next to Hotel Le Crillon Off of Avenue Steinmetz; CFA1,500-2,500; Open daily, 11am-10pm*

Indian Lady in Missèbo A former cook for an Indian family, Madame Eugenie Guinnakou serves authentic Indian meals in an upstairs salon. The experience, though at first awkward because it seems to be in her living room, is absolutely beautiful. There is a cool breeze and laid-back atmosphere. Madame Guinnakou also sells bottles of wine for about CFA2,000, a perfect accompaniment to the meal. *Tel: 97.57.23.76; Near Missèbo market; From CFA2,000*

Ganxi Maquis Here are several *maquis* and cafeterias packed together, toward the beach. They get very busy at lunch time, and some are also open for dinner. The typical menu includes mixed rice, fried plantains, fries, green salad with peas and onions, and fried fish or chicken. Typical *buvette* drinks are also available. The service is quite efficient, the food is great, and the value is hard to beat. Meandering street vendors create entertainment, displaying anything from padlocks and sunglasses to bootleg DVDs and bandanas. *Behind the Ganxi Market; CFA1,500-2,500, drinks CFA300-800; Open daily, 11am-11pm*

Lunch Cafeteria by the Hospital School One of Cotonou's best kept secrets, this outside food court is open only at lunch time. Each tantie prepares and sells her specialty; simply ask what's inside the cauldrons and coolers. Tailored for the medical students and researchers, the food and dining area are kept very clean. One can find beans and gari, rice and boiled vegetables, *pâte*, *igname pilé*, fish, chicken, beef, Fulani cheese, igname fries, omelets, spaghetti, fresh pineapple juice, sodas, beer, instant coffee, and tea. *Located within the concession walls of the Hospital school; From CFA1,000; Open Mon-Fri, 10am-4pm*

NIGHT LIFE

Cotonou's night life primarily takes place in the **Jonquet neighborhood**, appropriately nicknamed "*Quartier Rouge*" or the Red Light District. The main strip is lined with *buvettes*, Nigerian money vendors, kiosks, and a multitude of prostitutes and gigolos. There are several rather decadent bars in the area which are open all night, including **Playboy**, **Soweto**, and **2001** (*Deux mille-et-un*). All are located off of Rue des Cheminots, in the heart of Jonquet. There is usually no cover charge, and the atmosphere is booming with music and filled with women offering their nightly services. For those tough-skinned travelers in search of the real Beninese nightlife experience, this is the place. Jonquet, however, is dangerous at night with frequent muggings. To avoid any potential incidents yet still catch a glimpse of the action, visit during the day as it is just as busy and entertaining during the light hours.

Nearby *Quartier Guinkomé* also provides streetside bars and food stands that come to life in the early evening. **Hotel Accropole** is in this neighborhood, next door to **Le Repaire de Bacchus**. Other restaurants here are **Restaurant L'Amitié** and **Le Laurier**. For the more familiar version of a nightclub with disco balls, mirrors on the walls, and even karaoke, try **Hotel Le Chevalier**, or **Cristal Palace** at **Alex's Hotel**. Admission is about CFA3,500. The **Why Not Bar** is a very popular 'basement' club off of Avenue Proche where one can dance all night to European and African beats. The cover is CFA4,000, with drinks around the same price.

Ganxi and Avenue Steinmetz

Foley's Jazz Club, off Steinmetz Boulevard, has a comfortable, easy ambiance with live bands most nights and good mixed drinks. **So What! Bar** is a very popular place at the town center, near the Nouveau Pont and not far from Hotel le Crillon. This bar often has live West African music, and drumming lessons can be arranged here. The cover is usually CFA3,000-4,000 on Fridays, Saturdays, and nights when a live band is playing. **Titanic Bar** in Ganxi is across the lagoon from Hotel du Lac and provides a pleasant distraction with a great view of the water. There are live bands on Fridays and Saturdays. The **VIP Club** is next door, with a CFA7,000 cover charge that includes a drink.

Cadjehoun and Around the Airport

There is a popular *buvette* at *Carrefour Cadjehoun*, next to **Bon Pasteur** church and across from the Moov water tower. At nightfall, the parking lot next to the Catholic Church is filled with tables, chairs, and a hip young crowd with rows of parked motorcycles. *Tanties* sell cheap Beninese food such as *pâte* and rice dishes, fried yams and plantains, barbecued turkey wings, chicken, and salads. Street performers are frequent on weekend nights, like the shockingly flexible acrobats using car parts and metal basins as props. **Le Macumba** is a modern dance club just by the airport and popular with young expatriates. The Marina Hotel's club, **Le Téké**, has complimentary admission for hotel guests and is busiest on weekends or holidays; weeknights there are pretty quiet.

ACCOMMODATIONS

Many hotels do not provide mosquito nets but instead have a fan in the room, which help deter the mosquitoes. Higher-end hotels have air conditioning, and cheaper hotels will often, but not always, have screens over the windows. Some of the top end hotels such as Novotel, Marina, and Hotel du Port accept major credit cards and Euros, but it is safest to exchange money at the bank and have sufficient CFA francs to settle the bill. Due to frequent water cuts and power outages inherent throughout the city, most hotels have a plastic bucket as back-up in the bathrooms to use for bucket showers. If the bucket is not full upon arrival, be sure to fill it and keep it filled in case the water is cut when it comes time to shower or use the toilet. High-end hotels such as Hotel du Lac, Novotel, and Marina have their own water reserves and generators, so they usually remain immune to such outages. Room keys are commonly left at the reception desk upon leaving the building. If guests prefer to keep the key in their possession, it should be discussed with the receptionist. The guest is usually responsible for replacing the lock if the key is lost or stolen. *The following hotels have been listed by neighborhood.*

Avenue Steinmetz

 Le Crillon** This is a small and usually clean hostel. Sometimes the sheets are questionable, but for the price, it can't be beat. There is a small cafeteria stand across the sandy street. It is also next door to the travel agency Evénémenciel and the 'Secret Schwarma' restaurant. *Tel: 21.31.51.58; Off of Ave Steinmetz across from Carnival de Glace; CFA8,000; fan, private shower and toilet*

Hotel Benin Vickenfel**** The location is central and the rooms are small but quite comfortable, with satellite television, and good sized bathrooms. An internet café is adjoined. Vickenfel is one of the best deals in town for its category. *Tel: 21.31.38.14; vkfhotel@intnet.bj; On Avenue Steimetz; near Le Crillon; CFA30,000; a/c, private bath, TV*

Ayihoué Hotel**** Ayihoué Hotel offers clean rooms and hot water for bathing – the water is heated and brought to the room in buckets to mix with cool water. It is near the Lebanese burger and pizza restaurant Carnival de Glace, the 'Secret Schwarma' restaurant, and the travel agency Evénémenciel. This hotel provides shuttle service to the airport. It is also close to Leader-Price grocery store. *Ave Steinmetz, past the Societé Générale Bancaire Béninoise, or SGBB, and toward Missèbo market; CFA40,000; a/c, private bath*

Ganxi

Hotel de la Plage*** Hotel de la Plage is one of the oldest high-end hotels in Cotonou. The colonial-style architecture, pool and private beach, and internet café make for a pleasant experience. The room rate includes breakfast. Non-guests can use the pool for CFA1,000. *Tel: 21.31.25.61 / 21.31.34.67; Fax: 21.31.25.60; Near the main post office and the Embassy of Niger, close to Ganxi market; CFA25,000-40,000; a/c, private bath*

Haie Vive/Aéroport/Cadjehoun

Hotel Benin Marina (Sheraton)***** This lavish multi-national hotel chain has two superb pools, a sauna and massage parlor, landscaped gardens, a golf driving range, a business center, bars, a casino, excellent restaurants…just about everything imaginable. Major credit cards and Euros are accepted. Internet access is available at the business center. *Tel: 21.30.01.00; On the beach, off of Blvd de France, west of the city* *center; CFA120,000-355,000; a/c, hot water, private bath, telephone, TV, mini-bar, personal safe*

Novotel Orisha***** Novotel is a high-end multinational hotel with 100-plus rooms, a beautiful pool and a classy French restaurant. Main courses start at 6,000. The pool is open to non-guests for a fee of CFA3,000. Major credit cards are accepted. Internet access is available at the hotel business center. *Tel: 21.30.41.77; novotel.orisha@intnet.bj; Blvd de France, west of the city center. CFA70,000-110,000; a/c, hot water, private bath, telephone, TV, mini-bar, individual safe*

Hotel du Port**** This French hotel is charming and tastefully decorated with traditional and contemporary West African art. A 25-meter pool with swimming lanes and a diving board is surrounded by three stories of rooms. A bar and restaurant covered by a thatched roof serves delectable wood-oven pizza, European, and African cuisine. The hotel also boasts an underground nightclub, popular on the weekends. Next door, a lively salsa dance club offers dance lessons and is open to the public in the evenings. Internet access is available at the hotel business center. *Tel: 21.31.44.43; www.hotelduportresort.com; Blvd de France, beside the Port of Cotonou; CFA38,000-45,000; a/c, hot water, private bath, telephone, TV, mini-bar*

Croix du Sud**** Croix du Sud is a business class hotel with a 25-meter pool and a European restaurant. The bungalow rooms set amidst lush gardens are ideal for relaxation. In the basement of the hotel, there is a nightclub popular with the Lebanese crowd. *Tel: 21.30.09.54; Across from the Place des Martyrs on Avenue Jean Paul II, also accessible from Blvd de France; CFA33,000-48,000; a/c, hot water, private bath, TV*

Codiam Hostel* Codiam is within walking distance of surrounding upscale shops and restaurants in the Haie Vive/Cadjehoun neighborhoods. The rooms are very basic; the cheapest consist of a twin bed and shared shower/toilet. The hostel entrance is well-guarded and a wall surrounds the property. *Tel: 21.30.37.27; codiam@inet.bj; By Camp Guezo, not far from Haie Vive; CFA5,000-10,000; fan or a/c, private and shared baths*

Akpakpa

Hotel du Lac**** This is a great place to splurge at the beginning or the end of a trip through Benin, without going financially overboard. The rooms are spacious and luxurious. The restaurant overlooks the river and serves European dishes, pizzas, hamburgers, and seafood. Non-guests can use the swimming pool equipped with diving board at CFA2,500 per person. Wireless internet access is available. *Tel: 21.33.19.19; www.hoteldulac-benin.com; Located on the water, near Ancien Pont; CFA35,000-70,000; a/c, hot water, private bath, TV, phone*

Guinkomé/Jonquet

Les Hirondelles** This is a popular Peace Corps volunteer hotel. The staff is friendly, helpful, and accustomed to dealing with Westerners. The rooms are clean, though sometimes the bed sheets are not. The front desk agent will happily provide clean sheets, bath towels, soap, and toilet paper as needed. Les Hirondelles is conveniently located near the Ganxi market and good restaurants such as Le Repair de Bacchus and Le

Laurier. *Guinkomé, across the street from Le Chevalier; CFA6,000-7,000; fan, private shower and toilet, some rooms have a shared toilet*

Alex's Hotel*** This classy multiple-story hotel also has a hopping night-club and karaoke bar, Cristal Palace. *Tel: 21.31.25.08; Jonquet neighborhood, tall building indicated by a large 'ALEX'S' sign at the top of the building; CFA30,000-40,000; a/c, hot water, private bath, TV*

Le Chevalier**** This multi-story hotel and night club is newly built and quite pricey. It is a very busy place on Friday and Saturday nights. The music and party-goers of the dance club can make quite a bit of noise, especially for those staying at Les Hirondelles across the way. It is a good place for those seeking the ultimate Beninese-Lebanese night-life experience, and an opportunity for karaoke. Le Chevalier is easy to use as a landmark because of its lighted palm tree on the roof. Le Chevalier offers airport shuttle service to its guests. *Tel: 21.31.80.02; Guinkomé, across from Les Hirondelles; CFA38,000-70,000; a/c, hot water, private bath, TV, mini-bar, individual safe*

St. Michel

The St. Michel neighborhood can be a little sketchy after dark. It is recommended to arrive back to the hotel before nightfall.

Centre Paul VI (Six) Hostel* Centre Paul VI is a hostel run by Catholic nuns affiliated with Eglise St Michel. The rooms are clean and basic, and they are often booked for group stays and conferences. The nearby St Michel cathedral has daily services in Fon, Nigerian, English, French, and other languages. *Blvd St. Michel; CFA3,000; fan, mosquito net, private shower and toilet, some rooms have a shared toilet*

Petit Babo* Petit Babo offers cheap, spacious rooms ranging in style and size. The sheets may be questionable at times, but clean ones will be provided upon request. The multi-story building is donned with breezy balconies, which makes it a great place to relax in the evening and watch the neighborhood kids play soccer in the middle of the sandy streets below. A bar is located on the ground floor. The staff is quite friendly. *Located behind the Catholic Church St. Michel, off the paved highway; CFA3,000-10,000; fan or a/c, private shower and toilet.*

Ganvié

Ganvié, also known as the Venice of Africa, is a vast fishing community located in the lagoon waters of Lake Nokoué, just north of Cotonou. Its inhabitants are of the Tofinu lineage, related to the Adja people from Eastern Togo. Ganvié has become a popular tourist destination, where visitors can take a guided canoe ride through the village.

The village of Ganvié was established by the Tofinu people when Dahomeyan warriors raided their countryside for captives to sell to the European slave traders. Due to the Dahomeyan religious belief that battles could not be fought in or on water, the Tofinu refugees created a settlement in the middle of the lake. The Tofinu word *gan* means 'we are saved' and *vié* means community. The traditional bamboo houses stand on stilts above the shallow waters of the lake, and the villagers travel solely in dugout canoes. Women sell fish, fruit, and vegetables from their dugouts while men return from fishing excursions, their canoes laden with fishing nets. Fish are cultivated and bred within the barricades of trees and branches surrounding the village. The black canisters that are seen lugged around in canoes are full of pirated gasoline from Nigerian pipelines that is sold in recycled Coca-Cola bottles in the villages.

The Tour

A tour of Ganvié takes about two hours in a motorized boat, including a five kilometer ride to the village plus a couple stops in souvenir shops and refreshment stands. The official tourist office is located on the lake-side at Abomey-Calavi, about 20 kilometers northwest of Cotonou. Tours cost CFA7,000 per person with a motorized boat, and CFA4,500 per person with a sail-canoe. It is customary to tip the guide and conductor about CFA2,000. At least one of the guides can give tours in English. The inhabitants require a small fee before being photographed, which can be negotiated through your guide. To beat the day's heat, arrive early in the day.

GETTING THERE

A taxi ride from the Dantokpa *gare* to the Ganvié drop-off point in Abomey-Calavi costs about CFA300. A *zemidjan* costs around CFA700. The tourist office at the jetty is a short walk from the main road.

ACCOMMODATIONS

Auberge du Lac This hotel and restaurant near Lake Nokoué offers breakfast, lunch, and dinner. The rooms are small and rustic, with a fan. There are a few hotels on stilts in Ganvié as well. Hotel Chez M and Expotel Ganvié offer colorfully decorated rooms with bucket showers, toilets, mosquito nets, and the unique experience of sleeping over water. *Tel: 21.36.03.44; CFA5,000*

Niaouli

Niaouli is a small village off the north-south highway, five kilometers north of Allada and 70 kilometers north of Cotonou. It is home to the *Centre Regional de Recherche Agricole* (Regional Agricultural Research Center). Established in 1904, the center focuses its research on the flora and fauna of the surrounding virgin forest. Benin's native ecosystems are generally drier than the forests in Ghana and Nigeria due to the Dahomey Gap (see pg 44), but there are natural strips of denser and wetter Guinea forests through the lower half of Benin. The surrounding populations have compromised parts of these forests, but some relict stands remain. The *Centre de Recherche Agricole (Niaouli*

Research Center; Tel: 22.37.11.50; niaouliforet@yahoo.fr) offers guided tours (*CFA2,000/person with group rates available*). Visitors can climb the observation towers to watch and listen to the forest canopy wildlife: mon-monkeys, birds, butterflies, and more. The Niaouli forest is habitat to bush rats (*agouti*), dik dik antelopes, porcupines, green vervets, chameleons, turtles, pythons, green mambas, and cobras. The birds seen here include the African cuckoo falcon, the yellow-mantled weaver, the red-headed malimbe, and the naked-face barbet.

For those wanting to stay the night, the research center offers rooms with screened windows, fans, and shared toilets for CFA2,500/night.

GETTING THERE

From Cotonou, a taxi costs CFA600-700. The driver will stop in Atto-gon, by the dirt road leading to Niaouli. A *zemidjan* will complete the 3km trip for CFA200. The research station is on the left side of the dirt road. Register at the visitor's center, where guides with current knowledge of the research are available.

Allada

Allada is the site of the first kingdom formed by the Adja descendants of Tado, Togo. Today, it remains a bustling town with one paved road running through it. One dirt road leads directly southwest to Ouidah and was the original slave route used by traders from the ancient Allada Kingdom. A second dirt road points to the royal palace of the 16th King of Allada, located in the village of Togoudo. The royal palace is open to visitors, and the King's assistants can arrange a tour of the grounds and perhaps a visit to the King. A donation of CFA1,000-5,000 is expected. Guides at the palace can also set up a visit of Togoudo's sacred forest, home to several *fétiches* and the site of many vodoun ceremonies. There is an impressive Italian-run Catholic cathedral on the hillside just south of Allada, complete with a decorated bell tower and a private radio station. The magnificent mosaic tiles behind the altar in the church are imported from Italy, and majestic frescoes painted by Beninese artists adorn the palatial walls. Allada has a few basic guest houses with rooms from CFA5,000, and typical *maquis* along the paved road. Many taxi drivers stop in Allada to fill up on gas and buy food. Roadside vendors carry baskets and trays of giant grilled snails and crispy *agouti* legs with hot pepper purée. The region is known for its savory pineapples, especially those from the agriculture technical school at Sékou, just south of Allada.

GETTING THERE

Since buses do not stop in Allada, taxi is the only form of public transport. A taxi from Cotonou (40km) will run CFA500-600, while a taxi from Abomey costs CFA1,500.

Ouidah

Ouidah's town center is located toward the beach, off the main highway. One could easily miss the entrance to Ouidah if traveling by taxi, and mistake it for another suburb of Cotonou. Located about 40 kilometers west of Cotonou, Ouidah was originally a small village called Gléwé within the Kingdom of Xwéda. The villagers subsisted on agriculture, hunting, and fishing in the coastal lagoons. The Europeans first arrived here in the 16th century and later established a slave trade with the kingdom of Xwéda at the end of the 17th century. Once the powerful Dahomey Kingdom saw the economic value of the slave trade, it seized power of Ouidah in 1727 to take over trading with the Europeans. The Portuguese, Danish, French, and English all participated in this trade. In 1818, Francisco Felix de Souza, known locally as Chacha, was installed as the manager of the slave trade on behalf of the Dahomey Kingdom. Today, his descendents continue to hold an important status in Ouidah.

Ouidah is also considered the vodoun capital of Benin, if not the world. It hosts important ceremonies, with the grandest festivities taking place on January 10, the national vodoun holiday. The city offers a wealth of tourist attractions, including fortresses built by the early Europeans, the slave route leading to the Door of No Return, vodoun temples, and a selection of hotels along the coconut palm-fringed beaches. Knowledgeable guides at the historic Portuguese Fort take visitors on a city-wide circuit to explain the history and legends behind each monument and landmark.

> Bruce Chatwin's *The Viceroy of Ouidah* (1980) is a fictional account of the life of Francisco Felix de Sousa and the slave trade with Brazil.

GETTING THERE

A taxi from Cotonou costs CFA700. The Confort Lines bus stops in Ouidah. Arrange for tickets and drop off sites by calling Confort Lines main office in Cotonou (*Tel: 21.32.58.15*).

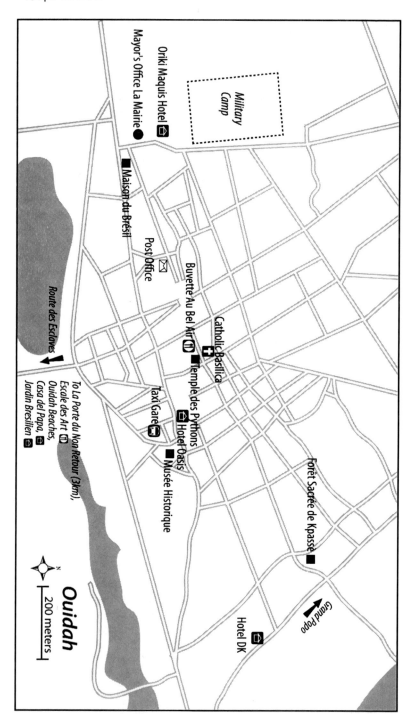

Mayor's Office La Mairie ●

Oriki Maquis Hotel 🏨

Military Camp

■ Maison du Brésil

Post Office ✉

Buvette Au Bel Air 🍴

Catholic Basilica ✚

■ Temple des Pythons

Taxi Gare 🚖

Hotel Oasis 🏨

■ Musée Historique

To La Porte du Non Retour (3km),
Escale des Art 🏨
Ouidah Beaches,
Casa del Papa, 🏨
Jardin Bresilien 🏨

Route des Esclaves ←

■ Forêt Sacrée de Kpasse

■

Hotel DK 🏨

(Grand Popo) ↗

N ↑

Ouidah
200 meters

SIGHTS AND ACTIVITIES

Le Musée d'Histoire de Ouidah — Fort Portugais
Ouidah History Museum — Portuguese Fort
The Portuguese fort was built by Joseph de Torres in 1721 and originally served as a missionary and slave trade base. The Portuguese retained control of the fort during the French colonization of the country until it was annexed in 1961 by the government of the newly independent Republic of Dahomey. Although the Portuguese burned the fort at the time of their expulsion, many of their maps, illustrations, and antique objects were recovered during the reconstruction of the fort in the mid 1960s. Today, recognized by its surrounding white walls, the once Portuguese Fort-turned-Historical Museum covers one hectare and contains the Portuguese representative's residence, a chapel, a military garrison, and military barracks. Most of the permanent collection is arranged by themes in the residence, covering the history of the fort, the Kingdom of Xwéda, the Kingdom of Dahomey, the slave trade, vodoun, and the cultural links between Benin and the regions of the Americas where slaves were shipped. The chapel houses temporary exhibits, and the museum has a boutique as well as a little craftsmen's village for souvenir shopping. *Tel: 22.34.10.21 www.museeouidah.org; Rue de General Dodd, east of the marketplace; Open Mon-Fri 9am-12pm and 3pm-6pm, Sat-Sun 9am-6pm; Entry fee: CFA1,000 for foreigners, CFA500 for Beninese; The rate includes a guided tour, some guides speak English.*

Festival de Films — Ouidah Film Festival
This film festival is usually held in January, linking the sister-cities of Ouidah and Melun, France. The festival is meant to promote new, original, and pertinent films on multicultural dialogue. Films in the festival comprise long works, such as movies or television shows, and shorter works of fiction, as wells as documentaries.

Jean Odoutan, who initiated this festival, also founded the *Institut Cinematographique de Ouidah (ICO),* the Cinematographic Institute of Ouidah, which is the first free African school of image, sound, and animated film. For more information on the festival, see www.festival-ouidah.org.

La Route des Esclaves
The Slave Road
The four kilometer sandy track leading from Ouidah to the beach was the route taken by thousands of captives boarding ships bound for the Americas. The road is lined with monuments of vodoun symbols and reminders of this dark piece of history. It begins at the Slave Auction, also called **Place Chacha**, located in front of Francisco Felix de Souza's residence. The slaves were selected here by the European merchants, chained, and marched down the road to the Tree of Forgetting, or **l'Arbre de l'Oublie**. Here, they were branded according to the mark of their purchaser and forced to walk around the tree to

symbolically forget their homes and families. Men were made to circle the tree nine times, and the women seven. Today, the tree has been replaced by a statue of the vodoun goddess Mamiwata. The next stop on the route is the Tree of Return or **l'Arbre du Retour**, planted by Dahomean King Agadja, where the slaves circled three times to ensure that their souls would return to their homeland after death. Before continuing to the ships, the slaves were kept for days or weeks in the tight quarters and obscurity of the **Zomaï Cabin,** meaning "where the light does not go." Many died there before even leaving Benin, and were buried in a mass grave, today memorialized by the six meter high **Mur de Lamentations**, or Wall of Remembrance. From here, the slaves finished their trek to the beach where they were loaded into longboats and piled inside the ships. This final stage is marked by an arched gateway covered in murals erected by UNESCO and known as the Door of No Return, or **La Porte du Non-Retour**. Two statues of vodoun Revenants, representing the spirits of the dead, await the return of the dead slaves' souls to the motherland. In 2003, The Gate of Return, or **La Porte de Retour**, was built further west on the beach in honor of the returned descendants of slaves. A museum there displays photographs and posters about the slave trade and the Diaspora. The entry fee is CFA1,000.

Le Temple des Pythons
The Python Temple
As proof of the peaceful cohabitation of religions in Benin, and also as a reminder of the struggle between natives and the early missionaries, the Python Temple sits directly across from Ouidah's Catholic basilica. The priests of the serpent deity Dangbé oversee the temple, which is shaded by towering sacred trees inundated with fruit bats. In commemoration of this venerated reptile, the temple houses dozens of languid pythons inside a dark circular room. Visitors can enter the room and stand among the pythons; the more daring can have a snake draped around their necks for a photo. *Across from the Catholic Basilica; Open daily, 9am-6pm; Entry fee: CFA1,000, plus CFA2,000 for a camera and CFA5,000 for a video camera.*

La Maison du Bresil
The House of Brazil
The former residence of the Brazilian Governor, this beautifully restored house showcases temporary art exhibits of vodoun culture and the African Diaspora. *Avenue de la France, on the west side of town; Open daily 8am-7pm; Entry fee: CFA1,000*

La Forêt Sacrée de Kpassè
The Sacred Forest of Kpassè
The sacred forest has sculptures and woodcarvings that illustrate the history of the territory. The forest was named after King Kpassè of the

Xwéda Kingdom, who is said to have fled from his Dahomean enemies and turned himself into an Iroko tree that still stands there today. *About one kilometer from the town center; Open daily, 9am-7pm; Entry fee: CFA1,000*

EATING AND DRINKING

There are several restaurants and bars in Ouidah's town center and along the Slave Road to the Door of No Return. The cheapest food can be found from the street stands around the market, with heaping plates of rice or *pâte* From CFA200.

Oriki *Maquis* Hotel This *maquis* also has two guest rooms for CFA6,000, but it is more recommended for dining. The restaurant has a popular bar and pleasant staff. Try the tasty chicken and fish with rice or fries. *Tel: 21.34.10.04; Rue des Palmistes, around the corner from the Maison du Brésil; Meals CFA700-1,500, drinks CFA300-800; Open daily, 10am-11pm*

Buvette Au Bel Air Au Bel Air is one of the typical *buvettes* around Ouidah where one can enjoy a cold drink after touring the museums. This place in particular has a pleasant shaded courtyard. *Center of town, around the corner from the Python Temple and Catholic church; Drinks CFA300-800; Open daily, 11am-11pm*

Restaurant Escale des Art This is a convenient and refreshing stop if traveling the Slave Road. The rice and *pâte* dishes are pretty good, with the usual accompaniment of fish, chicken, eggs, or beef. There are handicrafts on sale here as well, including jewelry, Batiks, and wooden sculptures. *Inside the Village Artisanal de Ouidah, along the Slave Road; Meals 2,000-3,000, drinks 300-900; Open daily, 11am-10pm*

ACCOMMODATIONS

 Casa del Papa***** This hotel is as club-med as it gets in Benin. It is a great place to unwind and be pampered after a back-country trip through Benin. The restaurant serves quality international and local cuisine. It is best to have a personal vehicle if staying at this hotel as *zemidjan*s do not come this far and a return trip would involve walking a few kilometers down the sandy road. A hired *zem* from Ouidah's town center costs about CFA1,000. If driving a rented vehicle, be aware that the road between the Door of No Return and Casa del Papa is sandy and vehicles commonly get stuck in sand pits. Chauffeur lodging is provided at the hotel for CFA10,000 per night, including meals at the chauffeur cafeteria. *Tel: 21.49.21.01 / 95.95.39.04; www.casadelpapa.bj; Seven kilometers from the Door of No Return, on the Route des Pêche; CFA35,500- 45,500; 61 rooms, ocean front or lagoon side, single/double occupancy with a/c, continental breakfast included, three pools, private beach, tennis courts*

Hotel DK**** This German hotel is a large and modern complex with a swimming pool. The restaurants serves meals for CFA4,000-8,000. *Tel: 21.34.30.40; On the Cotonou-Togo highway; CFA12,500-25,500; a/c, hot water, and satellite television*

Le Jardin Bresilien Auberge de la Diaspora *** The rooms at the Jardin Bresilien are set in attractive thatched bungalows. A restaurant serves international and local cuisine. The private beach with palm trees makes a beautiful and peaceful setting, and it is a cheaper alternative to the less accessible Casa del Papa for those without a private vehicle. *Tel: 21.34.11.10; e-mail: dyasporah@yahoo.fr; On the beach near the Door of No Return; CFA6,000-12,000; fan or a/c; private bath. Camping for CFA3,000*

Hotel Oasis ** This is the most central hotel in Ouidah, and the most conveniently placed for travelers without a vehicle. The manager is also the chef, and can provide good meals with advance notice. There is a lively bar on the ground floor. *Tel: 21.34.10.91; ouidahoasis@yahoo.com; About 300 meters west of the Portuguese Fort, toward the Python Temple; CFA8,000-14,000; single/double rooms with fans or a/c*

Les Jumeax – The Twins

The Beninese perceive the birth of twins to be an extraordinary phenomenon. This double birth is a sign of great fortune for a family. No matter what the family's financial situation might be, twins are always welcomed, and their mother is particularly favored during pregnancy. There is a coconut tree grove along the Route des Esclaves in Ouidah where families with twins celebrate their good fortune. An annual celebration is held there on the first Sunday in October.

In Benin, both twins must always be treated with absolute equality. In the event of death in childhood, the surviving twin child is informed that the other has gone to search for wood. From that point on, this twin will carry a doll representing their lost sibling. The doll is given gifts and food in keeping with the custom that the twins are to be treated equally. If both twins should die, the mother carries two dolls with her. The dolls are carried in a pocket or within the wraps of a *pagne*. Beninese tradition also demands that a mother with twins must have another child, to close the 'hole' formed by the double birth. The child following the twins will be named *Dossou* or *Dossi* in Fon, or an equivalent name in another native language.

Ouémé & Plateau

Bordering Nigeria, the Ouémé is an important *département* for international commerce and transport. Its largest city, Porto-Novo, is the government capital of Benin, and is a historical and current political hotbed. Arriving at Porto-Novo from Cotonou, travelers cross the Ouémé River, which reportedly has the third most fertile valley on the continent of Africa. Its origin is in the Atakora region, and it empties into the Atlantic Ocean at Cotonou. The *département* is also famed for the preparation of pork and *gari*, a spicy and filling meal that can be found throughout the region.

In 1999, the northern part of the Ouémé split off to form the Plateau *département*. This area is dominated by Nigeria and Yoruba-based ethnicities and cultures, creating another interesting corner in the composition of Benin's unique diversity. Though not as busy as Porto-Novo, Kétou provides a good amount of distraction for visitors with its particular traditions. Surrounding towns also contain markets and activities worth discovering.

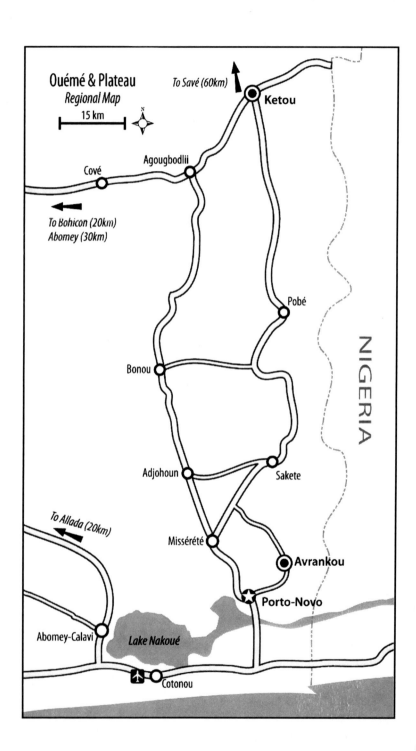

Porto-Novo

Porto-Novo lies on the Nokoué Lake Lagoon along the Ouémé River, 30 kilometers east of Cotonou and close to the Nigerian border. Before the Europeans arrived, Porto-Novo was called Hogbonou and belonged to the Yoruba Kingdom of Oyo, based in present-day Nigeria. The Portuguese settled Hogbonou in the 1500s, renaming it Porto-Novo as they implemented an important trading port. In 1863, the British based on the coast of Nigeria threatened to take over the territory, so the Porto-Novoan king agreed to sign a protectorate with the French. Later on, the French appointed Porto-Novo as the capital of the newly colonized Dahomey Kingdom. It is still the official capital of Benin and the third largest city with a population of about 230,000, after Cotonou and Parakou. 'Hogbonou' remains the name of the town in the local languages.

Today the city's center consists of charming brick roads, historic buildings, and impressive villas from the colonial era. The Yoruba culture of the ancient Oyo Kingdom prevails in the city and its surroundings. Another prominent ethnicity is the Gun (pronounced 'goon'), related to the Adja peoples of Tado, Togo. Porto-Novo's architecture and culture also has a strong Afro-Brazilian influence due to the returned descendants of slaves who settled there after emancipation in Brazil. The city is a center for the country's intellectual and political entities.

GETTING THERE AND AWAY

There are taxis and mini-buses to Porto-Novo at the Dantokpa Market *gare* in Cotonou for CFA500-600. To get to Kétou and Abomey, taxis depart from *Marché Ouando* and cost about CFA1,500. *Zemidjan* fares through the town center are around CFA150.

Porto-Novo sits ten kilometers north of the Cotonou-Lagos road. Taxis are available from Porto-Novo to Lagos for CFA2,700, or for a cheaper ride, take a taxi to the border crossing at Kraké and change vehicles for the rest of the trip to Lagos, as the Nigerian taxis are cheaper than in Benin. Bribes are often required at the border crossing. Ask the chauffeur about these charges when negotiating a taxi fare. Nigerian currency is available on the black market from the money vendors of the Jonquet neighborhood in Cotonou (see pg 84).

HOSPITAL

Centre Hôspitalier du Départment de l'Ouémé *Tel 20.21.35.90; Behind the National Assembly Building, next to Jardin des Plantes Naturelles*

Porto-Novo
500 meters

N

Carrefour Catchi
Maquis Catchi Ambiance
Financial Bank
To Quando (3km)
To Centre Songhaï
Supermarché
Le Panier
Hotel Dona
Péniche Patisserie
Complex Soufiano
BLVD EXTÉRIEUR
de Gaulle
Stadium
Place
Kokoyé
Atoké Roundpoint
Oganla
Taxi gare
Comme Chez Soi
Musée
Ethnographique
Post Office
Le Bar Mahi
Grande
Mosquée
Restaurant Akango
Aux Vents du Lac
Hotel Beaurivage
Hospital
Hotel Casa Dansa
Espace Toffa
Le Président
Grand Marché
Jardin des Plantes Naturelles
Java Promo
Eglise Notre Dame
Musée da Silva
Bank of Africa
Hotel Détente
Gas Station
Bus and Taxi gare
Musée Honmé
Royal Palace Museum
Buvette Escale du Pont
Lake Nokoué
To Cotonou (35km)
Patisserie Esperance

INTERNET ACCESS

The **Songhaï Center** is the best and most reliable source of internet in Porto-Novo, but the city has several other cyber cafés offering internet access for around CFA500 per hour.

SUPERMARKETS

There are three notable *supermarchés* in Porto-Novo: **Champion**, **Le Panier**, and **Universe 7**, which are all located on the Boulevard Extérieur, leading to *Carrefour Catchi*. These stores offer a wide variety of European products. For something more local, the produce market is held every four days near the mosque.

SIGHTS AND ACTIVITIES

The city can be divided into four main parts: the old, with its colonial buildings and narrow roads at the town center; the commercial, which contains the **Grand Marché** and many businesses, and extends toward the lagoon on the southwestern side of town; the administrative with government offices, on the west side; and the new residential districts along the eastern outskirts of town. The taxi *gare* is north of town center and is the most common taxi drop-off point. Many hotels and museums are within walking distance from here, though a *zemidjan* might be more convenient (costing around CFA150). The **Catholic Church Eglise Notre Dame**, in front of the Espace Toffa, is a beautiful building established by the first colonists in the late 1880s. The **Jardin Botanique** is also worth a visit with its displays of native plant species and sacred trees. These botanical gardens are located on the west side of town, near the hospital (*entrance fee for the gardens is CFA300, and guided tours offered for around CFA1,000*).

Musée Ethnographique de Porto-Novo
Museum of Ethnography
Established in 1962, this museum is housed in a French colonial building and specializes in the portrayal of the Guélédé ethnic group, which is related to the Yoruba. It displays masks, musical instruments, weapons of war, and traditional tools used by the various tribal groups of the Ouémé-Plateau region, as well as divination boards and items employed by Ifa priests. The elementary school next door to the museum is where former French President François Mitterrand began his educational career. *Tel: 20.21.25.54; On the west side of town, next to the Stadium Charles de Gaulle; Open daily, 8:30am-6pm; Entry fee: CFA1,000, including a guided tour*

Musée Da Silva des Arts et de la Culture
Da Silva Museum of Art and Culture
A superb example of Afro-Brazilian architecture, this building was built in 1890 as the residence of a family of returned descendants of slaves from Brazil. It houses a collection of miscellaneous remnants from the Da Silva family and other returning Afro-Brazilians, including photographs and old cameras. *Tel: 20.24.38.66; Rue Toffa, near the Bank of Africa; Open daily, 9am-6pm; Entry fee: CFA1,000*

Musée Honmè de Porto-Novo
Royal Palace Museum
Set within the royal palace of the former Kingdom of Hogbonou, the museum tours the residence of the kings and tells the story of the kingdom, focusing on the last sovereign king, King Toffa. King Toffa established the first relations with the French before colonization.

The museum showcases the alounloun musical instrument which creates the adjogan music, unique to the Porto-Novo area. This instrument and its music dates back to the founding of Hogbonou and its first king, originating in Allada. Initially used as a symbol of the king's power, the alounloun's use evolved into a musical instrument played to honor the Porto-Novoan royalty, living or deceased. The instrument is made of copper-clad iron, and is about a meter long with many metal rings. The rings slide along the stick, which creates the music. Today the alounloun is still used in formal, royal ceremonies. Adjogan music is also played in the Catholic churches in the area, though in this situation the royal insignia on the instrument is changed from the bird crest to a Christian cross. *Tel: 20.21.36.66; Open dialy; 9am-12pm and 3pm-6pm; Entry fee: CFA1,000*

 oueme & plateau

La Grande Mosquée
The Grand Mosque
This impressive Afro-Brazilian mosque stands out in the city, with its faded shades of yellows, reds, and blues. With permission from the Mullah and for a small fee, visitors can climb the tower and view the city of Porto-Novo and the Nokoué Lagoon from above. *By the market-place, on the northeast side of town.*

O.N.G. Vie Pour Tous
Life for All Non-Governmental Organization (NGO)
One of the first things a tourist will notice in Benin is the omnipresent black plastic bags littering the gutters, streets, fields, and trees. A small group of women decided to transform this otherwise eyesore into works of art. After collecting and washing the discarded bags, the women, using methods of crocheting and knitting, began to create dolls, hats, place mats, purses, and pretty much anything else they could think of to sell. Based on their success, the NGO Vie Pour Tous inspired simliar creative businesses in the neighborhood. There is a metal recycling shop where craftsmen transform spark plugs into insect figurines and tin cans into lamps. *Near the post office in the Oganla neighborhood.*

Espace Toffa
This large park plaza has a statue of the last king of Porto-Novo, Toffa. The name Jean Bayol comes from the first governor of the French Dahomey colony. There is also a large botanical garden nearby, created from the remains of the sacred forest of Porto-Novo. The garden was previously often used by biology students in field research for its rich diversity in indigenous plants. Many of the markets are in easy walking distance of Espace Toffa. *Near the entrance of town at the intersection Place de Jean Bayol.*

Charles de Gaulle Stadium
The stadium is a very popular place in Porto-Novo, frequented in the evening by teams of various sports, including basketball, handball, volleyball, boccie ball, and others. Entrance is free, and spectators are welcome. Both men's and women's basketball is jumping on Wednesday evenings. Locally organized teams who compete nationally, and sometimes internationally, practice and schrimmage while spectators and junior players participate from the sidelines.

Adjarra Market
The village of Adjarra (10km northeast of Porto-Novo) has a nice market held every fourth day. Apart from the typical market items, it offers unique types of tie-dyed and indigo fabric, traditional pottery, musical instruments, and various voodoo objects. Adjarra also houses a sacred voodoo temple of water called Zekpon. If traveling to Nigeria, Adjarra is definitely worth a stop.

EATING AND DRINKING

A specialty of the Porto-Novo region is *piron*, a version of the cassava-based *eba* served with pork. As in most large cities, Porto-Novo offers a tasty dining variety. The **maquis catchi ambiance** at the *Carrefour Catchi* has inexpensive and tasty Beninese cuisine From CFA700 a plate. Their specialty is *agouti*, the bush rat. **Restaurant Comme Chez Soi**, or Just Like Home, is at the *Ataké* round point, near *Bar Club Festival*, and serves meals for CFA600-1,500. **Le Bar Mahi** is a popular and recommended lunch spot, with great *igname pilé* for only CFA1,000. *Le Bar Mahi* is found between the Museum of Ethnography and the *Place Kokoyé*, open daily from 11am-10pm. **Péniche Patisserie**, at the corner of *Carrefour Catchi*, sells pastries for CFA500-800 and is open daily from 8am-8pm. The **Buvette Escale du Pont**, located near the gas station*/gare* by the lagoon bridge has typical Beninese fare for CFA500-1,000 a plate. **Bar Restaurant Aux Vents du Lac** is an upper-class type bar and restaurant with a pleasant courtyard set a couple kilometers northwest of the town center. Local and European meals there cost CFA2,000-5,000. Probably the most up-scale restaurant in Porto-Novo is **Le Président**, at the *Espace Toffa*. Meals range from CFA5,000-10,000 and the menu also boasts an extensive wine list. Other recommended eateries include:

Java Promo There is a breezy and comfortable terrace dining area, and local musicians play live on Sundays. The specialties are fish and chicken dishes, though this restaurant is also very popular for European-style steak with potatoes. *Tel: 20.21.20.54; Opposite Casa Dansa; Meals CFA1,500-3,000, drinks CFA300-800; Open daily, 11am-12am*

Panama Gates This new restaurant serves deliciously cold drinks and tasty grilled brochettes, or kebabs. There is an upscale air-conditioned restaurant inside. Eating and drinking outside is cheaper, where there is also music. *Within 200 meters of Place de Catchi; Meals CFA1,500-3,000, drinks CFA300-900; Open daily, 11am-10pm*

Restaurant du Jardin des Plantes Naturelles-JPN *(Restaurant of the Garden of Natural Plants)* This outdoor restaurant offers pleasant dining in the park, with local cuisine such as fish, chicken, couscous, and omelets. After eating, visitors can escape the heat of the day under the shade of many trees and tour the Botanical Garden. *West end of town, near the hospital; Meals From CFA1,500, drinks CFA300-800; Open Tues-Sun, 10am-9pm; Closed Mondays*

Patisserie Esperance *(Hope Bakery)* This breakfast and snack shop sells fresh baked goods, baguettes, and yogurt from a little hut. It is convenient for grabbing a bite to eat en route out of the city. *By the bridge at the southern entrance of Porto-Novo; Pastries CFA400-600; Open daily, 8am-9pm*

Restaurant Akango Akango is a stylish and central restaurant that offers local cuisine with indoor and outdoor dining. The tables even have tablecloths and the friendly waitresses provide menus. A recommended dish here is the poulet bicyclette, or African-style free-range chicken with akassa. *Tel: 90.93.15.58; South of the Museum of Ethnography; Meals CFA2,500, drinks CFA300-800; Open daily, 12pm-10pm*

NIGHT LIFE

Going dancing is always an interesting way to spend an evening in Benin. Porto-Novo offers many *buvettes* and restaurants full of ambiance, but the best places to dance are **Feelings Night Club**, attached to the *Complex Soufianou Hotel* northwest of town, and **Hotel Dona Nightclub,** on the north side of town near *Carrefour Catchi.* Feelings Night Club is open daily from 11pm-4am, has a CFA3,000 entrance fee, and attracts the young, well-to-do crowd of Porto-Novo with its American, European, and West African dance music. Dona Nightclub has the same hours and no cover charge, and is located on the terrace above the hotel. It is a lively place to have a drink and dance while enjoying the cool evening air.

ACCOMMODATIONS

Hotel Casa Dansa** This hotel offers some basic budget rooms. There is a quiet courtyard, and a small pond with caimans. The associated restaurant offers both higher-priced European cuisine (CFA5,000) and cheaper Beninese dishes. The bar and restaurant has a great music vibe in the evenings. *Tel: 20.21.48.12; Avenue Ballot, west side of the town center, near the Assemblée Nationale; CFA5,500-10,500; fan or a/c, hot water in some rooms, private shower and toilet*

Hotel Détente** This centrally located hotel offers clean, budget rooms with balconies. There's a great view of the lake and a large garden area with a terrace restaurant that offers three-course meals for CFA3,500. The markets and museums are within easy walking distance. *Tel: 20.21.44.69; At the south entrance of Porto-Novo, right on Lake Nokoué; Rooms From CFA6,000; fan or a/c, private shower and toilet*

Centre Songhaï*** The rooms are very clean and simple, and though not located downtown, there are many services available on site. The private, air-conditioned rooms are comfortable and reasonably-priced, and the dormitory-style rooms are the best budget option in town. There is a high-end restaurant that offers local and European cuisine, and an outdoor *buvette* and grill that serves barbequed pork with akassa and spicy crushed pepper, locally made fruit juices, yogurts, and ice creams. There is also a large high-speed internet café with an air-conditioned navigation room available for a slightly higher price. Songhaï-manufactured soaps, syrups, juices, and baked goods are available at the center's boutique. *Tel: 20.22.50.92; A couple kilometers north of town near Ouando Piscine; CFA4,000-20,000; private rooms or dormitory style, with fans or a/c, mosquito net*

Songhaï Centers

Named after the 12th century Malian empire that ruled much of West Africa, the Songhaï Center was established in 1985 by Father Godfrey Nzamujo in a suburb of Porto-Novo. With the help of local teenage dropouts, Nzamujo created a training center for the production, research and the development of sustainable agricultural practices. Today, the Songhaï Center continues to host conventions and training sessions that promote the implementation of sustainable farming techniques for the improvement of agriculture in Benin. Visitors can tour the lush gardens and observe the various farming methods in practice, such as large-scale composting, animal husbandry, snail farms, and fish cultivation. The Porto-Novo center remains the headquarters of the NGO, with agriculture centers, internet cafés, and boutiques also located in Cotonou, Savalou, Lokossa, and Parakou.

Musée da Silva Hotel*** The museum offers clean rooms, though it is beginning to look run-down. Because it is on a busy street, noise can be a problem. *Tel: 20.21.50.71; Rue Toffa, near the Bank of Africa; Rooms From CFA13,000; a/c, private bath*

Complex Soufiano*** The rooms are a bit small, but this would be the best place to stay if you want to experience a late night at Feelings Night Club attached to the hotel. *Northwest of the town center; CFA10,000-15,000; a/c, private bath*

Hotel Dona**** This is one of the newest and most expensive hotels in town. Painted a flashy pink, this hotel can get rather noisy with its bar/restaurant and nightclub. The restaurant serves European cuisine. *Tel: 20.21.30.52; contact@hoteldona.com; North side of town, near Carrefour Catchi; CFA17,000; a/c, private baths*

Hotel Beaurivage**** Beaurivage has a pleasant setup overlooking Lac Nokoué, with a large garden and comfortable rooms. The restaurant serves high-end European cuisine, though the service and food aren't always reliable. *Tel: 20.21.23.99; Boulevard Lagunaire, west of the town center; Starting at CFA15,500; double rooms with a/c*

Avrankou

Originally called *Avlankou*, this village was named after the death of a local plantain picker named Avlan. The word *kou* in the Gun language means death. As with several other town and city names in Benin, the French later altered the word to 'Avrankou' so that it was easier to pronounce. Located on the paved road between Porto-Novo and Nigeria, the village and its surroundings hold several sacred forests where traditional festivities take place. There is a large Catholic cathedral on the northern edge of the village, which was decorated by Beninese artist Félix Agossa (see pg 41), who also painted frescoes in the cathedrals of Lokossa, Allada, Dassa-Zoumé, and Godomé in Cotonou. Street stands and cafeterias can be found at the town center for a

oueme & plateau

cheap Beninese meal. There are no lodging options in Avrankou, so it is best to plan on staying in Kétou or Porto-Novo when visiting this area.

Kétou

Kétou is a predominantly Yoruba town with a rich spiritual history, involving the Nigerian Kingdom of Oyo and *Orisha*, the Yoruba form of vodoun. Kétou is also famous for its pile of trash. Known as **Aitan Ola**, this sacred garbage pile is a small mountain of waste that tells a fabulous tale of religious customs unique to the town. The paved road continues across Kétou toward Bohicon; this road is much less travelled, and taxis are scarce, but there are fewer potholes which makes it a more comfortable ride. Before traveling on, though, visit the royal palace and the Kétou markets.

GETTING THERE
Kétou, within the Plateau department, is about 140 kilometers northeast of Cotonou. Taxis from the Dantokpa market in Cotonou cost CFA2,500.

From Porto-Novo, take a taxi at the Ouando station. Vehicles leave frequently and cost about CFA2,000. The road between Porto-Novo and Kétou continues paved all the way to Abomey, making it the best road in the country since it's the least traveled. For quicker access to Kétou, take a taxi from Dantokpa to Ouando and then another vehicle from Ouando to Ketou. It takes a long time to fill a taxi for Kétou in Dantokpa, but a taxi to Ouando fills quickly. Taxis leave Dantokpa for Porto-Novo and Ouando every two minutes.

Kétou has one paved east-west road through its center, another road connecting Kétou to Illara in Nigeria, and a newly paved road connecting Kétou to Pobé and Porto-Novo, which is near completion.

Staying Safe

The community of Kétou celebrates its most powerful Orisha divinity, the Oro, during the month of August. These celebrations are sacred and completely forbidden to women. It is strongly advised to avoid Kétou throughout the celebrations, especially if not affiliated with any local community members. Foreign men should only attend if they know someone who can escort them. This also applies to other communities in the region which celebrate the Oro—Pobé in particular is known for its Oro sects. Only address the subject with very trustworthy and familiar people, and never use the word 'Oro' in public. Women in particular should never ask about it, and men should say *'fétiche'* rather than *'Oro.'* The guides at the Kétou royal palace can provide information on necessary precautions regarding the Oro.

There are three taxi *gares* in Kétou: one near the market for people heading south to Porto-Novo and Cotonou, one on the west side toward Bohicon, and another on the southern road that heads to Pobé.

Taxis to Bohicon in the west cost CFA2,000, and CFA500 to the Nigerian border 18 kilometers to the east.

Local *zemidjan* rides should not cost more than CFA150.

SIGHTS AND ACTIVITIES

The Royal Palace of Kétou

The palace houses the current king and is open to visitors. There is no official entry fee or tourist office, but guides are always available and in the vicinity. A donation of about CFA1,000 is expected. Visitors must remove their shoes before entering certain parts of the palace and ask permission to take photographs. The king is welcoming and of course must be treated with the utmost respect. There are many fetishes and shrines to observe throughout the palace, with their respective stories and sacred significance. *About 200 meters down a dirt road on the north side of town; Open daily*

The Sacred Door Akaba Idenan

Originally the site of the only entrance to the town of Kétou, this sacred doorway is fortified with traditional military walls and ditches. It is also the center for the Orisha cult of Kétou, and the area is laden with shrines, statues, and ceremonial sites. Because it is sacred, it is important for visitors to first seek permission or a local guide before approaching and taking photographs. The best way is to ask the king at the royal palace. He will ask for a fee of about CFA500-1,000 and provide a guide.

Aitan Ola - The Sacred Garbage Pile

Located near the Royal Palace, this Orisha shrine was established in the early days of Kétou's history. The mound of garbage sits over a sacred charm, said to offer protection to the Kétou Kingdom in time of war. When it was first buried, locals were given strict instructions to cover the charm with anything they could find—hence the garbage.

Kétou Markets

Kétou has three markets: the main market is every five days, a smaller market takes place two days after the main market, and a daily market is located near the western taxi *gare*. The main market is lively and attracts vendors and shoppers from throughout the region. One can find the typical foods and market items, as well as many intriguing and forbidden vodoun objects, such as the protection ring. Made from metal, these common vodoun rings can be bought at the market and 'charged' to protect the purchaser from maladies or maledictions. Other items include plant seeds, pulverized animal bones, and rodent

oueme & plateau

skulls. It is difficult to understand the meaning and function of all of these items, though most of them are used in sacrificial ceremonies for the divinities. Each divinity requires different ingredients, which in turn vary according to the reason for the sacrifice.

EATING AND DRINKING

The specialty dish in Kétou is *lafou*, a type of *pâte* made of cassava and corn flour. It is the main staple in the local diet and can be found in any food stall or restaurant around town.

Ave Maria This is the best place to eat in town. The owner is a very welcoming woman who loves foreigners. She makes *akassa, amiwo*, chicken, salad or just about anything with advance notice. *On the road to Porto-Novo, halfway between the high school and the customs checkpoint; Meals CFA500-1000, drinks CFA300-800; Open daily, 11am-10pm*

Maquis La Détente This bar and restaurant serves Beninese cuisine, including a good selection of fried fish. Salads are also available depending on ingredient availability. *Southern edge of town; Meals CFA500-1,500, drinks CFA300-800; Open daily, 11am-10pm*

Food Stall The *tantie* prepares excellent local dishes such as *akassa, amiwo*, and *eba*. Her cooking attracts people from all over town, especially at lunch time. *Across from the old City Hall; Meals CFA300-800; Open daily, 9am-8pm*

ACCOMMODATIONS

Motel Yokpodugbé This friendly, colorful and inexpensive hotel has a restaurant offering excellent jollof rice and fish. The rooms are clean and simple, and for a little extra, a room with a private bath is available. *Off the road that leads to the village of Ofia; Rooms CFA3,000; fan, television, shared bathroom; Meals CFA1,500-2,000, drinks CFA300-800*

Auberge de la Cité Auberge de la Cité prepares dishes such as grilled chicken, fish, couscous, and fries. The cook will make a hearty salad too, if requested a couple days prior. The rooms have shared baths, or a private bathroom for a little extra. *Just down the south-bound road from the taxi gare to Pobé; Rooms CFA3,000; fan, television, shared bathroom; Meals CFA600-1800, drinks CFA300-800*

Mono & Couffo

The Mono *département* is named after the river forming the border with Togo, from Aplahoué down to Grand Popo. A diverse area, the Kotafon and Mina are the most common ethnicities, though Fon, Watchi, and Adja people also live throughout the *department.* This region is fairly well developed because of the historical commerce along the river with the French colonists, and there are churches and schools dating back to the first missions in the 1880s. Originally a wooded area, especially the gallery forests along the Mono River, the region has seceded to the 'derived savanna' state of secondary growth woods, cultivated fields, and savanna grasses. Lokossa is the Mono capital; other prominent commercial towns are Grand Popo, Comé, and Possotomé. The Mono/Couffo region is generally referred to as 'Ajda,' which is the dominating ethinicity between the two *départements.*

The Couffo is also bordered by the Mono River and covers an area of 2,400km². This region has gentle hills and distinct red-colored dirt. Cotton is a common field crop, along with corn, cassava, and beans. The *département* was formed in 1999 when it split from the Mono department, with its administrative seat in Dogbo. The majority of the population speaks Adja, and other major languages include Fon, Kotafon, and Mina. It is known to be one of the least economically developed departments of Benin.

Grand Popo

Grand Popo sits right on the Cotonou-Lomé highway, 30 kilometers east of the Togo border and 85 kilometers from Cotonou. Barely more than a village, its population of about 2,000 is primarily Mina, and it is sprawled widely along the beach. Grand Popo was a major port during the slave trade and into the colonial era, but its importance declined drastically when the French built a deep-water port in Cotonou. Some of the colonial ruins are still visible, though much of the old town has been submerged by the encroaching ocean.

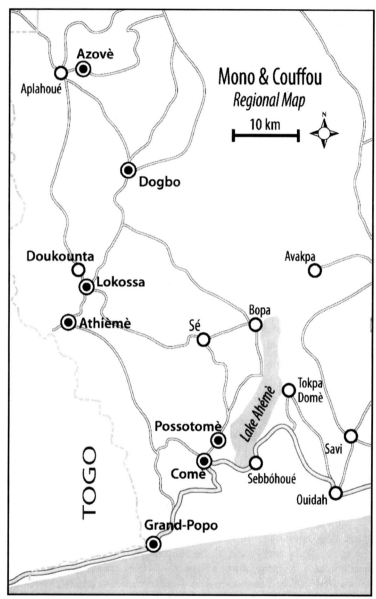

Toll booths mark the west entrance of the Grand Popo area. Women young and old sit along the road at the toll station selling red palm oil (called *aglan* in Mina), crabs, and *wagasi* from woven baskets. Surprisingly, fishing is not a major income activity for the natives of the area, but rather for the Ghanaian immigrants. Visitors can observe the fishing on the beach, as long lines of men and women haul enormous nets from the ocean, previously dropped from dugout canoes. Grand Popo is also the second largest onion producer in Benin, after Malanville in the northeast.

GETTING THERE AND AWAY

From Cotonou, hail a taxi at *Etoile Rouge* headed to Lomé—the ride should cost around CFA1,500. If there is no taxi to Lomé, take one from *Etoile Rouge* for Comé, which costs CFA800-1,000. There are two major taxi stops in Comé: tell the driver to stop at the intersection for Grand Popo, or else be prepared to walk back across the town. From Comé, a taxi to Grand-Popo costs CFA500-600. Stay vigilant and remind your driver to stop at the entrance of Grand Popo. From there, a *zemidjan* can continue through town to find a hotel.

mono & couffo

The old railway path picks up on the north side of the Mono River bridge just off the highway, and leads all the way to Athiémé. A *ze-midjan* or hired taxi can follow this route. Hail taxis heading toward Comé from Togo by standing next to the highway. These can be slow-coming, since most taxis fill up at the Togo border.

COMMUNICATIONS

The local government is currently negotiating internet availability, thus internet should be available at either the *Centre de Cooperation* between the Auberge and Villa Karo, or the *Centre Culturel Américain*, next to Villa Karo.

SIGHTS AND ACTIVITIES

Grand Popo is a great place for peaceful days lounging at the beach. While exploring the town, be sure to catch a soccer or basketball game at the local school or public stadium. Head over to the main drag to shop for souvenirs in the various handicraft cabins, especially **Aux Beaux Arts** near the Auberge and Farafina Boutique. The calabash lamps at Aux Beaux Arts are particularly interesting. The Grand Popo market is located at the base of the bridge crossing the Mono River, but it is fairly small since it is so close to the larger market of Comé. The **Villa Karo** is a Finnish-African cultural center which provides film nights, concerts, dance and language lessons, a museum, and a library.

Fishing Villages on the Coast

A series of coastal fishing villages sheltered by tall coconut trees extend to the Togo border. The beach front here is practically deserted during the day, and the waves are quite intense (swimming is not advised). An hour before sunset the fishermen return from the days work, fighting the waves to reach the shore. Some-times the *pirogues* overturn, and children waiting on the beach chase after fallen items like nets, buckets, and other lost gear. Once back on land, everyone helps pick the fish out of the nets, put the *pirogues* on shore, and roll up the nets. Wom-en from the market, or those just buying for the evening's meal, await the fishermen to barter for fresh fish.

La Bouche du Roi

A tour of the older, colonial-era part of Grand Popo and a boat trip to *La Bouche du Roi*, the 'King's Mouth', which is the mouth of the Mono river, can both easily be organized through the **Auberge de Grand Popo** (see accommodations). The tour of the 'old town' goes through several small villages and beautiful mangroves along the riv-er. On the river tour, pay attention to the tremendous currents, especially when swimming. The cost per person for these tours ranges from CFA2,500 to 5,000

Nonvitcha

Grand Popo is the place to be for Pentecost, known as *nonvitcha* in Mina, which takes place fifty days after Easter. Hundreds to thousands of visitors attend the weekend-long party and celebrate throughout the village. There are parties all Saturday night, with a Catholic mass befitting the size of the party. After mass, the celebrants and everyone else find a corner of the beach to have a picnic lunch—the beach is packed and it's a great time.

Across the border

Grand Popo is a small 'tongue' of land sticking into Togo; the Mono River here runs parallel to the coast before emptying into the ocean on the east side of the village. One can cross into Togo via a ferry to reach Agbannakin, a small village with colonial ruins and calm *buvettes*. This is reportedly the site of the Mina's last stand against the Fon in the territorial raids during the slave trade. The name *Agbannakin* is a shortened version of the true name of the town, a phrase representing how difficult it was to conquer the Mina: 'one cannot make *pâte* in a calabash.'

> **Togo Border Crossing**
>
> The official Togo border crossing, about 30 kilometers west of Grand Popo, is popular for its 'tax-free' zone with many products such as music CDs for CFA500, *yovo* vegetables, meat, bread, and other treats. Togolese visas are available here for CFA15,000. Togolese taxis to Lomé cost about CFA2,000 from this point.

EATING AND DRINKING

Awalé Plage and the **Auberge de Grand Popo** (see accommodations) each have good restaurants with Western and Beninese cuisine at a range of prices, though the Auberge seems to have a better reputation. Cocktails at the Auberge cost up to CFA4,000. Beer is sold only in small bottles, or *petite bouteilles*, and cost more than in the village *buvettes*. Other recommeneded spots:

Food Stand A *tantie* who sells *com*, a local dish popular in the Mono region (see Food and Drink on pg 64), sets up a rough-hewn table with a couple of oil lamps in the evenings, closing shop when the food runs out. *Along the main road between the Auberge and Awalé Plage; Plates at CFA300-600*

Bar Restaurant Bel Ibis Bel Ibis serves spaghetti and omelets, making it an ideal stop for those tired of *pâte*. *Right at the intersection of the brick road and highway, next to the zemidjan station; Plates CFA600-1,000, drinks CFA250-600; Open daily, 9am-10pm*

Blue Moon Opened in 2007, this chic restaurant provides up-scale service and excellent European cuisine. *On the road towards Togo, before Awalé Plage; Plates CFA3,000-7,000, drinks CFA600-1,500; Open daily, 12pm-10pm*

Sous les Nimes (Under the Neem Trees) This reputable *buvette* is ideally located, with an outdoor dining area under the shade that is degrees cooler and perfect for lunching. Try the fresh grilled fish with a side of rice and sauce. *Beneath a stand of Neem trees between the brick road and the highway; Plates from CFA500, drinks CFA250-700; Open daily, 11am-10pm*

Sea Turtles

From July to March, sea turtles come to the beach side near the *Bouche du Roi*. A local environmental organization collects the eggs each season. On January 9th, they release the baby sea turtles at the beach. Visitors in the region at this time have a great opportunity to see conservation in Benin.

ACCOMMODATIONS

Clean and affordable, the hotels of Grand Popo provide a relaxing distraction from the hustle and dirt of Cotonou, in a smaller setting than Ouidah. There are five hotels in Grand Popo: Lion Bar, Auberge de Grand Popo, Awalé Plage, Etoile de Mer, and Bel Azur. Lion Bar is located along the brick road, or *voie pavé*, running parallel to the beach, at about a CFA100 *zemidjan* ride from the main intersection. The Auberge lies beyond, about a CFA200 ride from the intersection. Awalé Plage and Bel Azur are located on the highway to Lomé.

Lion Bar Lion Bar is an ideal rest stop for backpackers. Beach mats are available for lounging, with parasols built into the sand. Soft drinks, beer, and cocktails are available at the bar. Plates can be prepared if ordered in advance. Lion Bar also has a bright red, green, and yellow painted vehicle that can be rented, with its driver, for tours through the Mono. *Just off the brick road, walk about 50 feet in the sand. Look for a sign in Rastafarian red-green-yellow next to the road indicating the path; Rooms from CFA5,000; Camping CFA2,000; fan, showers, and toilet*

Auberge de Grand Popo This beachfront guest house is set far back from the paved road and has a calm atmosphere. The colonial style Auberge has a restaurant overlooking the ocean, a swimming pool, and lounge chairs both on the beach front and poolside. European and Beninese plates are available for CFA2,500-7,000. The staff can help organize various tours and can also arrange private drum lessons. The Auberge is French-owned and is the first of a chain of hotels located in major towns across Benin, including Dassa, Parakou, Savalou, and Kandi. *Tel: 22.43.00.47; www.hotels-benin.com; On the beach east of the village center, CFA100-200 by zem from the beginning of the brick road; Rooms CFA13,000-23,000; fans or a/c in bungalows, ocean or garden view rooms; Camping available: with Auberge tent CFA5,000, with personal tent CFA2,000.*

Awalé Plage This guesthouse is situated in the middle of a tropical garden, with a private beach and swimming pool equipped with lounge chairs. The restaurant serves European cuisine under a *paillote*. The prices range from CFA2,500-5,000 or more per meal. *Tel: 22.43.01.17; awaleplage@yahoo.fr or awalegp@intnet.bj; Just past the main intersec-*

tion in Grand-Popo, on the road to Togo and just after the gendarmerie; CFA12,000- 20,000; tents at CFA5,000; fans or a/c

Hotel Bel Azur This German-owned hotel opened in 2005. There is a swimming pool and a private beach equipped with lounge chairs and parasols. The restaurant serves European and Beninese dishes for CFA2,500-7,000. Out of town toward Togo, this hotel is designed more for those with personal vehicles or a hired taxi. Though it has a business-style atmosphere, there is a great night club which is hopping on holidays and decent on an average Saturday night. *Far west end of the town, on the Lomé highway; From CFA15,000; spacious rooms with a/c, balconies, and ocean views*

Hotel Etoile de Mer Located beach front, the hotel courtyard is decorated with elegant bougainvilleas. The staff can help organize a boat tour of La Bouche du Roi. *Right at the junction in the middle of Grand Popo on the brick road.; CFA8,500-25,000; fan, kitchenette available, extra bed for CFA1,500*

Swimming Hazard

Although arguably the best beach location in Benin, the tremendous waves created from currents close to the bank make swimming a dangerous venture. Many reputable swimmers have been surprised by the strength of the waves in the ocean and the strong current at the mouth of the river. The waves can cause joint dislocation and even death. Swimming is greatly cautioned.

Comé

Comé, predominantly Mina, is a significant commercial town with a bustling market. It is an important transport junction for the southwest of Benin, and taxis will usually stop here before continuing either west toward Togo or north to Lokossa. Comé is most notable for its *ablo*-vendors, who chase relentlessly after slowing vehicles with their baskets full of food. These women often have children strapped to their backs and a load of *ablo*, or steam-baked corn bread, fish, and fried snails balanced on their heads as they race to be the first to sell. Cafeterias and food stands also line the road, making for a convenient lunch stop.

One recommened spot is **Tantie V Doublé**, or Aunt Double V (a*bout 100 meters south of the gare, indicated by a large sign; plates CFA500-2,000).* This *buvette* serves rice and *pâte* dishes throughout the day, along with cold drinks. There are large displays of packaged cookies and snacks for sale at the entrance. Though this stop is right along one of the busiest highways, it has a comfortable set-up.

GETTING THERE

From Cotonou, a taxi from *Etoile Rouge* costs about CFA800. From Lokossa, the ride should be CFA600-700, and from Grand Popo about CFA500.

Sé

The village of Sé is the next stop after Comé, for CFA200-300 more in a taxi, and is notable for its pottery market. Visible from the highway at the southern edge of town, many roadside stands display clay pots of various sizes. Vases for holding a day's worth of water, tea mugs, ashtrays, and many other objects are for sale. The **Pole Nord**, on the northern edge of town, is a magnificent two-story, open-air bar that is perfect for a refreshingly cold drink. This bar also sells typically tasty Beninese food, and is in the process of adding rooms for guest accommodations.

Possotomé and Lac Ahémé

Possotomé should be a familiar name once in Benin since this is the source of the bottled mineral water sold throughout the country (a bottling plant is located in the middle of town). This lakeside fishing community has become a popular tourist destination.

GETTING THERE AND AWAY

The best way to get to Possotomé is to first take a taxi to Comé. From there, take the asphalt road which goes directly to the lakeside village. A *zemidjan* ride costs CFA500-1,000, depending on the quantity of luggage. Renting a whole taxi costs about CFA5,000. The ride is very pleasant, with passing scenery of lush green groves and small villages.

SIGHTS AND ACTIVITIES

Ecobenin & Possotomé Area Tours

Ecobenin is a non-governmental eco-tourism organization based in Abomey-Calavi that arranges tours across the country including the parks in the north and other popular eco-tourist sites. The regional office in Possotomé (*Tel: 97.27.31.57, www.ecobenin.org*) is very active and coordinates many activities, from biking through lakeside villages and participating in community festivities, exploring the local sacred forests and viewing the monkeys and bird life with-

> **Guided tours of the Possotomé Region with Ecobenin**
> One tourist circuit , CFA5,000
> Two circuits, CFA9,000
> Three circuits , CFA12,500.

in, to visiting Possotomé's many artisans and learning about their craft. There is a small guest house run by Ecobenin where visitors can stay for a modest fee of around CFA3,000. Ecobenin also has camping available.

Possotomé lake tours are also given by local fishermen in their dugout canoes. A tour arranged by the **Palais des Jeunes** hotel costs CFA2,000 per person per hour, and CFA3,000 from **Chez Theo** and the **Village Club Ahémé**. Fishing is typically available for visitors on the tour, though it is not too productive since overfishing has resulted in a fish scarcity.

EATING AND DRINKING

The three hotels are the only actual restaurants in town; however street food and *buvettes* are available. The local specialty is smoked prawns and fried *agouti* or bushrat, served with *eba*, which is *gari* cooked in palm oil.

ACCOMMODATIONS

Palais des Jeunes This is the cheapest hotel in Possotomé, offering clean, basic rooms set around an open courtyard. The restaurant makes food to order for about CFA1,000 per plate. The staff is friendly and helpful in coordinating lake tours and providing information on the local markets. *Tel: 96.12.87; palaisdesjeunes@yahoo.fr; Just beyond the village center and close to the lake; CFA5,000; private shower and toilet*

Hotel Village Club Ahémé This hotel has 46 rooms of different categories surrounded by a lush garden full of birds. There is a high-end restaurant and bar, a swimming pool, and internet access for hotel guests. Lake tours can be organized by the staff. *Tel: 43.00.29 villageaheme@yahoo.fr; On the lakeshore; CFA12,500-22,500; a/c, private shower and toilet*

Chez Théo This hotel is a wonderful retreat with a clean and calm courtyard of flowers, trees, and a garden kitchen. Located on the bank of the lake, the dining area is over the water in a vast and beautifully constructed covered wooden deck. *Tel: 43.08.06 On the lakeshore, northeast of Hotel Village Club Ahémé; CFA10,000-18,000; fan or a/c, private shower and toilet*

mono & couffo

Lokossa

Lokossa is a rural city with a lot of businesses, though set well within a lower-economic population. Lokossa was originally called *Irokosa*, meaning 'under the Iroko tree' in Kotafon. It is the capital of the Mono region at the northern edge of the department. Dominated by the Kotafon ethnicity, the commune has a population of 70,000, with about 40,000 residing in the town itself.

GETTING THERE

From Cotonou, a taxi headed to Lokossa, or 'Adja' as the taxi-men refer to it, from *Etoile Rouge* costs CFA1,500. From Azové, taxis leave rather frequently and cost CFA700. From other destinations:

Comé: CFA600-700 taxi ride

Athiémé: CFA300-400 *zemidjan* ride

Dogbo: CFA400-500 taxi ride

Doukounta: CFA500 *zemidjan* ride, plus a fee for waiting the return trip, about CFA1,000

COMMUNICATIONS

There are a number of internet cafés in Lokossa, which are constantly moving or closing, with new ones often popping up. A few recommended internet cafés are La Madeleine Hotel, the Ciel Ouvert (across from the market), and the Centre Songhaï (behind the Maison du Peuple). Western Union services are available at the Ecobank in Lokossa.

SIGHTS AND ACTIVITIES

If seeking to experience life in a typical bustling Beninese town, then there are some key areas to see in Lokossa. Tour the market area and eat some of the fried snack foods sold throughout. Baobab juice, lemonade, and other chilled juices are sold out of calabashes by the market. Saturday and Sunday mornings, especially after church service, the women and children tend to gather in the city center wearing their best outfits. A small market profits from this informal congregation as the women purchase items for dinner while they socialize. There is usually a lot of action with students, including concerts, and athletic games. Students are frequent weekdays around lunchtime at the inner-city high school called 'CEG1,' found near the centrally-located statue of Lokossa's founder.

The cathedral, the largest Catholic church in the region, decorated beautifully with floor-to-ceiling art behind the alter, is worth a visit. This church was consecrated in 2005, and since has served the Catholic population of Lokossa every Sunday, and the Mono/Couffo regional population on holidays with visits by high-ranking church officials. The courtyard wall is lined with statues of the Stations of the Cross. There is an affiliated book store next door, which sells religious artifacts and school books.

Doukounta-Hippopotamus in Lake Doukon

Visit the small fishing village of Doukounta, found about five miles northwest of Lokossa, and take a boat tour of Lake Doukon. Guided by local fishermen, visitors observe a hippopotamus family that lives in this small fishing lake. The best times of day to visit are early in the morning and late in the evening, just after sunrise or before sunset. The guide hands out a brochure on the history of the project, a couple of pairs of binoculars, and leads the way to the boat. After the lake visit, continue to the village for a ceremonial shot of *sodabi* and interact with the villagers. The guided tour costs CFA2,000, which is paid at the end of the visit.

The Hippos of Doukounta

The small Lake Doukon is filled by periodic flood water from the Mono River. Several years ago during one of these floods, a very small hippopotamus population secluded themselves in the lake: two females and a male. One day, a pregnant hippopotamus was crossing the road in search of food. At the same time, a woman with her baby strapped on her back was walking along the road. A large truck rushed past the hippo and spooked the animal into a stampede, ultimately trampling the woman and her baby. Outraged, the community killed the pregnant hippopotamus. Years later, when the community had recovered from the accident, a Peace Corps Volunteer with a local non-governmental organization initiated an eco-tourism project on the lake. Tourists came to observe the hippos, guided by the local fisherman who are fluent in the local hippo behavior. At the beginning of 2008, the remaining female hippopotamus gave birth. The male died of natural causes later in the same year, leaving a protective mother and her playful hippo-puppy as the main attraction for the profitable eco-tour activity in an otherwise simple fishing village.

Visitors on Lake Doukon

mono & couffo

To get to Lake Doukon, ask a *zemidjan* in Lokossa, or a taxi if with a large party, to go to the village of Doukounta to visit Lake Doukon. The transportation will need to wait during the hippo tour since there is very little traffic along this dirt road. A full taxi should cost about CFA2,000, and a *zemidjan s*hould agree to CFA500-1,000 for the entire trip.

Kpinnou Bird Lake

Kpinnou is a small village located along the highway in the Athiémé *commune*. The small lake next to the village creates an ideal bird habitat. The variety of birds found on this lake is impressive, with ducks and other water fowl found in every corner. A great way to get out on the lake is to schedule a tour by contacting the local *chef d'arrondissement,* at the *Mairie* (town hall) in Athiémé, or with the manager of the Hunger Project in Kpinnou. Typically, a fisherman offers visitors the front, unused portion of his boat while he checks his nets from the back. Be sure to arrive at daybreak for the tour not only to see the birds, but because this is the usual time for fishermen to check the day's catch. The cost for this tour is CFA500.

A *zemidjan* from Lokossa would agree to the trip to Kpinnou, but this would be more costly because of the distance, nearly CFA1,000 or more. A taxi will charge CFA200-300 from Lokossa or the Athiémé intersection for the short ride to the Kpinnou Hunger Project building, a locally recognized landmark. Here, ask for a tour of the lake.

EATING AND DRINKING

Café-Bar du Coin This *buvette-maquis* serves cold drinks and a nice leaf sauce with tender rabbit or *wagasi,* along with a choice of chicken, goat, or eggs. It's an excellent spot to drink a cold beer, watching the day's business wind down and the evening crowd gather. *At the corner of the central intersection in Lokossa; Plates CFA1,000-2,000, drinks CFA250-700; Open daily, 11am-10pm*

Lunch Restaurant This little, nameless *maquis* serves fries and *amiwo, pâte,* and *akassa* with various sauces. It is a popular place for lunch, and has cold drinks and the added comfort of ceiling fans in a charming dining room. *Behind the Post Office; Plates CFA1,000-2,500, drinks CFA250-700; Open daily, 10am-3pm*

Restaurant Ambiancer Delicious *igname pilé* is sold here under a *paillote*. The dining area is small, but the restaurant's straw structure cools the place nicely. The manager and owner brings life to the name of the restaurant, as his charismatic demeanor creates a jovial ambiance. *Up the street from the Maison du Peuple and across the side street of the fabric factory; Plates CFA700-2,500, drinks CFA300-800; Open daily, 11am-10pm*

Supermarché Bel-Air Buvette Cold drinks are delightful at this open-air *buvette,* where tables and chairs are set out each evening on the sandy yard. The good music and crowd are a wonderful means of relaxation on clear, warm nights. *Past the cathedral, 50 meters to the left at the paved roundabout; Drinks CFA300-800; Open daily, 11am-10pm*

Bar Restaurant Les Collines Les Collines, the name reminiscent of that department well known for *igname pilé*, is one of the cleanest restaurants in Lokossa. Enjoy some of the best *igname pilé* outside of the Collines, with comfortable private dining as created between dividers made of woven palm leaves. *Past the Supermarché Bel-Air along the dirt road; Plates CFA700-1,700, drinks CFA300-900; Open daily, 11am-11pm*

Bar Restaurant Mefils This local spot serves cold drinks and various grilled meats including turkey, chicken, fish, and bush rat. Salads are also available. Everything is prepared by a *maman* and her family. The service is usually great, but can be slow on busy nights. *Up the dirt road, straight past the supermarket; Plates CFA1,000-2,000, drinks CFA300-800; Open daily, 11am-10pm*

Les Marmites de Grand Frère Catering more for planned parties and events, the staff will need advance warning to provide special dishes, though they do prepare basic plates daily. Grand Frère, the chef and owner, is by far the best cook (for Beninese and Western dishes) in all of Lokossa. *Tel: 93.46.62.72 / 93.66.69.51; About 50 meters down a dirt road directly across from the cathedral*

FanMilk Depot FanMilk is always good for a cold treat, with nearly all flavors available. The manager is a gentleman, and provides great service. *Next to the market; Open daily, 9am-7pm*

Markets

There are two markets in Lokossa: the typical market held every five days and the small *yovo* market where less common goods such as carrots, cabbage, eggplant, lettuce, and, canned vegetables are usually found daily. There are two supermarkets: **Supermarché Bel-Air** is located behind the cathedral, where goods such as yogurt, butter, milk, and a selection of wines and spirits are sold daily. The second supermarket is **Supermarché Aie-Peur** (Have Fear!), which is located down the dirt road past the Sonacop gas station on the highway to Cotonou. This supermarket has a good wine selection and even sells refrigerated hot dogs for those looking for a taste of Western food.

ACCOMMODATIONS

Hotel La Madeleine La Madeleine is the newest hotel in town, and fairly impressive. There are a number of rooms, some air conditioned and others with a fan. The restaurant, albeit expensive, serves decent Western and Beninese dishes. There is an internet café connected to the hotel with quality computers. Satellite televisions in each room offer many French, Ghanaian, and Nigerian channels. This hotel sits right next to the market and along a bustling thoroughfare to neighboring towns and villages. Despite its location, noise is generally not a problem.

There is a new hotel being built by the owners of Hotel la Madeleine along the highway on the southwest side of town. This is due to be completed by 2010. *Far end of market, headed out of town along a gravel road; From CFA10,000; fan or a/c, private baths, satellite television*

mono & couffo

Hotel le Baron This hotel is a common destination, and the *zemidjan*s know the place well. A zem ride here should cost no more than CFA200. The restaurant is equal to or better than that of La Madeleine, but is definitely a lot cheaper. The food here can be hit or miss, though, depending on the night of the week and the chef. *Tel: 22.41.18.80 / 22.41.14.64; Well off the highway, on the southern edge of town in the neighborhood known as Chez Pedro; From CFA7,000; fans or a/c, private bath*

Athiémé

The charm of Athiémé is in the air of the Mono River and the colonial ruins. Athiémé was the colonial capital of the Mono region beginning in the early 1900s, when it was economically and politically more important than Cotonou or Lokossa. A railroad transported produce, creating commerce and an ethnically diverse area from Accra, Ghana, through Togo, to Athiémé and Grand Popo in Benin (then Dahomey). The railway lines were removed when the trade collapsed during the communist era in the 1960s, but the remaining path serves as a road between Athiémé and Grand Popo, linking many villages in between.

The international commerce during the first half of the 1900s induced strong diversity resulting in five different ethnic groups, each with their respective language, within the jurisdiction of the Athiémé commune. The Mina people, also called Guin, are descendants from Ghana and dominate the town, while the Kotafon people tightly surround Athiémé. Six kilometers northwest of Athiémé reside the Watchi, and eight kilometers to the east a form of Adja is heard. Fon, the dominant language in the south, is spoken throughout the region.

Disputed History

Athiémé has a unique history in that its founder is disputed! Ancestry is the root of belonging in Beninese culture, thus varying settlement stories are sensitive topics. According to legend, a man named Adity Donou fled tribal wars between the Fon people in the 1800s and settled an area he named *Adanlokpé*, meaning 'Where the Anger Stops.' His nephew, Akoubalaty, followed him and settled an area closer to the river, in the Samba trees. 'In the Samba trees' translates to *Atihéweme* in Mina, the area now known as Athiémé. The French colonists arrived via the river in the mid 1880s, thus finding Akoubalaty and his settlement first. The disagreement lies in which of the two founders should be credited for the establishment of the town. Today, *Adanlokpé* is a neighborhood of Athiémé. The residents of any neighborhood are sure to recount some version of this story, depending on where their alliance lies.

GETTING THERE

From Lokossa, a *zemidjan* ride to Athiémé costs around CFA400, give or take according to the starting point in Lokossa.

From Cotonou, take a taxi from *Etoile Rouge* toward Adja, or Lokossa. The driver will stop at Zounhoué, which should cost CFA1,500. A *zemidjan* will complete the four kilometers on the dirt road to Athiémé for CFA200.

SIGHTS AND ACTIVITIES

Visit the river at the west end of town. In Athiémé, the river is a popular site for catching a bit of fresh breeze, doing laundry, or participating in any other river-side activity. A few families live on the Togo side of the river and cross the water regularly for school and business. One can explore the Togo side of Athiémé by taking one of the readily available canoes for a small donation (CFA100-200 should suffice).

There is an official river crossing point located past Athiémé and through the neighboring villages of Agniwedji and Lokossavi. Many local merchants traverse the Mono River here to buy goods in Lomé, Togo. The crossing fee is CFA100-200. There is a small Togolese town and market farther down the road. Show identification to the border guards and explain the visit. On the return trip, be sure to bring a small gift for the guards since technically a Togo visa is required. An Italian development organization has promised to construct a bridge at this river crossing.

Be sure to ask permission to take pictures and say hello to the passers-by, for Athiémé has great personality. Soccer games and political rallies are dear in this town. If either are manifesting, take care to pay attention for at least the entertainment it brings.

mono & couffo

Where's the Pâte?

Don't expect to find *pâte* for sale at lunch or dinner time, as legend forbids that it be sold in Athiémé. Reportedly, Adity Donou asked for *pâte* one day upon returning from work in his fields. When the vendor asked him to pay for it, Donou was appalled and declared that neither he nor any of his descendants should ever have to pay for *pâte* in their own town. *Akassa* and *pâte rouge* are sold instead.

EATING AND DRINKING

Located in front of the mayor's office, Eugenie's **La Puissance de Goût**, or 'The Power of Taste,' is the most popular eatery. Eugenie sells food Monday through Saturday from about 10:30am until the food runs out (usually around 3:30pm). A plate of rice and/or beans, *akassa*, or *telibo* with sauce and hard-boiled eggs, meat, fish, or *wagasi*, costs CFA300-500. She also serves drinks. Other food can be found throughout the town at any time of day.

There are a couple of *buvettes* in Athiémé. The most popular is the **Cooperant** with its solidly built cement *paillote*, located next to the *Maison des Jeunes.*

Azové

Locally called 'Azovi,' this bustling city is the commercial capital of the Couffo, due to its location along the highway and its junction to Abomey. The market is scheduled in coordination with the Lokossa, Klouékanmè, and Dogbo markets. Internet access remains elusive in this town, though hotels, restaurants, and *buvettes* provide plenty of distraction for locals and visitors.

GETTING THERE
The road between Abomey and Azové is not frequently traveled. It is much easier to find transportation from Azové to Abomey, rather than the other way around. Taxis and *zemidjan*s for Abomey await passengers at the northwestern-most intersection in Azové. Vehicles fill rather quickly on market days and cost about CFA1,000. Representative of the economic status of this region, the vehicles are in poor condition and make vehicles bound for Cotonou appear luxurious. The route toward Abomey is enjoyable as it passes through lengthy spans of unpopulated forests and farmland, about a two hour ride. There are only a few small villages lining this section of highway, so patience is the virtue-of-all-virtues during those inevitable vehicle breakdowns.

> Taxis from *Etoile Rouge* in Cotonou to Azové cost CFA1,800-2,000.

SIGHTS AND ACTIVITIES
The main attraction in Azové is the vast market in the center of town. It takes place every five days and boasts an important textile section, with an endless selection of fabrics on display. From Azové, there are several possible excursions or day trips to discover surrounding villages.

Togo Border
One can take a *zem* or bicycle to the Togo border beyond the village of **Aplahoué** and view some of the meagerly populated rural communities, not frequented by tourists. The border is about 15 kilometers from Azové and is most commonly used for large trucks, though some private vehicles pass through. A little *buvette* is installed there on the Togo side, with sodas and typical Togolese beers. It's easy to skip across the border for a drink and then jump back to Benin. There is very infrequent public transportation through this area, so a *zemidjan* would have to be hired for the return trip as well (this should cost a

total of about CFA1,500). The Togo side of the road is very rough, especially in the rainy season.

Local Villages

A great way to experience the inner countryside and rural life of the Couffo region is to explore the local villages and towns. **Djakatomé** is a small town south of Azové with an even smaller heritage museum. Though there are no official guides, informal village tours are available with a polite request. A taxi from either Dogbo or Azové costs CFA200-300, and a *zemidjan* costs CFA600.

Klouékanmè is located well off the main highway between Azové and Abomey and has a substantial regional market worth visiting. On market days, taxis cost CFA500 from Dogbo and CFA800 from Azové.

EATING AND DRINKING

Azové houses many bars. One recommended spot is the yellow painted *buvette* at the southern entrance of town, by the round-about past the **Supermarché Immaculé**. Various food stands line the streets, with *tanties* selling *pâte* dishes or beans and *gari*. A specialty in this town is *klouikloui*, which are dry, crunchy rings of fried peanut butter. *Klouikloui* is popularly eaten with *gari* or corn *bouillie*, and can be found at many roadside stands.

ACCOMMODATION

Le Plateau A simple hotel with basic amenities, Le Plateau is within walking distance of Azové's market. There is a pleasant café with coffee and cold drinks. *On the road to Aplahoué and Togo, northwest of the intersection for Abomey; From CFA6,000; fan, private shower and toilet*

Dogbo

Dogbo is an important commercial town. Oranges are a popular produce in the market, as well as red palm oil, s*odabi,* and beautiful hand-dyed indigo fabrics (ask for the 'tissu bleu de Toviklin'). The hustle and bustle of the market make it an exciting place to be, though the traffic has a particularly bad reputation. Reportedly at least one accident happens every market day.

From Lokossa a taxi should cost around CFA500 to Dogbo, and from Azové, CFA300.

SIGHTS AND ACTIVITIES

On a day trip to Dogbo, one can tour the market, followed by a visit to the small village of **Dogbo-Ahomé** where the King of Dogbo resides. Here, the continuous runoff from an artesian well has created a unique wetlands ecosystem adjacent to a sacred forest. The forest is forbidden to outsiders, but the artesian well, the spectacular flowers, and an opportunity to see the king make the trip worthwhile. A *zemidjan* ride out of the Dogbo market to Dogbo-Ahomé costs about CFA200.

Zemidjans at the Dogbo market can also give tours to the neighboring village of **Midangbé**. A former iron smelting site, this village is characterized by large piles of ore deposits and rudimentary smelting tools. There are caves which are said to have been used for sleeping, storage, or for hiding from various slave raids. Some old men in the village have attempted to mine mercury by hand. Not all *zemidjan*s can conduct a proper tour of Midangbè; one way to check is to ask them is they are familiar with the story of *les trous des hommes a queue*, or 'the holes of the men with tails.'

What's in a Name?

The town name of 'Dogbo' is an onomatopoeia. According to legend, a giant calabash fell from the sky and landed at the top of a hill (near the current mayor's office). As it rolled down the hill, something inside the calabash made the sound *dogbodgobdogbodogbo*. At the bottom it cracked open against a large tree, releasing a man and a woman, each with one arm and one leg. The couple worked together to build a home. Hunters who traveled through the region were so well received by the couple that they settled there and eventually built a town.

EATING AND DRINKING

The Dogbo market food stalls serve chick peas in palm oil, a highly recommended local specialty. A plate costs a mere CFA100-200. Beans and rice stalls are easy to find. More established *buvettes* and restaurants are locted past the market on the paved road toward the high school and mayor's office.

The Holes of the Men with Tails

One day foreigners began selling iron tools at the Dogbo market. Thought to have come from the north or perhaps Ghana, they arrived at the marketplace before everyone else, and they were always the last to leave. Villagers thought this behavior was odd and began to investigate the area of the market where the iron tool sellers set up shop. They discovered holes in the ground and assumed that these strange foreigners must have tails that they hid in the holes while sitting down. To unveil their secret, the story goes that the villagers filled the holes with red palm oil to attract fire ants. As expected, the 'men with tails' yelled and jumped, running out of the market.

Zou & Collines

The Zou département is located in the central region of the republic of Benin, covering an area of approximately 5,100km² with a population of around 630,000. The population is mostly Fon and Mahi, though Bohicon and Abomey are as multi-ethnic as any other large Beninese town. The historical capital of Benin, Abomey, is the main point of attraction in the Zou.

The Collines département covers an area of approximately 14,200km² with a population of around 500,000. The Collines, or 'hills' in French, is a region characterized by large plateaus dominated by ranges of rolling hills. For centuries, these hills were inhabited by local populations fleeing their brethren from the southern kingdom of Abomey, who sent warriors to seek slaves and sell them to the traders on the coast. The granite laden hillsides served as convenient fortresses for the refugees and today stand as reminders of this dramatic history.

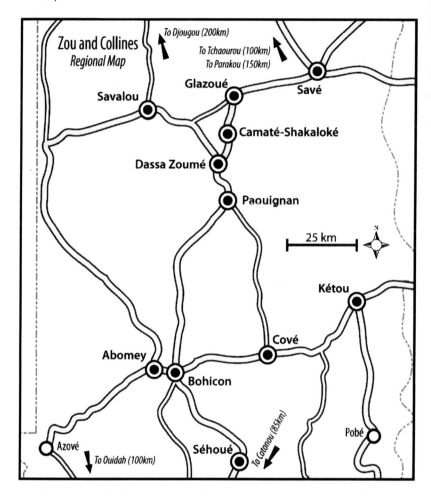

Zou and Collines Regional Map

To Djougou (200km)
To Tchaourou (100km)
To Parakou (150km)

Savalou
Glazoué
Savé
Camaté-Shakaloké
Dassa Zoumé
Paouignan

25 km

Kétou

Cové
Abomey
Bohicon

Azové
To Ouidah (100km)
Séhoué
To Cotonou (85km)
Pobé

Sèhouè

Situated about halfway between Cotonou and Bohicon, this little town is renowned for its fruit vendors. Cars and trucks are always parked along the road as passengers fill up on pineapples, bananas, oranges, plantains, papayas, and tomatoes. Women and children carrying heavy baskets of produce instantly crowd around a slowing vehicle. They seem to stop at nothing to make a sale, so much so that they often trample one another or breakout into fights. This is a great place to purchase fresh pineapple before continuing to the arid north, where fruit is much harder to find. Some taxi men do not habitually stop here, but will do so upon request. As soon as a vehicle stops, women thrust handfuls of bananas and oranges into the car, insisting on their superior quality. There are great deals in Sèhouè if buying in large quantities: ten medium-sized, deliciously sweet and juicy pineapples can sell for CFA1,000. Vendors will usually allow potential customers to taste their products before buying in bulk.

Bohicon

Bohicon lies 130 kilometers north of Cotonou, just east of Abomey and along the north-south highway. The town was founded in the 20th century when the French constructed the Cotonou-Parakou railway. A train station was built, followed by the establishment of a major marketplace. Today, Bohicon is intersected by two paved highways, connecting the north-south (Cotonou to Niger and Burkina Faso) and the east-west routes (Togo-Nigeria). Due to its crucial location, Bohicon has become a veritable crossroads of international trade. It is the third largest trade center in Benin, after Cotonou and Parakou. Bohicon also has a significant handicraft commerce, with several artisan shops lining the paved road leading west toward Abomey.

GETTING THERE

A bush taxi or bus from Cotonou at *Etoile Rouge* costs about CFA1,500. Taxis typically drop off their passengers at the gas station near the railway crossing. Teams of *zemidjans* in purple and orange shirts crowd new arrivals, offering their services.

SIGHTS AND ACTIVITIES

Bohicon has a large daily market in its interior, and there are multitudes of food vendors and kiosks lining the streets. Because it is an important taxi stop, the north-south highway is full of food stalls offering fruits and snacks, including bags of oranges, fried corn cakes, soy biscuits, and bread of all sorts and sizes. On the road to Abomey one can find the Bank of Africa, Ecobank and other banks, a large post office, cafeterias, a grocery store with European products, internet cafés, and the grand mosque. This commercial town is constantly bustling with chaotic traffic and vendors wheeling heavily loaded pushcarts. *Zemidjan* men, taxi drivers, and merchants tend to be aggressive and most visitors avoid spending more time than necessary here.

EATING AND DRINKING

Maquis Tanti Gabon Conveniently positioned on the north-south highway, this nationally renowned restaurant is a popular lunch and dinner stop for travelers. The friendly Gabonese staff offers cauldrons of African foods from which to choose, and a wide selection of cold beers and soft drinks. There are craft shops selling traditional wooden sculptures and mortars of all sizes in the vicinity. Tel: *22.50.00.75 / 22.50.13.80; At the south entrance of Bohicon, by the big round point and near Hotel Dako; Meals CFA600-2,000, drinks CFA300-900; Open daily, 11am-10pm*

Jardin de l'Hotel de Ville De Bohicon (City Hall Garden) This vast garden with tables in the shade is a quiet recluse from the noise and heat of the town. Togolese *tanties* serve cold drinks and basic rice dishes. Street stalls nearby typically offer fried yams, plantains, and bean or wheat beignets at midday. *On the road to Abomey, close to the market; Meals CFA1,000, drinks CFA300-800; Open daily, 12pm-10pm*

Maquis Malodie Amid street stands heaped with pineapples and oranges, this *maquis*-cafeteria is a nice, affordable spot for breakfast or lunch. Nescafé, tasty omelets with fried peppers and tomatoes, and other typical Beninese cuisine are served throughout the day. *On the street corner, near the train station; Meals CFA500-1,500, drinks CFA300-800; Open daily, 8am-10pm*

Cafeteria Stand This little no-name cafeteria stand has friendly staff and generous portions. Nescafé and Lipton tea are served in bowls with sweetened condensed milk and large pitchers of hot water. The attentive and accommodating cooks will prepare omelets or spaghetti upon demand. This is also a great spot to sit in the shade of the metal awning and watch the busy Bohicon merchants pass by on the street, or chat with the mechanics from next door. *On the road to Abomey, across from the Bank of Africa; Meals CFA200-1,000; Open daily, 8am-8pm*

Hotel Dako Restaurant This is the place to go for a little splurge and a taste of international cuisine, or simply to enjoy a cold beer beneath the shade of the *paillote* while watching Beninese television. The restaurant staff is friendly, and can provide good advice on touring the region. *Tel: 22.51.01.38; South entrance of town, near the round point; Meals 4,000 and up, drinks CFA500-1,500; Open daily, 8am-10pm*

ACCOMMODATIONS

Hotel Dako The large hotel complex is hard to miss, with a pink-painted gateway and large signs. Hotel Dako offers dozens of spacious, clean rooms, a swimming pool, and night club. Due to its central location within Benin, the hotel is popularly used for conventions and business conferences. The bar and restaurant, set under the shade of a *paillote*, offers international specialties. *Tel: 22.51.01.38; At the south entrance of town, by the big round point; CFA10,000-25,000; a/c, private bath*

Abomey

Abomey is the former capital of the Kingdom of Dahomey. The commune of Abomey covers about 140km^2, with a population of 17,300. While the rural populations of this commune continue to live chiefly off of agriculture, the urban neighborhoods of Abomey specialize in handicrafts.

GETTING THERE

Behanzin Monument

Abomey is situated 130 kilometers north of Cotonou. Taxis from *Etoile Rouge* usually drop off passengers in nearby Bohicon for CFA1,500. A *zemidjan* from Bohicon to Abomey costs CFA300-400. Direct taxis from Cotonou to Abomey exist, but are less frequent, and should cost about CFA1,700. Buses coming from the north or south drop passengers off at the Bohicon bus station. A *zemidjan* from there to Abomey costs about CFA500.

A taxi from Azové in the southwest costs CFA600. Vehicles headed to Adja-land from Abomey are not frequent and can take a long time to fill up. Many travelers take the quicker yet more expensive and much less comfortable option of hiring a *zemidjan* for the 45 minute ride to Azové. This costs around CFA1,500.

INTERNET

There is an internet café in the post office in the center of town. There are also a few places on the paved road leading out of Bohicon towards Abomey. As in the rest of the country, internet access here is ever changing.

POLICE AND HOSPITAL

Both the police station *(Tel: 22.50.00.12)* and the hospital (*Tel: 22.50.00.61*) are located on the paved road between Bohicon and Abomey.

SIGHTS AND ACTIVITIES

Behanzin Monument

A towering monument of King Behanzin stands at the east entrance of Abomey. His outstretched palm signals 'halt,' and symbolizes the king's efforts to fend off the French just before they conquered and colonized the Dahomey territory. The statue is surrounded by a triangular park dappled with trees and park benches.

zou & collines

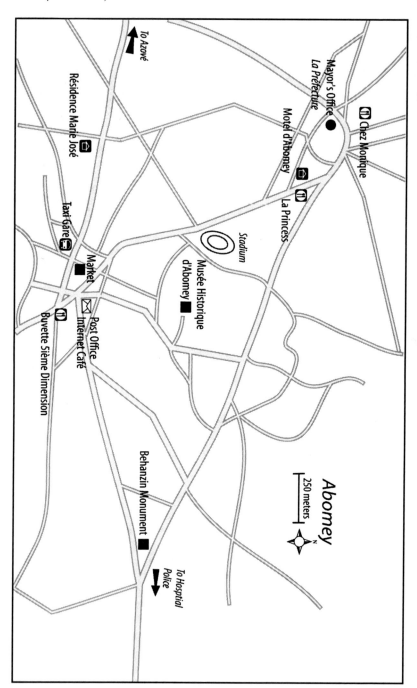

Musée Historique d'Abomey
Historical Royal Palace Museum

Situated in the heart of the ancient city, the red clay walls of the multiple kings' palaces built in the 17th century attest to the era of the powerful Dahomey Kingdom. The first palace was established by King Houègbadja in 1645. Each successive king built a new palace next to his predecessor's. When King Gbehanzin added his residence in 1889, the twelve palaces encompassed an area of 44 hectares, entirely surrounded by a ten meter-high wall. Many of the palaces were destroyed in 1892 when King Gbehanzin set fire to Abomey and fled as the French took control of the city and conquered the kingdom. In 1943

Visitors at the Palace Museum

zou & collines

the French established the Royal Palace Museum within the most intact remaining palaces, those of Kings Guezo and Glélé. In 1985, the 44 hectares of palace remains were listed as a UNESCO World Heritage Site. Many international organizations have initiated restoration and protection measures on the ancient palace walls. The museum is one of the best organized tourist sites in the country.

Knowledgeable guides take visitors through the two hectares of historical buildings full of artifacts, wooden thrones, vodoun statues, *fétiches*, decorated earthen huts, war objects, and anecdotes on the centuries of events that occurred within those walls. The museum tour finishes in the craftsmen's courtyard. The kings of Abomey had their own craftsmen with a series of workshops attached to the royal palace. Today, ornate brass sculptures, royal patchwork tapestries, handwoven drapes and hammocks, and other art objects are sold. The craftsmen use the same techniques and tools their ancestors used centuries ago. *Tel: 22.50.03.14; ahononlenoard@yahoo.fr; Open Mon-Sun, 9am-6pm, Closed on New Years Day; Non-Beninese: Adults CFA1,500; Children CFA1,000; Beninese: Adults CFA500; Children and students CFA300; All visits are guided with tours lasting about 2 hours; French and English guides available; No photos or audio recording allowed.*

EATING AND DRINKING

Motel d'Abomey This hotel restaurant serves both European and African cuisine, including fresh salads and chicken curry, in a dining room decorated with royal patchwork tapestries. *Tel: 22.50.00.75 / 22.50.13.80; North of the town center, near the Place de la Préfecture; Meals CFA2,500-4,000, drinks CFA600-1,000*

Bar Restaurant Chez Monique Serving typical local cuisine, Chez Monique is best known for its fried *poulet bicyclette* (African free-range chicken). The *pâte* rouge and fries are great too. Food should be ordered in advance as it can take some time to prepare. *Tel: 22.50.01.68; Behind the mayor's office; Meals CFA2,500, drinks CFA300-800*

Résidence Marie Joseé African and European specialties are served at this hotel restaurant. The garden atmosphere is relaxing and quite pleasant. *Tel: 22.50.02.89; Toward Lokossa, west of the market; Meals CFA2,000-4,500, drinks CFA500-1,000; Open daily, 8am-10pm*

La Princess This *maquis* sits in a triangle between two roads. It is a great spot for an evening drink in the open air. The *tanties* sell typical and budget Beninese food from their cauldrons, most often chicken and rice. If staying at the Motel d'Abomey located across the street, La Princess is a good dining and drinking alternative from the more expensive hotel restaurant. *Across the street from Motel d'Abomey; Meals CFA700-1,500, drinks CFA300-800; Open daily, 12pm-10pm*

Buvette 5ème Dimension (The Fifth Dimension) This lively bar and restaurant is set in a pleasant garden. Loud music abounds. *Near the market, at the town center; Meals From CFA1,500, drinks CFA300-800; Open daily, 11am-12am*

ACCOMMODATIONS

Auberge Chez Monique Chez Monique is a family-owned establishment that offers simple and clean rooms. There is a great nature scene, with pet monkeys, crocodiles, and small antelopes in the yard. Local artisans sell crafts and souvenirs in the shade of the large garden. There is even a makeshift ping-pong table and a boccie ball court. The bar and restaurant is an excellent spot for a refreshing drink after visiting the royal palace museum. *Tel: 22.50.01.68; near the Place de la Préfecture; CFA5,500-8,500, camping CFA3,000 per person; fan, private shower and toilet*

Motel d'Abomey This is a higher-end lodging option in town, with round bungalows split to form two spacious rooms. The lobby offers comfortable sofas and satellite television, and the elegant restaurant serves tasty European and African cuisine. The staff can assist in arranging a *zemidjan* tour of the city, including visits of the royal palace sites complete with stories about the kings and the battles against the French. **Prestige Nightclub** is attached, with a CFA2,000 entry fee. *Tel: 22.50.00.75/22.50.13.80; North of the town center, near the Place de la Préfecture and mayor's office; CFA10,000–40,000; fan or a/c, private shower and toilet, satellite TV*

Résidence Marie Joseé This is a shaded and calm retreat, far from the noise and bustle of the town center, with gardens and clean rooms. The hotel owners rent vehicles for day use and can organize guided tours of Abomey and surrounding areas. There is internet access available for CFA1,000 per hour. *Tel: 22.50.02.89; Toward Lokossa, west of the market; CFA6,500-18,500; fan or a/c, private shower and toilet, some rooms have hot water and tubs*

Cové

Cové is a large village populated primarily by Mahi people and located on the dirt road between Bohicon and Kétou. The Mahi language is similar to Fon and, according to tradition, these people actually stemmed from the Dahomey Kingdom as a rebel group that created separate settlements. Cové is most known for the yearly Gélédé Masked Festival celebrated by the Yoruba people, another dominating ethnic group in the region. Beninese and foreigners come to watch the vibrant masked dancers depict daily activities that include honoring the role of women in their society. The Gélédé Festival is a tradition that dates back to the 15th century, and the masked dances are only performed by village men who have been initiated through intricate rituals into the relevant secret society. These men are qualified to play the sacred ceremonial instruments and to fall into a dancing trance as they personify the spirits and the female characters being honored.

Environmental Concerns in the Collines

The landscape of the Collines was originally wooded savannah, but the pressure of the increased population has resulted in deforestation at an alarming rate. Agriculture is the principal activity throughout the rural region. Cotton monocultures have been the main source of agricultural revenue, but climate change and over-cultivation have greatly diminished soil fertility and caused increasingly poor cotton harvests. In 2005, the Beninese National Assembly took into account this imposing agricultural problem as they evaluated each of the country's twelve *départements* for their economical values; the Collines department was designated as one of the key regions of interest for tourism.

Paouignan

Apart from the fishing villages near the Ouémé River Bridge, Paouignan is the first town in the Collines Department when traveling from the south. The population is mostly Mahi, with a mixture of Fon, Idaatcha, and a strong presence of Fulani. The market, which takes place every five days, is regionally significant as it draws people from surrounding villages. Paouignan is the place to purchase *gari* and *tapioca* as arrays of towering plastic bags full of the white cassava products sit on wooden stands along the highway. Big bags of *gari* are sold for CFA600-1,500. Just north of the town, the **Paouignan Auberge** stands alone amidst fields by the highway. The staff are quite friendly and serve delicious chicken and fries, cold sodas, beer, and fruits juices.

Dassa-Zoumé

The commune of Dassa lies in the center of the Collines *départment*, with the seat of the commune in the town of Dassa itself. It is known for its 41 Sacred Hills, a range that stretches about 40 kilometers between the towns of Glazoué and Paouignan. Each of these hills are said to have once been inhabited by fleeing natives evading capture during the slave trade. The ruins of these settlements remain, hidden in the wild landscape and protected by the revered vodoun divinities. The number 41 is a sacred vodoun number; there were actually more than 41 hills inhabited during the slave trade. The majority of the population is Idaatcha, related to the Yoruba of Nigeria. A close second is the Mahi.

> The Dassa market is located up the hill, to the east of the main round point. It takes place every five days, and offers all the typical market items.

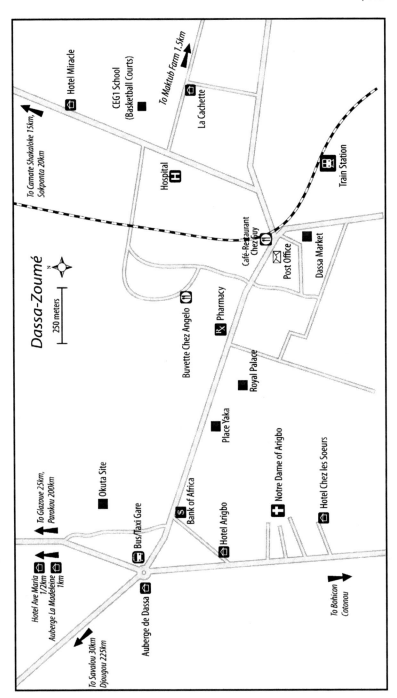

Dassa-Zoumé

250 meters

To Camate Shakaloke 15km, Sokponta 20km

To Maktub Farm 1.5km

Hotel Miracle

CEG1 School (Basketball Courts)

La Cachette

Hospital

Train Station

Café-Restaurant Chez Guy

Post Office

Dassa Market

Buvette Chez Angelo

Pharmacy

Royal Palace

Place Yaka

To Glazoue 25km, Parakou 200km

Okuta Site

Bank of Africa

Notre Dame of Arigbo

Hotel Chez les Soeurs

Bus/Taxi Gare

Hotel Arigbo

Hotel Ave Maria 1/2km
Auberge La Madeleine 1km

Auberge de Dassa

To Savalou 30km
Djougou 225km

To Bohicon
Cotonou

GETTING THERE

The town of Dassa-Zoumé, popularly referred to as Dassa, is located 230 kilometers north of Cotonou. It lies on the main highway leading north, directly at the intersection where the paved road diverges northeast to Parakou, and northwest towards Djougou.

A bush taxi from *Etoile Rouge* in Cotonou costs CFA3,000-4,000, while buses depart each morning at 7am from the same location for CFA2,000 or CFA3,500 for the air-conditioned buses.

From Bohicon, bush taxis heading to Parakou or Djougou line the right side of the main north road. The rate for Dassa is CFA1,000-1,500. From other destinations:

> Bus from Bohicon: CFA1,000.
> Bus from Parakou: CFA3,000-4,000
> Bush taxi from Parakou: A vehicle leaving from the marketplace costs about CFA3,000-4,000

Bush taxis and buses drop off passengers at the main round point of Dassa, where a team of *zemidjans* in green and yellow shirts await. The maximum rate to go across town on these motorcycle taxis is CFA300. One can also take a *zemidjan* to surrounding villages at a negotiated rate.

HOSPITAL

Dassa has a large regional hospital located on the dirt road leading northeast towards Camaté and Sokponta.

BANK OF AFRICA

Just up the hill from the Mayor's office, on the paved road leading from the main round point to the center of town; Open Mon-Fri, 9am-12pm and 3pm-5:30pm; Western Union services available.

SIGHTS AND ACTIVITIES

Royal Palace of Dassa

The royal palace is still home to the current King of Dassa. Although he holds no official power with the government, the King is regarded as a religious and political entity. The Palace is usually open for guided visits, though the current king, King Egbakotan II, does not reside there permanently. Guides present themselves at the palace entrance and give tours of the residence, including the greeting room where lies the king's throne and a vast collection of patchwork banners representing each king who ruled in the long history of the Dassa Kingdom. As with all royal palace tours, the guides recount colorful stories about the different kings and their reigns. *Center of town; Guided tour: 2,000-3,000; Open daily*

Place Yaka and the Ogoun Divinity

Place Yaka is a highly sacred site located on the *Hill of the Omandja-goun*. Only direct descendants of original inhabitants of this mountain reside in the rocky hillside neighborhood. All visitors must seek permission from the residents to hike up the mountain and be escorted by a guide. Only French-speaking guides are available for an organized tour. Guides are available to take visitors through the neighborhood and up the steep slope to the main shrine of the Ogoun Divinity, vodoun god of iron. The visit is rich in stories and breathtaking vistas of the town. *Center of town, next to the Royal Palace and the Maison du Peuples; Guided tour: CFA3,000; Open daily*

Notre Dame of Arigbo

This giant basilica is hard to miss when arriving in Dassa from the south. It sits at the foot of a hill, surrounded by vast fields and peaceful, tree-lined paths. Tourists are welcome to visit the church, brilliantly decorated by local artists. Behind the cathedral sits a large shrine set in the granite boulders, where the Virgin Mary is said to have appeared. This shrine has become the destination of a yearly pilgrimage. Thousands of adepts congregate around the basilica each August, transforming all of Dassa into a crowded religious camp.

Mystic History of Idaatcha-Land

The spiritual story of the region begins in western Nigeria. The Yoruba gods of Egba, Ilé Ifé and Abèokuta, had become angry with the local population for their lawlessness and neglect. Consumed with their material problems, the humans had abandoned the altars of the divinities. This prompted the gods to emigrate to more worthy and welcoming lands as they searched for a place with the right spiritual vibrations. Their exodus brought them to the region of Dassa. Pleased with the spiritual climate, they did not hesitate to settle there. Dassa became the promised land of the Yoruba divinities.

Four principal gods came to settle the region: Ogoun, god of iron and war; Arira, god of thunder and lightning; Sakpata, god of smallpox and maladies; and Arigbo, divine source of water, nativity, and old age. From Dassa, the gods continued their journey to discover cities and kingdoms in southern Benin, such as Abomey and the sea town of Ouidah. They continued onwards in their voyage to Haiti and Brazil via the slave trade, where they evolved into the vodoun entities of Hèviosso, Ogoun and Sakpata. Meanwhile, the gods maintained their principal seat in Dassa.

In time, the Catholics also discovered the strong spiritual presence in this granite haven. At the base of the hill where the majority of the Yoruba gods chose to settle definitively, there was an apparition of the Virgin Mary. Dassa thus became the site of the largest pilgrimage in West Africa. The first Catholic population named this sacred site Notre Dame d'Arigbo, or Our Lady of Arigbo, representative of one of the local divinities. This site serves as an important symbol of the juxtaposition of traditional and western beliefs which permeates the entire country.

zou & collines

Behind the shrine, a stairway leads to a magical conclave of granite boulders with the Stations of the Cross installed in the rocks.

Okuta Site

This outdoor museum of rock sculptures is located at the base of the hill at the northeastern entrance of town. The site is run by the **Okuta Association**, established by local artist Felix Agossa in March 2008. Okuta (which means *rock* in Idaatcha) promotes cultural development and the collaboration of local artists. The Association has an office in the *Maisons des Jeunes*, a youth center at the main round point, where artists work together, exchange techniques, and train apprentices. In December 2008, Okuta launched the first major rock sculpture symposium in Benin. A group of artists from West Africa and Europe convened for three weeks to carve masks into the boulders at the main site. These works of art can be viewed at leisure, along with the contemporary monument and sculptures decorating the entrance. The second edition of the Rock Symposium is set to take place in December 2009.

> Okuta is partnered with Blank Canvas Concepts, LLC in Miami, Florida, which actively works to finance international residencies and symposiums in West Africa, allowing artists from diverse backgrounds to collaborate and learn together.

Basketball at the CEG1

The biggest of the three high schools in Dassa is on the northeast side of town, not far from the hospital. A functional and well-used basketball court was built on the grounds by the soccer field in 2006. Girls and boys of all ages train with the physical education teachers on weekday evenings and sometimes Saturday mornings. Visitors are always welcome to play a game or two.

Bétékoukou-Hippo River Tour

About 30 kilometers east of Dassa, the village of Bétékoukou has a large-scale agro-pastoral farm. A bit farther east along the Ouémé River is a small fishing village and river crossing for merchants traveling to and from nearby Nigeria. There is a significant hippopotamus population in this section of the river and visitors can either rent a car or hire a *zemidjan* from Dassa to Bétékoukou, where local fishermen are available for a *pirogue* tour (CFA3,000/person, 2 hours) of the Ouémé. It is best to go in the dry season during the early morning hours when the hippos gather in the deeper parts of the river—making them easier to spot—and the fishermen have not left for the day. Once the fishermen find the hippos, they bang their paddle against the side of the *pirogue* to prompt the animals to stick their heads out of the water. The vibrations caused by the banging actually irritate and confuse the hippos, making them search for the source of the sound. The fishermen are accustomed to these dangerous creatures and know the importance of keeping a safe distance. It is crucial, however, to understand that hippos are quite unpredictable and can swim very fast. If frightened or aggravated, they will attack. An alternative to the *pirogue* tour is to view the hippos from land. Some *zemidjan* men in Dassa know the way to the best viewing spot along the river, but it is best to first go through the fishermen's village and seek permission in order to avoid any conflict or surprises.

EATING AND DRINKING

The specialty dish in Dassa is *igname pilé*, which can be found in many locales around town. Restaurants also serve rice, *pâte*, or *akassa*, with boiled eggs, fried fish, chicken, *wagasi*, beef, pork, or *agouti*.

Popular sauces are spicy tomato, *gumbo*, peanut, sesame, or green-leaf, similar to spinach. Choices vary each day. Ask the *tanties* to know what is in each pot. Restaurants along the main road and round point charge CFA1,000-2,000 per plate. Road-side stands in Dassa's center charge CFA300-900 per plate.

> Bars or *buvettes* are found all around town, serving beer and sometimes fresh palm wine and *sodabi*.

 Auberge la Madeleine A popular *buvette* is attached to the hotel and a legendary *igname pilé* cook serves under the *paillote*. The restaurant gets quite busy at lunch time, as many Dassa business men and women gather here for a delicious plate of *pilé* and their choice of *wagasi*, rabbit, chicken, *agouti*, or *biche* (miniature bush deer) with peanut sauce. *At the north entrance of town, on the highway leading to Parakou; Meals CFA600-1,500, drinks CFA250-800; Open daily, 12pm-10pm*

Auberge de Dassa The Auberge restaurant serves both French and African cuisine for breakfast, lunch, and dinner. Some particularly interesting dishes include the ostrich omelet or grilled crocodile. There is a full bar and although drinks tend to be high-priced, it is probably the best place in town for a cocktail or martini. *Tel: 22.53.00.98; At the main round point, by the road leading to Savalou; Meals CFA3,000-6,000, drinks CFA600-2,000; Open daily, 8am-11pm*

La Cachette This restaurant and bar is cozy and inviting, with art and tapestries hanging from the walls. There is satellite television behind the bar. Grilled rabbit and rice is the specialty, but other Beninese dishes are available. *On the northeast side of town, off of the main dirt road leading to Camaté and Sokponta, just south of the CEG school; Meals CFA2,500-3,000, drinks CFA250-700; Open daily, 11am-11pm*

 Buvette Chez Angelo – La Fleur des Collines (The Flower of the Hills) This former maternity ward from colonial times has been transformed into a marvelous *buvette* sprawled over a series of granite boulders. A modernized *paillote* was recently built on top of the rocks. The *buvette* offers a pleasant view of the city and surrounding hills, especially at sunset. One can either sit at the selection of tables and chairs around the grounds, or simply lounge on the flat rocks with a refreshing drink. *Set*

deep in the middle of town, north of the paved road, behind the pharmacy; Drinks CFA250-750; Open daily, 10am-12am

Café-Restaurant Chez Guy This restaurant and bar is at the center of the busiest crossroad in Dassa. The cafeteria and bar serves typical breakfast and spaghetti dishes, as well as beer and soft drinks. A woman serves good and cheap *pâte* and rice dishes from her food stand inside the restaurant. In the rainy season, she can also prepare salads upon request. *Across from the market; Meals CFA300-700, drinks CFA250-750; Open daily, 8am-12am*

ACCOMMODATIONS

Hotel Arigbo Hotel Arigbo offers basic, budget rooms. The lobby has comfortable chairs in front of a satellite television often playing West African music videos. The hotel kitchen serves breakfast, lunch, and dinner with a European style menu. *Southern entrance of town, before the main round point; CFA6,000-12,000; fan or a/c, private shower and toilet*

Auberge de Dassa Part of the reputed French-owned chain of Auberge properties, the Auberge rooms are in a U-shaped building with doors around the outside, which open toward the restaurant. There is a great shaded patio with wooden tables and chairs, perfect for reading a book and enjoying a cold drink or coffee.

A special attraction is the Auberge Ostrich Farm in the fields behind the hotel. Most of the ostriches have been relocated to a larger farm in a village ten kilometers south of Dassa, but a few remain and can be observed from the hotel yard. The restaurant sometimes serves ostrich-egg omelets (when available). *Tel: 22.53.00.98; At the main round point, by the road leading to Savalou; CFA11,500-18,00; fan or a/c, private shower and toilet*

Hotel Chez les Soeurs Set back from the paved road, this peaceful guesthouse is well-kept and run by the nuns of the cathedral next door. The rooms are quiet and spacious, with high ceilings. Breakfast is available, as well as cold non-alcoholic drinks. *Located beside the Arigbo Cathedral, at the south entrance of town; CFA10,000; a/c, private shower and toilet*

Hotel Ave Maria Set apart from the town center, the hotel sits on a sandy path in a residential area. The rooms are simple and clean, with full baths in each. There is a small food stand across the way, and the hotel kitchen can provide meals upon request. *North side of town, near the two paved roads leading to Parakou and Savalou; CFA7,500-14,500; fan or a/c, private shower and toilet*

Auberge La Madeleine The rooms here are rudimentary, but a good budget location especially if looking for a place set away from the town center. The attached restaurant and *buvette* get pretty lively at lunch time. *At the north entrance of town, on the highway leading to Parakou A6,000; fan, private shower and toilet*

Hotel Miracle This three-story circular building was built in 2007, so the rooms are new, clean, and relatively luxurious. Each room has a name labeled on the door, such as Hope, Love, and Prosperity. The top floor provides pleasant views of the neighborhood. *On the northeast side of* *town, along the dirt road leading to Camaté and Sokponta and north of the CEG school and hospital; CFA12,000 and up; fan or a/c, private shower and toilet*

Auberge La Cachette This hidden little restaurant and hotel has pleasant and basic rooms with friendly staff and a unique decor. The owner, Luc, raises rabbits and caimans, which he would be happy to show. *On the northeast side of town, off of the main dirt road leading to Camaté and Sokponta, just south of the CEG school; CFA8,000; fan, some rooms have shared baths*

 Maktub Farm Owned by local biology teacher Armand Tobossi, this paradisiacal eco-lodge is also a sheep and rabbit farm. The rooms are in modernized mud houses with thatched roofs and simple indoor plumbing. Meals are prepared upon request and a delicious breakfast menu includes housemade cassava bread, preserves, and fruit juices. The kitchen is often well stocked with a variety of vegetables, and has cold drinks. Maktub farm also organizes visits of the Dassa region, hikes in the hills, and festive musical gatherings under the straw huts in the evenings. *Located in the east outskirts of Dassa, this farm is not easy to find without an experienced guide; Rates are by donation, suggested at CFA5,000; mosquito net, shared and private baths*

Camaté-Shakaloké

This quaint village of about 2,000 inhabitants is a jewel hidden in the landscape ten kilometers northeast of Dassa-Zoumé. Situated at the foot of three rocky hills, the site is as beautiful as it is peaceful. The village was initially formed when three settlements of *Idaatcha* peoples descended from hiding in the hillsides after the turbulent era of the slave trade. Over a hundred years later, the three groups have merged into one village, though they continue to distinguish themselves by neighborhood. Each is named after the hill they had once inhabited: Camaté, Shakaloké, and Oké N'la.

GETTING THERE

Camaté lies ten kilometers northeast of Dassa, on a dirt road. A *zemidjan* ride from Dassa costs CFA500-700. Taxis generally do not take this route.

Camaté is 13 kilometers southeast of Glazoué. A *zemidjan* costs CFA600-800. Taxis run to and from Camaté on Wednesdays, which is Glazoué's market day, at a cost of CFA400. From Sokponta, Camaté is 5 kilometers southeast and a *zemidjan* costs CFA300. Finding transportation out of Camaté, however, can be difficult, so it is best to arrange a pick-up in advance if following a tight schedule. Traffic is most frequent on Wednesdays (Glazoué market) or Dassa market days (every five days).

SIGHTS AND ACTIVITIES

Connaitre et Proteger la Nature (CPN), les Papillons
Know and Protect Nature, the Butterflies
Tel: 95.42.34.28/97.32.00.95; onikpol@yahoo.fr

CPN les Papillons is a non-governmental organization located just outside the village. Founded in the year 2000 by two villagers, Léandre Onikpo and Hyacinthe Adamassou, the organization is a branch of CPN International which promotes environmental education and protection. CPN les Papillons works actively with the village and surrounding schools to educate the community on the importance of environmental conservation, as well as the development of ecotourism. The organization's passion for nature is manifested in its tranquil and beautiful site. An abundance of trees, beds of plants and flowers, and colorful sculptures by local artists decorate the grounds. The site is equipped with three guest rooms (CFA5,000/night), each with showers and modern toilets. The office building has also been turned into a bunkhouse with multiple beds (CFA2,000/night). There is a restaurant and bar, with a local cook who prepares traditional meals (from CFA1,500). The cook, Agathe, or *Inan-Jacques*, is best known for her *igname-pilé*. With its large pavilions and open spaces, CPN les Papillons is perfect for hosting retreats or family getaways. The staff at CPN is available for guided tours of the region and throughout Benin.

A French-speaking CPN guide will take visitors on an interactive village tour (CFA5,000/day) of Camaté. Visit each neighborhood, interact with the villagers, and observe their daily activities. Some of the tour highlights include:

Sodabi distillery: See how palm wine moonshine is made locally.

Blacksmith workshop: Watch how hunting rifles and other tools are fabricated.

Ifa priest: A local vodoun diviner, or *babalawo*, can teach about his trade or read individual destinies.

Shakaloké bone-healers: The traditional healers of Shakaloké are nationally famous for mending broken bones through a regimen of massages, herbal infusions, strict diet, and therapy. Visit their center for the opportunity to observe a healing session.

Hiking in the hills: Guides lead hiking excursions into the three hills surrounding Camaté, as well as some of the other 41 hills in the Dassa region. Each hill has its own story and vodoun fetishes, and one can walk among the ruins of the ancient hilltop settlements. It is important for visitors to respect the sacred boundaries and to seek a village guide before climbing.

Gravel making is a primary economic activity in Camaté-Shakaloké. Walking down the main pathway, noise from the pounding of granite can be heard from all directions. Entire households labor with stone hammers at slabs of rock harvested from the surrounding hillsides. Piles of gravel lie at the village entrance, as the inhabitants await the next gravel truck in hopes of selling another load. If one adult works nonstop for two days, they can fill up an entire metal drum and sell it for the mere equivalent of US$2. Throughout the long dry season, this activity becomes the only constant source of revenue, and the hillsides have become heavily exploited quarries, augmenting erosion problems.

Glazoué

Glazoué is an important international market town 30 kilometers north of Dassa along the paved road to Parakou. The market takes place every Wednesday, with merchants traveling from as far as Togo and Nigeria to sell their produce. From Tuesday evening to late Wednesday afternoon, this sleepy town comes alive as trucks and taxis bring loads of vendors with their masses of produce to sell in an otherwise empty marketplace. All types of goods can be found here, varying with the seasons. Yams and red hot peppers are available in colossal amounts. There is a *shakparo* (the Idaatcha word for *tchoukoutou*) section for those wishing to try a taste of the sorghum

Making gravel in Camaté-Shakaloké

zou & collines

beverage, and several food stands offer delicious local cuisine. Near the paved road and next to the permanent boutiques at the edge of the market, a few women sell *atièkè*, a traditional dish from the Ivory Coast made of *gari*, hot peppers, onions, palm oil, and fried fish. In the middle of the *gare*, some women sell *baguettes* sandwiches of avocado and fish for CFA100. There is a particularly large *yovo* clothing section along the road, with vendors from Niger and other northern countries. The Glazoué market is also a perfect spot to see the Fulani, or *Peuhls*, in all their splendor. These nomadic herdsmen and women attend regional markets to sell their cheese and to socialize. Always dressed in their best clothes on market days, their particular styles and fine features are quite striking. The un-betrothed girls wear especially bright fabrics full of pink, red, and blue hues. Colorful beads dangle from their hair, waists, and wrists, and their hands and feet are dyed magenta; a brilliant display for attracting prospective husbands.

GETTING THERE

It is best to go to Glazoué on a day excursion from Dassa. A *zemidjan* between the two towns costs at least CFA1,500, but may be less on market days. Glazoué *zems* wear purple and green shirts, in contrast to the yellow and green of those from Dassa. A taxi costs about CFA600. If traveling directly from Cotonou, a taxi from *Etoile Rouge* costs CFA3,000-3,500. From Parakou, the trip costs around CFA3,300.

The bus lines generally only stop in Dassa, but a stop in Glazoué could be negotiated.

EATING AND DRINKING

Cafeteria This quiet restaurant with friendly staff serves coffee, tea, and tasty omelet sandwiches in the company of a couple of affectionate cats and dogs. It is perfect for a breakfast or lunch away from the noise of the market and reckless traffic on the paved road. *Along the brick road leading east on the north side of town; Meals CFA400-1,000, drinks CFA250-700; Open daily, 8am-10pm*

Pantagruel Built in 2007, this European-style bakery and restaurant with shiny glass windows is impossible to miss. The bakery offers tasty croissants, pastries, and fresh coffee. The lunch and dinner menu is a cross between French and African food, including fresh salads and sandwiches, but many of the items are not regularly available. The dining room is air-conditioned. *On the paved road, just north of the marketplace; Meals CFA2,500-5,000, drinks CFA600-1,200; Open daily, 8am-10pm*

La Pantagone This casual and often busy place serves a cheap and wide selection of *pâte*, rice, fish, chicken, eggs, and, *wagasi*. They also have a nice selection of green leaf and tomato sauces. An air-conditioned dining room is available for a small fee. *Adjacent to the Maisons des Jeunes of Glazoué; Meals CFA300-700, drinks CFA250-700; Open daily, 11am-10pm*

Savè

Savè is another railroad town, about 35 kilometers north of Glazoué on the highway to Parakou, and just 30 kilometers west of the Nigerian border. It is recognized by three round-topped hills of solid rock, called *Les Mamelles de Savè*, which can be seen from miles away (the French word *mamelles* means breasts). The main language spoken here is another derivative of Yoruba called *tchabé* (also spelled *chabi*).

The most interesting activity here is hiking the *Mamelles*. There is also a royal palace off of the road to Nigeria where one can pay respects to the king and tour his palace.

GETTING THERE
From Cotonou, taxis heading north from the *Etoile Rouge* cost CFA3,500-4,000. A taxi from Parakou costs CFA2,500, and the cost from Glazoué should be CFA300-500.

ACCOMMODATION

Hotel Idadu The rooms are quite basic and the staff at Hotel Idadu are available to provide information on visiting the town and hiking the hills. *Tel: 22.55.01.14; Center of town, at the 'y' intersection on the north-south highway; CFA7,000-12,000; fan or a/c, private shower and toilet*

Toll stop

On the highway to Parakou, a couple kilometers north of Savè, there is a CFA500 toll stop. Young women line the road by the toll booth, selling bags of sliced papaya, *ronier* palm roots with chunks of coconut, and large bags of roasted peanuts. The *ronier* and coconut mixture is a suprisingly tasty and very fibrous snack. The Beninese say *ronier* roots are a sexual stimulant for men.

Savalou

The Savalou commune covers an area of 2,700km^2, and is divided into 14 *arrondissements*, or districts. The seat of the commune is in the town of Savalou, 45 kilometers northwest of Dassa on the highway to Djougou. Agriculture is the main rural activity, with corn, yams, and cashews as the most important crops. Cashews are a particularly significant source of revenue for Savalou residents. There is a cashew processing plant at the northeast end of town. There are numerous cashew tree, or *anacardier*, plantations between Savalou and Bantè to the north. Several kiosks and small supermarkets sell bottles of the roasted nuts, and even cashew butter.

The primary ethnic groups are the Mahis, related to the Fon, and the Ifés, related to the Yoruba. There is underlying friction between the people of this region and the rest of the *département* because this town has such a strong Mahi and Fon presence. This mild hostility has its roots in the slave trafficking era when the Fon of Abomey raided the Collines region for captives to sell to their European counterparts.

Savalou sits at the foot of a large rock outcrop; the paved road goes around the base and continues north towards Djougou. A dirt road leads west to the Togo border, about 38 kilometers away.

GETTING THERE

A bush taxi from Dassa to Savalou costs CFA700-1,000. The return trip to Dassa can be difficult to find, especially later in the day. The best place to catch a south-bound taxi is the round point on the southern end of Savalou, at a CFA150 *zem* ride from the town center. *Zemidjans* also make the trip, at around CFA1,500. A taxi to Djougou from Savalou costs CFA4,500.

SIGHTS AND ACTIVITIES

Annual Yam Festival

Each August, around the 15th, Savalou celebrates its traditional yam festival. A large fairground is set up in the center of town, with performances from national and local music groups, and several stands selling handicrafts and snacks.

Centre Songhaï Internet Café

As with all Songhaï Centers around Benin, this place offers the fastest and most reliable internet connection around for CFA400 an hour. The boutique attached sells refreshing Songhaï fruit juice and baked goods. The center is located near the south entrance of town, a couple hundred yards from the paved road.

Sacred Caimans of Todjitche

The village of Todjitche is a CFA300 *zemidjan* ride north of Savalou, where various vodoun shrines are located and villagers will recount the significance of each one. A pond with several sacred caimans is the main attraction of this sleepy village.

Fetish de Dankoli

Located several kilometers east of Savalou, along the highway to Djougou, this is probably one of the most impressive (and is said to be the most powerful) vodoun fetishes in the country. Based at the foot of a giant tree, the *fétishe* is adorned with hanging white sheets and grotesque mounds of organic matter including palm oil, animal parts, and blood. It is 'open' every day to any believer who wishes to ask for help and guidance from the spirits. A *vodounsi* is constantly on-site to assist in the ceremony. Those making a request to the gods must first buy a wooden peg from the priest and hammer it into the tree, all the while whispering the request to themselves, and promising the gods that once the wish is granted, they will return to make a sacrifice in thanks. Then, they must drizzle palm oil and spit mouthfuls of *sodabi* onto the fetish while they continue to whisper their requests. Finally, a donation of at least CFA1,000 is placed next to the wooden peg on the tree. The request is supposed to be granted within the year, after which one must never forget to return and give thanks by sacrificing a chicken, sheep, goat, or cow.

EATING AND DRINKING

Gabonese Cafeteria This little cafeteria is the perfect place for a cheap, satisfying meal such as an omelet sandwich, spaghetti, or even salad. Nescafé, Lipton tea, and the usual selection of cold sodas and beers are available. *On the west end of town, where the paved road curves east; Meals CFA300 and up, drinks CFA250-700; Open daily, 8am-11pm*

Le Zenith Maquis This yellow-painted *maquis* serves cold drinks, yogurts, and superbe *igname pilé*. It is just across the road from the Songhaï Internet Café. *At the south entrance of town, on the paved road; Meals CFA500 and up, drinks CFA250-800*

ACCOMMODATIONS

Auberge de Savalou A former administrative office of the town, the Auberge de Savalou belongs to the chain of French-owned hotels also present in Dassa, Grand Popo, Parakou, and Kandi. The restaurant is similar to others in its chain, serving French and African cuisine at about CFA3,000 per plate. *Tel: 22.54.05.24; Near the Savalou hospital, off the paved road leading through the town center; CFA7,500-4,500; fan or a/c, private shower and toilet*

zou & collines

Alibori & Borgou

The Borgou *département* covers an area of 25,300km². The capital of the region is Parakou, the second largest city in the country after Cotonou. The Borgou is most likely the first northern *département* a visitor will encounter coming from Cotonou. Not only is the air less humid, but the pace of living is slightly slower, especially outside of the city limits. The local languages in this region are different from the south and a foreigner's title changes from *yovo* to *anasara* or *batouré*. The predominating ethnicities are Bariba and Dendi, though the Fon are still well represented, as are the Yoruba. The culture is therefore slightly different, with its own traditional and religious ceremonies. Rather than *sodabi*, the popular alcoholic beverage in the Borgou is *tchoukoutou*, a home-made millet brew sold ubiquitously in market stands.

The Alibori *département* was created in 1999, when it divided from the Borgou. It covers an area of nearly 26,000km², making it the largest *département* in Benin. The population of 356,000 is spread thinly across the vast savanna lands, mostly comprised of Fulani, Bariba, and Dendi. The dominant crop is cotton, with cotton factories in Kandi and Banikoara. Due to the prevalence of Fulani and their herds, *wagasi*, or Fulani cheese, is widely available in this region. The seasons play a large role in how and when to visit the Alibori: March and April are the hottest, with temperatures reaching 120°F, while May through September rains fall heavily, making roads mostly impassable. The *harmattan* months, from November to early March, are the best months to plan a visit.

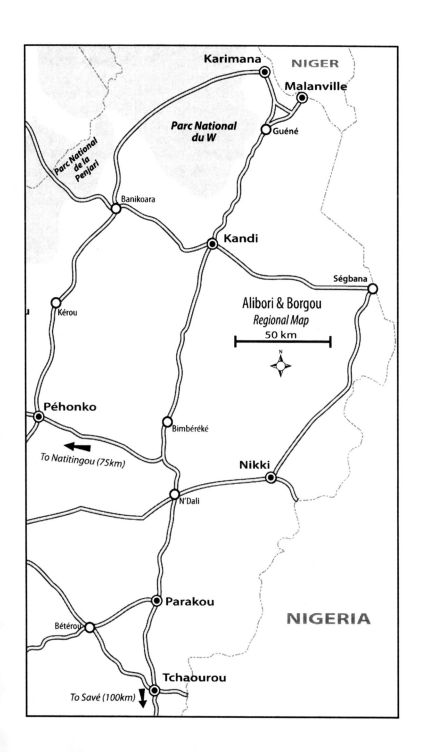

Tchaourou

Located 59 kilometers south of Parakou on the north-south highway, Tchaourou is the birthplace of current Beninese President Yayi Boni. Apart from its primarily agricultural activities, this town is known for its involvement in fuel trafficking with nearby Nigeria. The main ethnic groups are Bariba, Yoruba, and Fon. The Fulani herdsmen are also numerous in the town and its surroundings. The market takes place every Monday and is located just behind the *boucherie,* or butcher, in the middle of town. The market offers a great selection of items, from traditional fabrics to fresh fruits. Some hard-to-miss points of attraction are **Yayi Boni's houses** on the southern edge of town. His first house is a lavish, two story white structure surrounded by a pink fence and a statue of a golden pot and cowrie shell (his political symbol) in the yard. Just behind that house is his new home, an even grander building that looks like it belongs in Southern California. Tchaourou has an important cashew factory, about three kilometers south of town, right off the highway. Free tours of the facility are negotiable, but note that no pictures are allowed. If looking for a meal or a place to stay, the best option in town is the **Auberge Joie de Vivre**, indicated by a sign on the southern edge of town. The Auberge has a great bar with regular drink prices, and there is a food stall across the street. The rooms are basic and reasonably priced, and some rooms have a/c.

Parakou

Parakou is the second largest city in Benin, with an estimated population of 190,000. Despite its size, the feel of the town is quite different from Cotonou or Porto-Novo. Streets are wider, buildings are more spread out, and there are more open fields within the city limits. The major industries here are cotton, textiles, peanut oil, and brewing at Parakou's own SONAPRA brewery. The name Parakou is derived from the Dendi phrase that means *'La ville de tout le monde'* or 'everyone's city.' The name adequately depicts the wide variety of ethnicities which reside here: Bariba, Dendi, Somba, Fon, Gun, Mina, Dita Mari, Djerma, Ibo, Yoruba, Nagot, Hausa, Warma, Touareg, and *Peulh,* (or Fulani). Each group typically has its own neighborhood. Parakou is a great place for travelers to recharge before continuing their travels through the north of Benin or onwards. There are several markets to explore, each with their own theme, and an array of hotels, bars, and restaurants in which to relax and pass the long, sweltering afternoon hours.

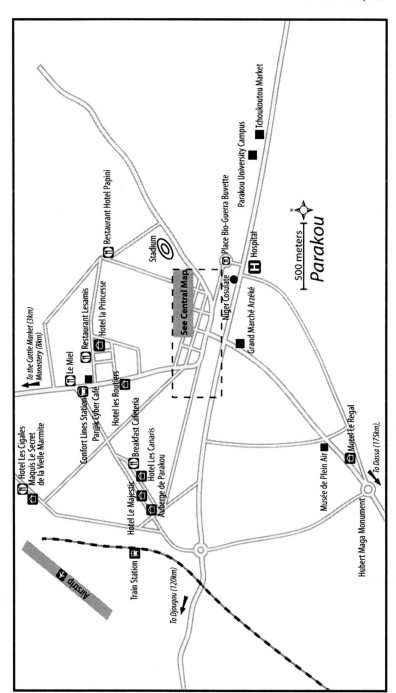

To the Cattle Market (3km)
Monastery (8km)

Restaurant Hotel Papini

Stadium

Tchoukoutou Market

Parakou University Campus

Place Bio-Guerra Buvette

Hospital

Niger Cosulate

See Central Map

Restaurant Lesamis

Hotel la Princesse

Le Miel

Grand Marché Arzéké

Confort Lines Station

Par@k Cyber Café

Hotel Les Routiers

Hotel Les Cigales

Maquis Le Secret
de la Vielle Marmite

Breakfast Cafeteria

Hotel Les Canaris

Hotel Le Majestic

Auberge de Parakou

Musée de Plein Air

Motel Le Regal

To Dassa (175km)

Hubert Maga Monument

Train Station

Airstrip

To Djougou (120km)

500 meters

N

Parakou

GETTING THERE AND AWAY

Parakou is 410 kilometers north of Cotonou and 315 kilometers south of the Niger border at Malanville. There is also a paved road leading west to Djougou, 130 kilometers away. A bus from Cotonou costs CFA6,000 while a taxi costs

> **Airport**
> This dusty airstrip is currently not used for public transport. President Yayi Boni's plane flies in once in a while.

around CFA7,000. From Dassa, a taxi costs CFA3,500. From Djougou, a taxi costs CFA2,500. From Malanville, a taxi costs CFA4,500 A bus from Natitingou costs CFA3,500.

There are *zemidjans* everywhere, in yellow and green shirts. Rides around the city cost CFA100-300. The **Confort Lines** bus station is near the 'y' intersection north of the city center, across from the Par@k Cyber Café. **Benin Routes** bus station is across from the Bank of Africa and Financial Bank.

The train station is on the southwest edge of town, near the airstrip. It is the last stop on the Beninese railway from Cotonou.

HOSPITAL

Nationally important nursing and medical schools are affiliated with the Parakou Hospital, and there are several pharmacies in town. *Tel: 23.61.07.17 / 23.61.07.13; On the dirt road leading east of the Arzéké Market.*

COMMUNICATIONS

Par@k Cyber Café is the best-known internet café in town, with a rather constant connection. Located on the paved road leading to Malanville, north of the Bank of Africa and across the street from the Confort Lines bus station. Navigation costs around CFA500 per hour. There are cellular phone booths all around town.

BANKS

Ecobank, Bank of Africa, SGBEE, and Financial Bank are all located at the town center. Ecobank and Bank of Africa are open through the lunch hour and both have Western Union facilities. There are ATM machines that accept Visa cards at both Bank of Africa and SGBEE.

CONSULATES

Niger Consulate
Tourist visas to Niger are CFA22,000 and require a completed application with two photos. If lucky, the visa may be issued the same day. *Tel: 23.61.28.27; On the road leading to the hospital.*

SIGHTS AND ACTIVITIES

Hubert Maga Monument
At the southern entrance of town when arriving from Cotonou, a bronze monument of Hubert Maga, Benin's first president, stands in the center of a large round-about. Maga was born to a peasant family in Parakou in 1916, where he began attending school. He eventually continued his education in Abomey, Bohicon, and Porto-Novo, as well as in Dakar, Senegal. Though firmly raised Muslim, Maga converted to Roman Catholicism in his twenties, which was especially rare in those days. He had much political influence among the uneducated due to his years of teaching, and he formed the Northern Ethnical Group political party. Maga also held many positions in the French National Assembly. After negotiating Dahomey's independence, Hubert Maga was proclaimed the country's first president in 1960.

Musée de Plein Air
Open Air Museum
Constructed to display the architecture and layout of traditional Bariba households, a tour of the museum's round cement structures takes visitors through a series of themed rooms. Exhibits of traditional Bariba clothing, an ancient loom, musical instruments, household pottery, and weapons of these tribes serve as an introduction to the cultures of the north. Several other cement huts on the grounds remain empty and unused as a drought in finances cut short some of the original ambitious goals for the museum. Pricey decorated calabash bowls and wooden sculptures are for sale in the guide office. *At the south entrance of town, on the highway from Cotonou and up the hill from the Hubert Maga round point; CFA1,500; Open daily, 9am-5pm*

Tchoukoutou Market, *Chak-i-ti-boum*
The *Chak-i-ti-boum* market consists of a collection of grass huts and specializes in traditional sorghum beer called *tchoukoutou*, or simply *tchouk*. Men and women alike spend Saturday afternoons and evenings here, socializing, drinking, and eating barbecued beef and pork. They select a hut and sit on the wooden benches while the *tchouk* vendor brings a calabash bowl to serve them. The beer costs CFA50 per bowl. For an added kick to the mild alcoholic beverage, some people enjoy a spoonful of hot pepper powder mixed in. This little additive has been adequately named *le démarreur*, or 'the starter,' as it definitely gets the blood circulating. This market is a common place for singles to

alibori & borgou

meet a partner. Women should not go there alone without anticipating associated behavior from men. *On the dirt road leading east, after the hospital and just past the Parakou University Campus; Open Saturdays 4pm-9pm*

Cattle Market

One can observe the herds of cattle for sale by their Fulani owners. A regular market is attached, with newly renovated vendor stands. Shea butter, sold here in big chunks at CFA50, is great for moisturizing skin or for treating hair (shea butter is sold at sky-rocket prices by brand name cosmetics stores in the U.S. and Europe). Other typical northern products such as kola nuts, spices, and baobab leaf powder for sauces are found at every corner. *On the far north end of town, along the highway to Malanville*

Grand Marché Arzéké

This covered market is open every day and is much like the Dantokpa market in Cotonou. Endless stalls of goods include agricultural products, such as corn and beans, and fruits, vegetables, and spices.

> Be sure to get permission from the vendors before photographing amongst the bustling atmosphere.

Wagasi and various meats are also available. Clothing and fabrics, both of *yovo* and local style fill baskets and tents, open to rummaging shoppers. Nigerian CDs, household items, kitchen utensils, and pottery claim another corner of the market—especially intriguing are the beautifully carved Fulani and Bariba calabash bowls.

Centre Culturel Français

French Cultural Center

Much like its sister-center in Cotonou, the French Cultural Center in Parakou has a library and a gallery space with rotating exhibits. It is an excellent source for tourism information on the Borgou and Alibori region. Newspapers, magazines, and other media are available to the public with proper identification. There are frequent concerts, lectures, films, and plays depicting West African history and culture. Animated tennis and basketball courts are attached to the cultural center, open to anyone wanting to watch or get in on a game. *Center of town, near Cinéma le Borgou; Open Tues-Sat, 9am-6pm plus scheduled events*

Mosque

About half of the Parakou population is Muslim, thus the Grand Mosque at the city center is a notable landmark. Noted for its fortress-like structure and turrets with dark red window panels, the structure is striking, and worth a visit.

Univeristy Campus of Parakou

Past the hospital, on the dirt road leading east. This is part of the university network in Benin, an extension site from the campus in Abomey-Calavi by Cotonou. The school focuses on forming professionals within the needed fields of development in Benin, including economic, social, intellectual, and cultural. The university houses a variety of departments: agronomy, medicine, technology, law and political science, and economics and management. A third campus is located in Natitingou, called the Normal School, where teachers are trained. The Parakou campus is complete with a cafeteria, residence halls, a research library, and arenas for cultural and athletic activities. Students are a good source of entertainment, either in casual conversation or as a means to discover the evening's activities.

Monastery

Surrounded by charming gardens, tree-lined paths and flower bushes, this monastery is a great place for a quiet stroll. The main attraction is the monastery boutique, where there is an array of fresh juices, handmade soaps, balms, candles, fruit wines, syrups, and natural remedies all fabricated by the religious community. The kiosks and supermarkets in Parakou also sell the monastery juices and syrups, whose contact information is found on the product labels. It is best to call and make sure the boutique is open before making the trip.

> Located a few kilometers outside of the city, along the highway to Malanville. It is easiest to go in a rented car or hired taxi as a *zem* could get expensive and would be nearly impossible to find for the return trip.

EATING AND DRINKING

Parakou is full of cafeterias, roadside food stands, and *maquis*. Nearly all the hotels have excellent restaurants and offer French cuisine. The following are recommended:

Lunch Maquis A banquet table of steaming cauldrons and several *tanties* offer all sorts of delicious Beninese cuisine. This is a popular lunch spot with reasonably priced rice, *pâte*, *igname pilé*, vegetables, and various sauces with different meats. Beer and soft drinks are also for sale in the big dining room area equipped with a television always set on ORTB or LC2. *By the intersection at the center of town, next to Financial Bank; Meals CFA500-1,500, drinks CFA250-800; Open daily, 10am-4pm*

Restaurant Hotel Papini Even though it is called a hotel, this quaint and flowery establishment only offers two rooms for CFA9,000-15,000. The restaurant, on the other hand, has great pizzas as well as pasta and European dishes served in an outdoor dining area. Whole pizzas cost CFA3,000 *Northeast of town center; Meals CFA2,000-3,000, drinks CFA300-1,000; Open daily, 12pm-10pm*

Restaurant Les Amis There is a spacious dining room and full bar under a *paillote* with an extensive French and Lebanese menu at moderate prices. The schawarmas, falafels, and fresh salads are great. *Near Hotel La Princesse; Meals CFA2,000-3,500, drinks CFA500-1,000; Open daily, 12pm-10pm*

Maquis Le Secret de la Vielle Marmite (The Secret of the Old Cooking Pot) This *maquis* is another popular lunch spot. *Tanties* serve tasty, budget-priced *pâte*, rice, and *igname pilé* with a wide selection of meats, cheese, fish, and sauces. The atmosphere is clean and friendly, and cold beverages are also available. *Next door to the Hotel Les Cigales, near the airport; Meals CFA600-2,000, drinks CFA300-1,000; Open daily, 12pm-10pm*

Le Miel (also known as Patisserie La Borgoise) Le Miel is a bakery and restaurant with wonderful pastries, sandwiches, salads, ice cream, as well as a full menu. There is a pleasant dining room upstairs. *Along the Route de Transa, near P@rak Cyber Café; Meals CFA1,500-2,500, drinks CFA300-800; Open Mon-Sat, 7:30am-11pm*

Place Bio-Guerra *Buvette* – **La Fraicheur** This popular *buvette* is set right in the middle of the vast roundabout. Several tables and chairs are spread out in the shade, and the atmosphere is breezy and relaxed. There is the possibility of ordering grilled spiced pork to accompany the drinks, or a huge plate of chicken and fries for CFA2,000. The drinks are always cold. *At the Bio-Guerra round point by the Parakou hospital; Meals CFA2,000, drinks CFA250-800; Open daily, 12pm-12am*

Local Favorite

At the round point closest to Hotel Papini, there is a good salad, chicken, fries, and fried fish joint that is popular with the locals.

ACCOMMODATIONS

Hotel la Princesse The rooms are basic and clean, ranging in comfort and style according to price. There is a restaurant and bar in the hotel. *Tel: 23.61.04.16; North of the town center; CFA8,000-18,000; fan or a/c, private shower and toilet*

Hotel Les Cigales Clean rooms and a restaurant offering delicious European cuisine including pizza makes this a good choice. Food should be ordered well in advance. A plate costs CFA2,500-4,500. The bar and dining area is uniquely decorated with colorful African fabric and wooden sculptures. This is a great place to wile away the hot hours of midday, listening to music with a cold drink and a stack of cards. The bar and restaurant also gets quite lively in the evenings, particularly weekends. *Tel: 97.89.11.98; West end of town, right by the airport; CFA6,000 and up; fan, mosquito net, most rooms share a common bathroom*

Hotel Les Canaris This hotel has been renovated and relocated from its original spot across the street since 2005. The rooms are clean, with pastel green doors set around a central cement courtyard. There is a *buvette* attached to the hotel. The staff is friendly, albeit a bit sleepy. Just up the road, a corner cafeteria is a convenient spot for a cheap breakfast omelet and coffee. *Tel: 23.61.11.69; Off of the road between the airport and the Bank of Africa, well indicated by signs; CFA6,000-11,000; fan or a/c, mosquito net, private shower and toilet*

Auberge de Parakou This branch of the French-owned Auberge chain offers seven spacious and clean rooms with tiled floors. There is a terrace restaurant and bar next to a large garden of tall trees. Tasty European cuisine is available for CFA2,500-3,500. The shade here is a rare and pleasant reprieve from the intense heat of Parakou. The bar has satellite television. *Tel: 23.61.03.50; Between the train station and Hotel Les Canaris; CFA10,000-16,000; fan or a/c, mosquito net, private shower and toilet*

Hotel Le Majestic This large, Lebanese-owned hotel is one of the most luxurious in Parakou. It is a great value for travelers seeking a little pampering. The best rooms are those with a flowery balcony overlooking the neighborhood. European cuisine is served at the restaurant for CFA3,000-4,000. An added bonus is internet access on the property. *Tel: 23.61.34.85; www.lemajestichotel.com; Near the train station and Auberge de Parakou; CFA12,000-29,000; fan or a/c, private baths, some rooms have a balcony*

Motel Le Regal This is one of the first places visitors will see when arriving from Cotonou, and it is also a good spot for a snack and a cold drink. The rooms are basic and clean, and a particular attraction is the large and seemingly frustrated caged baboon in the courtyard. *Tel: 23.61.26.82; South entrance of town, between the Hubert Maga round point and the Musé de Plein Air; CFA7,500-12,500; fan or a/c, private shower and toilet*

Hotel les Routiers Les Routiers is reputed for being the most high-end hotel in town, and it is quite popular with expatriates. The setting is peaceful and beautiful, with lush gardens and bougainvilleas. There is a pool, open to non-guests for CFA1,500. The expensive but excellent restaurant serves exclusively European food for CFA5,000-7,000. This hotel also houses the French vice-consulate office. *Tel: 23.61.04.01; On the paved road leading to Malanville, just north of Bank of Africa and south of the Par@k Cyber Café; Rooms and suites, CFA24,000- 40,000; a/c, hot water, and private baths*

N'Dali

N'Dali lies 60 kilometers north of Parakou, on the north-south highway. There is a major customs check point here, for the regulation of all north-south commercial traffic. It is a crossroads between the highway and the dirt road leading to Nikki and nearby Nigeria.

Nikki

Nikki is the historical Bariba capital of the northeast. It is the seat of an ancient royal palace that still presides over a vast territory, including a large part of northeastern Nigeria. At the height of the dry season, the effects of the encroaching desert are apparent in this quaint town of dusty paved streets. For travelers sticking to Benin's paved roads, a side trip to Nikki may be the best opportunity to visit a culturally charged locale that is relatively untouched by tourists. This town provides a glimpse into some of Benin's authentic, rural agricultural town life. Despite being off the main roads and rather over-overlooked by tourists, Nikki has a bustling daily market and town center, and offers all of the basic amenities an adventurous traveler would need for a day trip or overnight stay.

GETTING THERE

A bush taxi from Parakou costs CFA2,500. Transportation to and from Nikki is usually pretty reliable, with as many as a dozen regular departures from Parakou beginning around 8am, and return trips departing from Nikki as late as 6pm. A taxi exchange may be required in the junction town of N'Dali, where the dirt road to Nikki branches off of the highway. This dirt road is usually decent, although in the rainy season it can be particularly pothole ridden and slow-going.

SIGHTS AND ACTIVITIES

Palais Royal
Royal Palace
The royal palace of Nikki is surrounded by clay walls and sparsely shaded by enormous trees teeming with giant fruit bats. The Muslim king reigns over a vast territory surrounding Nikki. He is a calm and gracious man, open to visitors who wish to bid hello and take a photograph with him. He does not speak French, but many of his children who attend school serve as French translators for brief exchanges with His Royalty. It is best to see the king on a Friday, when noblemen and royalty from all corners of the Borgou kingdom come traditionally dressed to greet the king or bring issues to his attention. To arrange a visit with the king on this or any other day, go to the mayor's office, whose *Chef de Culture* can provide directions and a guide. *East side of town; Free but a donation of CFA500-1,000 is suggested; Open daily*

Musée de l'Ancien Palais Royal
Museum of the Old Royal Palace
The ancient site of the Royal Palace of Nikki has been transformed into a museum. The museum is still a work in progress, but the curator and his assistant give a good tour and are always pleased to see visitors. Because few foreigners venture here during most of the year, the museum guard will invite you to sit in the shade of a tree while someone fetches a guide for the tour. The museum offers a series of old houses, Bariba artifacts, ornately carved wooden doors, and the marked graves of ancient kings. *Farther east of the town, on the road leading to Nigeria; CFA1,000; Open daily*

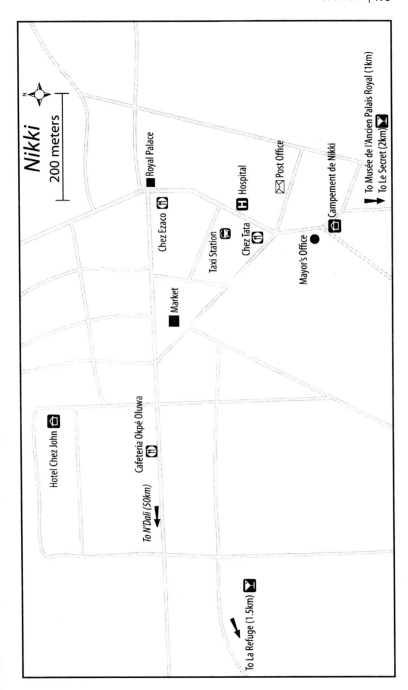

Nikki

200 meters

N

Royal Palace

Chez Ezaco

Taxi Station

Chez Tata

Hospital

Post Office

Market

Mayor's Office

Campement de Nikki

To Musée de l'Ancien Palais Royal (1km)
To Le Secret (2km)

Hotel Chez John

Cafeteria Okpé Oluwa

To N'Dali (50km)

To La Refuge (1.5km)

La Fête de la Gani

This spectacular festival of Bariba horsemen takes place each spring and lasts about one week. The dates vary each year according to the moon, but the festival usually takes place in March or early April, around the birthday of the Prophet Mohammed. If traveling in the north around the month of April, this is a celebration not to miss. The Nikki taximen at the Parakou *gare* will be able to provide specific dates and information for the Gani. Nikki's streets become flooded with visitors and vendors from the region, and foreigners of all countries come to observe the elaborate displays of decorated horses and their riders.The king with all of his dignitaries parade around town as the ceremonial grounds vibrate with the thrum of drums, trumpets, and the clamor of spectators. Other events often include craft shows, dances and musical events, and even a 5k run! If staying the night in Nikki during this time, be sure to make a hotel reservation well in advance because rooms fill quickly.

Horsemen of Nikki

If visiting Nikki outside of the Gani Festival period, one might wonder where all the horses and their cavaliers are located. There are no obvious stables to be seen, and most of the horseback riding takes place out in the fields or on the hunting grounds. The horses are actually stabled in the familial concessions, and are kept behind closed doors when not being ridden. Any teenage school student with adequate language skills will be able to guide visitors to a home with a stabled horse. With a little negotiation, the rider will be happy to show his horse and conduct a bareback tour of the town, or down a peaceful dirt road to the town's large water reservoir. The horses are highstrung and accustomed to dancing parades, so it is best that the owners stay nearby to avoid runaway escapades through the neighborhood. A recommended donation for a horseback tour is CFA3,000 per person, depending on the length of the ride. Keep in mind that the horsemen usually leave early in the morning to work in the fields and come back at nightfall, so a visit should be arranged a day in advance.

EATING AND DRINKING

Roadside stands offer local fried snacks, or rice dishes. In the morning and at lunchtime you can find *igname pilé*, the signature dish of the north, served with a tomato sauce and fresh local cheese or meat. Ask around for a stall serving *igname pilé*, or just follow your ears to where you hear the rhythmic pounding of the yams. Despite its small size and Muslim majority, Nikki houses a good number of bars. Some of the best watering holes include **La Refuge** (on the way to the *barrage*, or reservoir), **Le Campement**

The most Western dining options in Nikki are Chez John's Hotel and La Belle Princesse, where one can get a choice of meat with fries, rice, or couscous for CFA1,500-3,000 (across from the Mayor's office), and *Le Secret* (a bit hidden, past the customs checkpoint, right off the road going to Tchikandou/Nigeria), where from the roof you can enjoy a drink while watching the sunset.

Cafeteria Okpé Oluwa A polite and friendly gentleman cooks up spicy omelet sandwiches, spaghetti, and coffee or tea from his modest roadside cafeteria. *At the southwest entrance of town, by the road to N'Dali; Meals CFA200-600; Open daily, early mornings (7am) and evenings*

Chez Ezaco Ezaco and his lovely family will prepare all the classic cafeteria dishes. At times, homemade yogurt is also available. *Near the royal palace; Meals CFA200-600; Open Mon-Sat, 7am-10pm*

Chez Tata This hole-in-the-wall restaurant is run by a Fon lady and is a favorite of locals. She serves up delicious garbanzo beans (*pois chiche*) in palm oil—usually they're freshest at lunch—as well as other traditional plates. *The eastern edge of the meat market, just behind the old radio tower; Meals CFA200-600; Open Mon-Sat, 7am-10pm*

ACCOMMODATIONS

Hotel Chez John This hotel was built to accommodate the flood of visitors who come once a year for the Fête de la Gani. Apart from that week long festival in the spring, the hotel remains open but quite empty.
This two story building houses clean and basic rooms at a great bargain. A deluxe room with a/c is being built and should be ready to house guests for a higher fee in 2010.
   A restaurant and *buvette* are attached to the hotel. The *tanties* prepare tasty Beninese meals including hearty breakfast omelets, rice or couscous dishes, and chicken and fries from CFA1,000 per dish. It is all made to order, so guests should place requests in advance. A hopping underground night club at the hotel is popular with the locals on weekend nights. *From the west entrance of town, the first dirt path to the left before the marketplace. Indicated by signs; CFA5,000 and up; fan, private shower and toilets*

Campement de Nikki A series of comfortable bungalows dot the dusty hotel courtyard. An open air restaurant offers basic Beninese cuisine, and is the favorite watering hole of local functionaries and visiting NGO workers. *West side of town, across the intersection from the mayor's office; CFA5,000 and up; fan, private shower and toilets*

Kandi

Kandi, on the north-south highway 200 kilometers north of Parakou and 110 kilometers south of Malanville, developed as a rest stop along the ancient caravan routes. The settlement became an important cheifdom under the rule of the Bariba King of Nikki. The main entrance to the 'W' National Park is at Alpha Koara, 40 kilometers north of Kandi. One can also enter the park at Kofonou, 15 kilometers from Karimama, or at Sampeto via Founougo. Kandi is the capital of the commune, equipped with a post office that also has Western Union services. Post office hours are Monday through Friday, 9am-12pm and 3pm-5:30pm.

GETTING THERE

A bush taxi costs between CFA2,500-3,000 from Parakou and CFA1,500 from Malanville.

PARC NATIONAL W

National Wildlife Park 'W' (Pronounced 'dooble-vé')

Created in August 1954, *Parc National 'W'* became a UNESCO World Heritage Site in 1996. It is a UNESCO Trans-boundary Biosphere Reserve, and supports West Africa's largest wildlife populations. The park covers an area of one million hectares, covering parts of Benin, Burkina Faso, and Niger. Over half of the reserve is in Benin, with 250,000 hectares in Burkina Faso and 220,000 hectares in Niger. The park is named after the bends of the Niger River in this area, in the shape of the letter 'W'. The Niger River is the third largest river on the continent of Africa, its ancient path an important flyover landmark for migratory birds. Over 350 species of birds have been identified in the park, and is thus an internationally recognized Important Birding Area (Ramsar).

The dry season between December and April is the best time to observe wildlife. It is home for a significant ungulate, or hoofed mammal, population, such as buffalo and warthogs. It also has a large population of African elephants and some hippopotamuses. West African manatees, though very rare, have been identified in this region. Cats include cheetahs, leopards, lions, caracals, and servals. Also notable are baboons and aardvarks.

The wetlands, important to so many forms of life, also perform a critical role in water quality and availability in the region by trapping and filtering the ground water. The rainy season displays a lush version of the landscape, with more watering holes and diverse flora. Humans have lived along the pre-historic Niger River bed since Neolithic times. Today, the Fulani inhabit parts of the park and herd their cattle throughout, while Bariba and Dendi farmers cultivate fields around the perimeter. There is constant friction between the humans utilizing the natural resources and those attempting to conserve. The current major environmental threats to the park territory include poaching, illegal farming, brush fires, and toxic fishing methods. Park authorities struggle to manage the natural resources, while also attempting to accommodate those necessary activities for human livelihood. *Tickets can be purchased at the park entrance or in Kandi. There is no public transportation to the park entrance, and it*

There are hunting zones in Park W accessible to registered local and international hunters.

is forbidden to enter on foot. Visitors must have a four-wheel drive vehicle in good condition with several spare tires and extra fuel before entering this wilderness practically void of humans and roads. Tel: 23.65,01.95; www.parc-w.ne; CFA10,000 for foreign tourists, CFA6,000 for Beninese visitors; Sport-fishing liscence costs CFA3,000

Alfa Koara Water Hole

Located right on the edge of a **Park W** hunting zone, this water hole is a great place to see elephants and other wildlife like baboons, antelope, and elephants venturing from the park. The best time of year to visit is at the end of the hot season before the rains begin, usually in April. There is an observation platform run by CENAGREF, with an entry fee of CFA5,000, plus an additional CFA500 for a camera and CFA1,000 for a video camera. It is best to get there early in the morning or at sunset to see the most animals, and be sure to bring a pair of binoculars. The easiest and best way to get there is with a hired taxi or vehicle. Otherwise, a bush taxi driver will most likely charge the full rate to Malanville for this drop off. Finding a taxi back may also involve long hours of waiting on the side of this lonely highway stretch. *On the highway to Malanville, 40 kilometers north of Kandi, roughly an hour's drive.*

Les Chutes de Koudou

These waterfalls are on the Mékrou river, a rainy-season stream. Found within the park and near the Burkina Faso border, the area has been developed enough to allow for comfortable tent-camping and wildlife viewing. Because of the stream's ephemeral nature, the vegetation and animal life that dominates in this area thrive for a short period. The remoteness of the location adds adventure to any safari. Lions, elephants, and hippopotamuses frequent this area.

Point Triple

Located on the west side of the park, The *Point Triple* is where the countries of Benin, Niger, and Burkina Faso meet. There is a rough track here that runs between Park Pendjari and Park W, but it is passable only with an all-terrain vehicle and a driver familiar with the area.

alibori & borgou

CENAGREF (Centre National de Gestion des Reserves de Fauna)

An integral participant in the development of National Park W, the Kandi CENAGREF office staff can provide a 4x4 vehicle and guide, as well as hotel and camping reservations in the park. *Tel: 23.63.00.80; South side of Kandi*

ACCOMMODATIONS

In-Park Accommodations

Campement de Chutes de Koudou This remote camp is run by the French Auberge chain. To reach this point, a 4x4 vehicle is recommended in the dry season, and necessary in the rainy season. The camp is comprised of 11 tents, permanently installed on teak structures with roofs. Reservations can be made from the Auberge de Kandi or the CE-NAGREF office. Though there is no electricity, radio communication is possible between the camp and Kandi over the park guide network. The camp also has kayaks to tour the Mekrou River. *Kandi office tel: 23.63.02.43; voyageur@intnet.bj; 120 kilometers northwest of Kandi, via Banikoara and just past the Sampéto entrance; CFA20,000; Extra bed CFA3,000; mosquito net, private shower and toilet; Meals CFA4,000*

Staying across the border

There are other campsites on the Burkina Faso and Niger side of the park. These include Point Triple, Tapoa, Karey Kopto, Boumba, and Mare. Arrangements can be made through CENAGREF in Kandi.

Kandi Accommodations

Auberge de Kandi Set in a vast courtyard of multiple buildings, the rooms are pleasant and simple. There are a total of seven rooms, five of which have a/c and two with a fan. Some rooms have satellite television. The outdoor restaurant and bar under a *paillote* is always open and serves African and French cuisine. Meals cost around CFA4,000, and this is the only place in Kandi with beer on tap. The hotel staff can arrange a tour of the Chutes de Koudou. *Tel: 23.63.02.43 / 93.05.21.90; voyageur@intnet.bj; Almost two kilometers north of town, on the road to Malanville; CFA10,500-17,000; fan or a/c, private shower and toilet*

Auberge La Rencontre This hotel has a friendly atmosphere and ten clean rooms with a double bed. There are satellite TVs in each room. There is a nice rooftop bar and restaurant, but be sure to order food in advance. *Tel: 23.63.01.76; Near the gare, on a side street off the paved road. Turn right two streets after the Pharmacie Na Siara, or one street after Inter-City Lines if coming from the south; CFA7,500-14,500; fan or a/c, private shower and toilet, some rooms have shared baths*

Motel de Kandi There are about 12 total rooms, which are a good value and clean. The restaurant serves breakfast for CFA1,500 and main courses for CFA3,000. *Tel: 23.63.03.03; North of town, on the road toward Malanville; CFA8,000-18,000; fan or a/c, private shower and toilet.*

Auberge la Pension de l'Alibori This centrally located hotel has eight rooms with double beds. Two of them have a/c, but they don't always work. If they do, the price is CFA12,000. There is a good restaurant on site, but be sure to order meals in advance. *Tel: 90.02.39.25; In the center of town on the old road to Banikoara and near the Banikoara taxi gare; CFA6,500-12,000; fan or a/c, private shower and toilet*

EATING AND DRINKING

There is a wide choice of bars and *buvettes* around Kandi, most of which are concentrated around the marketplace. *Maquis* **Aefi,** at the southern roundabout near the cotton factory, sells drinks and a tasty assortment of food: rice, *pâte*, *wagasi*, turkey wings, chicken and fries, or chicken and couscous. Another recommended *buvette* and eatery is the *maquis* **C'est Ça Même** (also called *La Terrace*), located just south of the marketplace. This *maquis* is particularly popular with the functionaries of Kandi. The **Tropicana Nightclub** is popular on a weekend evening with a cover charge of CFA2,000.

Guéné

Guéné is located at a fork in the road 26 kilometers south of Malanville. The paved road to the east leads to Malanville and the border with Niger, while the dirt road to the northwest goes to Karimama.

The main attraction in Guéné is the market every Thursday, which is known for its livestock. Fulani and other traders come from afar to trade cattle, sheep, and goats. This is a great place to find Fulani clothing and accessories, as well as the beautifully carved calabash bowls which Fulani use to carry milk.

Malanville

Malanville sits at the end of the north-south highway through Benin, right along the Niger River which forms the border with Niger. A bridge connects the two countries, with the Niger town of Gaya just on the other side. The Nigerian border is also not far to the southeast. Malanville is an international town with a heavy Arabic and Muslim influence, and all cohabit peacefully with Christians and *Voudounsi*. A market renowned throughout the Sahel region animates this northern town each weekend. Malanville becomes inundated with merchants and Fulanis in their brilliantly colored clothing. Tourism is a growing sector here, due to its proximity to the Park W and the Niger border.

GETTING THERE AND AROUND

Inter-City Lines buses from Cotonou cost CFA12,000 and take about 13 hours.

A taxi to Cotonou can be found in the early morning hours, though few people choose to brave the entire journey in one trip. The cost is CFA12,000 and takes at least 13 hours if all goes well. A bush taxi or bus to and from Parakou costs CFA4,000.

A taxi from Kandi costs CFA1,500. The drivers sometimes ask for the fare at the beginning of the trip to buy fuel.

Malanville is 35 kilometers downstream of Karimama, connected by a very rough dirt path that can be passable on motorcycle. The ride would be an adventure to say the least, as it is quite sandy in the dry season, and eroded in the wet season. One can take a *pirogue* between Karimama and Malanville on market days. The most efficient way to get from Malanville to Karimama is to take a taxi to Guéné on the highway for CFA1,000, and then another CFA500 taxi ride to complete the trip to Karimama.

ACCOMMODATIONS

Sota Hotel In association with the Majestic Hotel of Parakou, the Sota Hotel offers classy accommodations. This hotel has a swimming pool, a boccie ball court, and a small playground. Niger River tours by *pirogue* can also be arranged. The attached restaurant Le Calao offers African and European meals, while the bar Le Baobab serves mixed drinks in the evenings. Meals range from CFA2,500-4,500. *Tel: 97.64.97.48; CFA18,000-22,000; fan or a/c, private baths*

La Rose des Sables This hotel has pleasant and comfy rooms, recently renovated. The restaurant next door has hearty meals for about CFA3,000, including fresh grilled fish from the river. The staff can arrange tours into Park W, camel rides, and boat trips up the Niger River. *Tel: 23.67.01.25; On the southern edge of town, near the gare; CFA12,500-22,000; fan or a/c, private showers and toilets.*

Motel Issifou This is the best budget option in town, with clean, basic rooms and large baths. The restaurant serves local meals at CFA1,500. *Off the paved road, at the southern end of town; CFA5,500; fan, private showers and toilets.*

EATING AND DRINKING

The cuisine in Malanville is a mixture of African, Arabic, and European. There is a simple and clean restaurant that serves great rice, chicken, and fries on the east side of the street toward the Niger River Bridge. Meals cost about CFA2,000 a plate. **Hotel Issifou** serves decent chicken-and-chips, while many food stands line the paved road near the *gare*. *Buvettes* also abound in this part of town.

Karimama

This village is the seat of the northernmost *commune* of Benin. Bordered by the Niger River on the north and east and the National 'W' Park on the west, Karimama has much to offer those seeking a taste of the natural state of things. For great bird watching, tour the *Ile des Oiseaux* or Bird Island, and *Ile d'Eté*, Summer Island, by *pirogue*. Both islands are disputed territories between Benin and Niger; Niger currently claims the *Ile d'Eté*. One can take a leisurely six hour *pirogue* ride to Karimama from Malanville after the market closes on Friday afternoon; witness massive wooden canoes filled to the brim with merchants, 200 pound bags of corn and millet, basins of fruit and fried treats, and even cattle. For an excursion into Park 'W', ask at the hotel in Bello Toungo where a few of the guides speak English. The hotel can also arrange a visit to *Le Docteur* (the current mayor of Karimama, nicknamed 'The Doctor') to see his zoo with Niger crocodiles, snakes, and massive Sahelian land turtles. There is a bird hunting camp in Kompa, a village 25 kilometers from Karimama. Contact CENAGREF (*Tel: 23.63.00.80*) for more information.

GETTING THERE

A bush taxi or *zemidjan* from Guéné costs about CFA1,000, and is a 45 kilometer ride.

ACCOMMODATIONS

There is a small hotel in the village of Bello Toungo, two kilometers south of Karimama. It is run by the mayor and offers modest rooms and pit latrines. The hotel is generator-powered with electricity from sunset until about midnight. Meals can be provided upon request. Tourists can also stay at the CENAGREF base, or at the mayor's office where there is a welcome center (*centre d'acceuil*).

Swimming near waterfalls in the north

alibori & borgou

Atakora & Donga

The northern regions have notably calmer atmospheres compared to the south—bargaining and negotiating are less intense, and the people have a more relaxed demeanor. Yams almost exceed corn in market importance, and the *igname pilé* served with *sauce d'arachide*, or peanut sauce, is said to be the sweetest in the country. Many Fulanis herd their cattle throughout the countryside, selling milk and *wagasi*. Djougou is the capital of the Donga *département* and an important town in the north. The Donga *département*, bordered by Togo on the west, split from the Atakora in 1999, and has a population of about 396,000.

The mountainous Atakora *département* is home to many of Benin's wonders, including waterfalls, two-story worked-earth homes (the Tata Sombas), and the *Parc National de la Pendjari* (Pendjari National Park). The Atakora mountain range runs laterally from Togo into Benin, creating the beautiful rocky landscape of this region. The sub-desert terrain of the Sahel is especially obvious in the Atakora, with less rainfall and more scrubland vegetation. The capital of Atakora is Natitingou, the proclaimed hometown of former Beninese President Mathieu Kérékou.

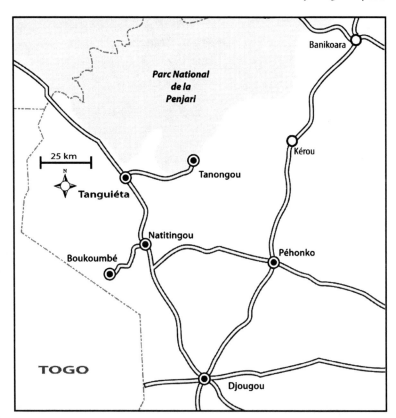

Djougou

The largest city in northwest Benin with a population of about 229,000, Djougou is an important market town. Buses and taxis stop here en route between Parakou and Natitingou. If traveling from Savalou or farther south, the climate changes to the typical hot and dry of the Sahel region. The majority of the community here is Muslim.

GETTING THERE

Bus

The bus stops in front of the *Maison des Jeunes* in the center of town.

> From Cotonou CFA6,000
> From Parakou CFA2,500
> From Natitingou CFA1,500

Bush Taxi

Taxis are very frequently loading for Natitingou, Parakou, Cotonou, and nearby Kara in Togo.

From Cotonou CFA7,000
From Savalou CFA4,500
From Parakou CFA2,500
From Natitingou CFA1,500

HOSPITAL
Tel: 23.80.01.40; West of the town center, on the road to N'Dali.

SIGHTS AND ACTIVITIES

There is a reputed handicraft trade in Djougou, including woven fabrics, jewelry, and sculptures. One can visit the little boutiques around town. Northwest of the market, the Zembougou-Beri neighborhood houses silver jewelers and blacksmiths who meld recycled metal into large ladles, royal canes, and ornaments. On the west end of town, near the hospital, traditional weavers sell beautiful shawls and wraps from their workshop. Another craftsman nearby fabricates unique leather flasks and little boxes. Just west of the market, an artist displays his abstract paintings in his little studio. The **regional market** takes place in the center of Djougou every five days. The **Djougou Royal Palace** is located off the road to Togo, where the king welcomes visitors in exchange for a small gift—a suggested donation is CFA1,000.

North of Djougou, the hillside **Tanèka** villages off the highway near Copargo are worth a visit. These semi-nomadic communities have established settlements of stone-walled huts with shale covered courtyards. Only the *féticheurs*, elders, and children remain in the village while all able bodied persons travel as seasonal workers. The village *chef* carries a long, curved pipe made of copper, which is constantly lit. Though the community is friendly, visitors should enter with particular caution and respect, and of course ask permission before taking photographs. Inquire at one of the hotels in Djougou or Natitingou for a local guide to take you into the villages.

EATING AND DRINKING

There are several foodstands and *maquis* around town. Some recommended *maquis* are **La Rencontre des Amis** (Meeting Place for Friends), **Le Sans-Rancune** (Without a Grudge), and **Le Flamboyant**. The bar/restaurant **Le Quasar**, near Motel de Djougou, offers a generous variety of local and European dishes for CFA2,000. It also has an internet café with a navigation rate of CFA600 per hour. For a refreshing drink on the road, try **L'Escale des Routiers** (Driver Stop), a pleasant *buvette* on the highway leading out of town to Parakou.

To Tanèka Villages
To Natitingou
La Rencontre des Amis (1km)

Hospital

Market

Post Office

Soccer Stadium

Maison des Jeunes

Royal Palace

$ Bank of Africa

Djougou

N

300 meters

Motel de Djougou

Le Quasar

Motel du Lac (3km)
Auberge La Princesse (1km)
Hotel La Residence (1km) Catholic Church

ACCOMMODATIONS

Motel de Djougou The Motel offers standard rooms and bungalows arranged in a flowery courtyard garden, complete with a roaming flock of guinea fowl. This is a good budget choice. The hotel restaurant serves local cuisine for CFA3,500. *Tel: 23.80.00.69; Located near the highway to Parakou; CFA5,000-12,000; fan or a/c, private shower and toilet*

Hotel La Residence La Residence is a large hotel, with dozens of quite decent rooms. There is a restaurant and a swimming pool, open to non-guests for CFA300. *South side of Djougou, on a side road leading to Auberge la Princess; CFA8,500-12,500; fan or a/c, private shower and toilet*

Auberge La Princesse La Princess is a basic little hotel and restaurant that offers clean rooms. *Tel: 90.04.33.16; On the south end of town; CFA6,500-12,500; fan or a/c, private shower and toilet*

Motel du Lac This French owned hotel is the most high-end option in town. The rooms are spotless and large, complete with balconies, a view of the lake, and satellite television. The owner, Madeleine, is quite helpful in providing information on visiting the region, such as the best way to go to the Tanèka villages and when to see the king. She promotes local craftsmen and keeps a collection of their work on display. The restaurant has great French specialties, too. *Tel: 23.80.15.48/97.07.01.76; Southern entrance of Djougou, on the road to Savalou; CFA10,500-17,500; fan or a/c, private bath, TV*

Pehunco

Escape the regular tourist track by stopping in Pehunco. Also known as Ouassa-Pehunco, this is a major intersection and market town off the beaten path between Parakou and Natitingou. *Tchoukoutou* is prevalent in the rural spots of town, and along with the Fulani population are the associated *wagasi* and jewelry, especially the bracelets, commonly found in the local markets. Typical for national holidays, though also at other times throughout the year, there are ceremonies and parades with the regional king's horse. Pehunco is an ordinary village of the north, and although not much for tourists, is an enjoyable spot for the few *yovos* who arrive.

GETTING THERE

Because Pehunco is a rural town, taxis to and from usually only leave once per day. All of the roads are *terre rouge*, or red dirt, so the ride is bumpy and break downs are nearly inevitable. The market takes place every four days and plays a large role in the accessibility of transportation, though *zemidjans* are more likely to be ready and willing to make the trip for double the cost. Taxis from Djougou (CFA1,500, one hour), Natitingou (CFA3,000, two and a half hours), and Parakou (CFA3,000, three hours) only leave for Pehunco once the vehicle is full of passengers. To avoid waiting hours at the *gare* for the vehicle to leave, commission a *zemidjan* to deliver the message once the car is full. There is a slight possibility that the *zem* will forget, but an offer of CFA200 to do this will serve as a good reminder.

> In the north, the rainy season is the worst time to travel to towns only accessible by dirt tracks, as the roads wash out and fill with potholes.

There is typically a taxi that leaves Pehunco for Natitingou around 10pm, though that depends largely on the number of passengers. There is also a car that leaves Pehunco to Parakou, usually pulling out by 11pm.

> Please remember that night travel anywhere in Benin can be quite dangerous and is not recommended.

ACCOMMODATION

Hotel Prestige If opting to spend the night in Pehunco, Hotel Prestige is really the only choice. The rooms are clean and basic, and the staff is friendly. Friday and Saturday are dance nights and can get noisy. *CFA6,000-7,000; double bed with fan*

Natitingou

Natitingou is sprawled across a wide valley within the rocky Atakora Mountains. With a population of about 75,000, this increasingly cosmopolitan town is inhabited by the Waama, Ditamari, Dendi, Fon, Fulani, and many other ethnicities. It has a roughly equal amount of Christians and Muslims, with a strong vodoun presence. Natitingou is the most prominent town in the Atakora department, with internet service, supermarkets, hotels, and good eateries. It is also the jump-off point for many of the surrounding tourist destinations, such as Boukoumbé, the Tanongou Falls, and Park Pendjari.

There are several European NGOs based in the town, with supermarkets, internet cafés, and quality hotels and restaurants to support the local and tourist population. **Pharmacie Tissanta** is near the center, on the main paved road running through town. The Natitingou market takes place every five days and generally has fruits and vegetables of one sort or the other year-round. **Supermarché Quidata**, situated just across the street from Financial Bank and next door to the Post Office, has a wide range of products and European foods, including a surprising cheese and fruit selection.

The Indian store (known as *Chez les Indiens, Chez les Syriens, or Chez les Libanais*) is overall the best and cheapest supermarket and electronics/building supply store. **Divin Protecteur** is a small supermarket that isn't as well stocked and is slightly more expensive, but it is conveniently open until later in the evening.

HOSPITALS

Although there are two hospitals in Natitingou, the regional **Hospital St. Jean de Dieu** in Tanguiéta is recommended if needing medical assistance as they are generally better equipped and have European doctors.

Hôpital de Zone

This hospital has two Chinese surgeons, which is why it is also called *l'Hôpital Chinoise. Tel: 23.42.14.17/.23.82.12.43; On the main road, just north of the town center and south of the police station.*

Hôpital Module

Tel: 23.82.21.52; South of town, along the highway

INTERNET

There are three recommended cyber cafés in Natitingou with satellite connections. The cost is CFA400-500/hour, and they are generally open daily, 9am-10pm. One is located in a blue building across from the CeRPA, at the north end of town along the highway. Another is just south of the road to Hotel Kantaborifa, on the highway. The third is on the second story of the pink building across from the northern end of the stadium.

BANKS

Financial Bank
One can also exchange Euros and U.S. Dollars here, but the exchange fees are high and the process is lengthy. *At the central round point and across from the post office; Open Mon-Fri, 9am-12pm and 3pm-5:30pm; ATM available*

Ecobank
By the taxi gare in the center of town; Open Mon-Fri, 8am-5pm, Saturday 9am-1pm; ATM accepts Visa

GETTING THERE AND AWAY

Bus
There are many bus companies in Natitingou: Intercity Lines, Tunde, NTS, Confort Lines, Coton Bus, Benin Routes, and La Poste. The Confort Lines office is across from the entrance to the main Stadium. Tunde buses leave from the taxi *gare*. Intercity Line buses leave from their office across Pharmacy Tissanta, and La Poste leaves from the post office. They all depart southbound at 7am except for NTS, which leaves at 6:30am, and Tunde, which leaves sometime between 6:30-7:30am. Intercity, NTS, Tunde, and La Poste buses are all air-conditioned and a little classier than the rest, though La Poste has the smallest seats and is not as comfortable. Confort Lines is the oldest of the bus lines in Benin and the vehicles tend to be in worse condition, and break down more often.

Only Intercity and Confort Lines go to Parakou (CFA3,000). Intercity has two departure times for Parakou: 8am and 3pm. Confort Lines only leaves at 8am. This bus continues on to Cotonou (CFA7,000, full day's ride including a lunch stop) and then to Porto-Novo. A bus to Djougou costs CFA1,000.

Bush Taxi
Taxis going to Tanguiéta (CFA1,000) pick up passengers on the highway just north of Quidata Supermarket. Taxis going to Djougou (CFA1,500) are on the highway just south of the Évêque. Both of these leave several times every day. Most taxis for other destinations depart from the taxi *gare* and leave once a day.

SIGHTS AND ACTIVITIES

Musée Regional de Natitingou
This museum has an interesting ethnographic display of musical instruments, traditional clothing, architectural miniature models, and historical artifacts from the region. *Located between Hotel Bourgogne and*

the Police Station; CFA1,000 per visit; Open Mon-Fri: 8am-12:30pm and 3pm-6:30pm; Sat-Sun: 9am-12pm and 4pm-6:30pm

Handicrafts

There are several recommended boutiques along the road to Hotel Tata Somba, including Le Carrefour des Artisans, Tresors D'Afrique, and Nouvelle Galerie. These stores sell typical West African crafts, from wooden sculptures and jewelry to Dogon doors from Mali, carved calabash bowls, and leather bags. Another craftsman named Lawa has a nice workshop just south of Hotel Bourgogne. *On the brick road between Hotel Tata Somba and the highway*

Chutes de Kota (Waterfalls)

Tucked away in the hills about 15 kilometers southeast of Natitingou, the *Chutes de Kota* are not as tall as the Tanongou Falls (see pg 198), but make for an equally pleasant adventure. To arrive, pedal a bike, ride in a car, or hire a *zemidjan* (CFA2,500, one-way). The road gets curvy and rocky, so if traveling by car, go in a 4x4 jeep because bush taxis may not make it. The easiest way to get there is to follow the highway ten kilometers toward Djougou, then turn left on the dirt road to Kouandé. After three kilometers, a sign on the right indicates a narrower dirt road to the falls. There is a small visitor's center set up at the entrance, though the guard is not always present. If he is, an entry fee of CFA200 is usually required. From here, a hiking path goes down the steep slope to the bottom of the falls, where a shaded pool is open for swimming. Depending on the season, the path can get overgrown and is difficult to see, so take care not to get lost.

Kouandé

Located 50 kilometers east of Natitingou, Kouandé is the historical capital of the Bariba peoples in the Atakora. The Kouandé Kingdom was founded in the 18th century by Worou Wari, the son of a prince who had fled the Kingdom of Nikki in the east. One can get there by bush taxi for CFA1,500, or CFA2,500 by *zemidjan*. The trip from Natitingou takes about an hour. The **royal palace** of Kouandé is an interesting place to visit. A tour includes a visit with King Bagana Sorou III and re-counts of the region's legends. There are rooms from CFA4,000 at the **Motel des Princes**. The hotel restaurant serves local cuisine and cold drinks. Another great dining place is the *maquis* across from the *gendarme* station.

EATING AND DRINKING

Le Tour Le Tour offers a fantastic view of Natitingou, cold drinks and hearty dishes of meat or cheese with couscous, fries, rice, or spahgetti. Food may not be available at all hours of the day, so be sure to check in advance rather than arrive on an empty stomach. *Up the road from Hotel Kantaborifa, indicated by a sign; Meals CFA1,000-3,000, drinks CFA300-800; Open daily, 12pm-11pm*

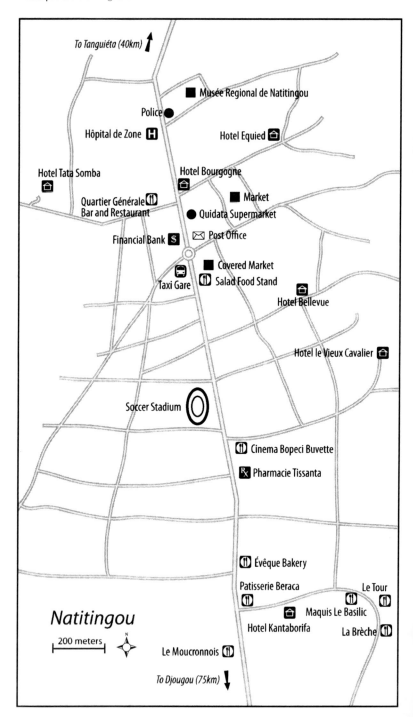

To Tanguiéta (40km)

Musée Regional de Natitingou

Police

Hôpital de Zone

Hotel Equied

Hotel Tata Somba

Hotel Bourgogne

Quartier Générale Bar and Restaurant

Market

Quidata Supermarket

Financial Bank

Post Office

Covered Market

Salad Food Stand

Taxi Gare

Hotel Bellevue

Hotel le Vieux Cavalier

Soccer Stadium

Cinema Bopeci Buvette

Pharmacie Tissanta

Évêque Bakery

Patisserie Beraca

Le Tour

Maquis Le Basilic

Hotel Kantaborifa

La Brèche

Natitingou

200 meters

N

Le Moucronnois

To Djougou (75km)

La Brèche *(The Breach)* This restaurant offers the unique opportunity to dine in or on top of a Tata Somba, an experience not to be missed if visiting Natitingou. A plate consists of meat (including beef, goat, or rabbit, chicken, or guinea fowl) or fish of the day served with couscous, fries, rice or spaghetti. Cold drinks and *tchoukoutou* are served. This is an excellent option for savoring the evening air and viewing the surrounding scenery. The food is delicious and the staff is friendly. *Up the road from Hotel Kantaborifa, near the breach of the hill overlooking the city; Meals CFA2,000 and up, drinks CFA300-800; Open daily, 12pm to 11pm*

Maquis Le Basilic The tables are set in an attractive courtyard with flowers. There are delicious African specialties and the possibility of ordering a nice salad or pizza, but be sure to order in advance. *On the dirt road past Hotel Kantaborifa; Meals CFA4,000 and up, drinks CFA300-800; Open daily, 24 hours*

Cinema Bopeci Buvette The *buvette* attached serves cold drinks, Tampico, and yogurt. Fried snacks, rice and beans, and quality *igname pilé* are prepared by *tanties* under the trees by the road. There are few tables but most people simply eat from the wooden benches. *On the paved road, south of the town center; Meals CFA400-600, drinks CFA250-700*

Taxi Gare Several women sell bread, bags of snacks, and rice and beans by the *gare*. There is a small and pleasant cafeteria that serves coffee, omelettes, and bread with generous portions of butter or Laughing Cow cheese. *Center of town, by the paved road; Snacks from CFA100-500*

Salad Food Stand Between 3pm-6pm, a woman sets up her food stand in front of the little market across the street from the taxi *gare*. Her specialty is fresh salad. *Center of town, across the street from the taxi gare; CFA300-700*

Quartier Générale Bar and Restaurant This *maquis* and *buvette* is one of the most popular bars in Natitingou. The service is amazing and the location is conveniently central. The family that runs it will do their best to accommodate any request, even if food requires a bit of a wait. Omelet sandwiches, a plate of couscous, fries with guinea fowl, or chicken are all available. Quartier Général also has a good variety of beers and soft drinks. At night, the owner turns on a video projector and shows ORTB, music videos, or soccer games on TV. *In the center of town, on the brick road leading to Hotel Tata Somba; Meals CFA500-1,500, drinks CFA250-800; Open daily, 11am-11pm*

Kiosque Bar This bar is very popular with the Beninese and foreigners alike. There's a woman who makes delicious salads for CFA500 or *pâte rouge* for CFA100. A man by the Kiosque also grills and sells meat. *Next door to Quidata Supermarket; Meals CFA500-1,000, drinks CFA250-800; Open daily, 11am-11pm*

Bar Restaurant This restaurant cooks up great pizza, spaghetti, steaks, and more. They even deliver! *Across the street from Pharmacie Tissanta; Meals CFA1,000-3,000, drinks CFA300-800; Open daily, 11am-11pm*

Igname Pilé Stand This is a great place to eat quality, inexpensive *igname pilé* accompanied with *wagasi* cheese or meat. They also serve cold drinks. *Across from the post office, south of Quidata Supermarket; Meals CFA300-1,000, drinks CFA250-800; Open daily, 11am-11pm*

Cafeteria Le Ronier This cafeteria serves restaurant quality food with generous amounts of vegetables in most dishes. The owner, Daniel, is a remarkable local chef that can prepare multicourse meals with advance notice. *Just south of SBEE, about 10m off the paved road; Meals CFA500-2,000; Open daily, 8am-10pm*

Patisserie Beraca This little bakery offers a good selection of baked goods including croissants, sweet and salty pastries, yogurt, non-instant coffee, soda and beer. *On the highway, just north of the road that goes to Hotel Kantaborifa; Pastries and meals CFA500-2,500, drinks CFA300-800; Open daily, 24 hours*

Évêque Bakery (Diocese) The évêque is a good place to go for breakfast, with fresh baguettes available at CFA100, as well as yogurt and an assortment of pastries. There is a pricier restaurant upstairs, and even a church affiliated bookstore around the back *In front of the Diocese of Natitingou, along the main paved road; CFA500-1500; Open daily, 8am-8pm*

NIGHT LIFE

The Belgian owned restaurant and nightclub **Le Moucronnois** is at the southern edge of town. The menu includes tasty beer marinated steak or rabbit at a cost of CFA3,000. The discoteque cover charge is CFA2,000 and a couple clean, basic rooms are available for CFA6,000.

ACCOMMODATIONS

Hotel Tata Somba*** This luxurious hotel, with an architecture inspired by the Tata Sombas, is currently the only accommodation with a pool in Natitingou. There are even tennis courts on the grounds. The restaurant serves African and European cuisine, including a platter of charcuterie or cold cuts, and an exquisite chocolate mousse for dessert. The hotel staff can arrange reservations for the three hotels in and around Park Pendjari: Relais de Tanongou, Campement de Porga, and Campement de la Pendjari. *Tel: 23.82.11.24 / 23.82.20.99; Northwest side of town, at the end of the brick road off the highway indicated by a sign; CFA30,000 and up; a/c, private bath, satellite television, telephone; Extra bed CFA3,000; Breakfast CFA3,000, Dinner CFA6,500*

Hotel Bourgogne*** This hotel is centrally located with clean and comfortable rooms. The restaurant, though pricey, serves superb African and European specialties, including duck ravioli and ice cream. *Tel: 23.82.22.40; On the main road just north of the market, indicated by a sign; CFA10,500-25,500; fan or a/c, private bath, some rooms have hot water; Breakfast CFA2,500; Lunch or dinner CFA5,500*

Hotel Bellevue*** Once used as a police headquarters, this hotel was built in the colonial style of the 1950s. The rooms are in smaller buildings surrounding the central mansion that houses the dining room. The hotel offers a pleasant hilltop view of Natitingou, and vibrant bougainvilleas shade the terrace. *Tel: 23.82.13.36; Up the dirt track from the Cinema Bopeci, indicated by sign post; CFA8,000-15,000; fan or a/c, hot water, private baths; Extra bed CFA2,500; Meals from CFA2,500*

Hotel Kantaborifa** This hotel has comfortable rooms and a breezy courtyard restaurant. A full meal usually consists of salad, a main dish, and some fruit. *Tel: 23.82.11.66; On a dirt track at the south end of town; CFA6,500-14,500; fan or a/c, private shower and toilet; Meal CFA3,500*

Hotel le Vieux Cavalier** This is a good value stop, with comfortable air-conditioned or ventilated rooms, a bar, and a shaded courtyard restaurant. The owners rent out 4x4 vehicles for trips to Boukoumbé or Park Pendjari for CFA45,000 per day. *Tel: 23.82.13.24; East of the cinema, indicated by a sign; CFA5,500-8,000; fan or a/c, private shower and toilet*

Hotel Equied* This is one of the most budget accommodations in town. Rooms are clean and spacious, although there is no door separating the bathroom from the sleeping room. The owner also sells an impressive little collection of handicrafts. *Tel: 90.03.33.68; Located north of the market, several hundred meters off the paved road; CFA3,500; fan, private shower and toilet*

Boukoumbé

Located 45 kilometers west of Natitingou, Boukoumbé is close to the border with Togo. Boukoumbé has a significant market, and it is home to one of the regional Fulani whipping ceremonies. **Mount Koussou-Kovangou**, the highest point in Benin, is nearby. The most famous attraction to this town is the **tata sombas**, the traditional two-story, fortress-like habitations built by the Dita-Mari, or Betamaribé ethnic group. The structures were so built to provide a lookout for oncoming dangers such as enemy tribes or dangerous predators. The first level houses the family's livestock- cows, goats, sheep, and chickens, while the upper-level is for the family. Grains are stored in silos made with palm leaves on the top level, safe from wild animals and roaming livestock. Families live in clusters of neighboring tata sombas. According to tradition, when a son is ready to build his own home he

Fulani Whipping Ceremonies

The nomadic Fulani (*Peuhl* in French) herders of the Sahel hold an annual flagellation ceremony as a rite of passage into manhood, usually in the months of the dry season. These rituals are typically held in the marketplaces of towns in northern Benin, such as Boukoumbé and Ouaké, near the Togo border. As a testament to their courage and worth, the young Fulani men must stand motionless as their elders slash them across the torso with tamarind whips, cutting the skin, creating welts, drawing blood. The Fulani women gather around, clapping and singing to the rhythm of drums, as the candidates come to the center of the circle, stripped from the waist up. Under the scrutiny of the audience, the candidates must endure the torture of the whip while singing songs of praise and defying corporal agony for the sake of their manhood.

climbs to the rooftop of his parents' tata somba and shoots an arrow into the distance to designate where he will build it. The door of the home always opens to the west, the believed direction of life, and there are usually a series of animistic altars by the entrance, each family with its particular vodoun deity. The tata sombas are made of pounded earth, decorated with lines and designs around the outside.

GETTING THERE

Taxis from the Natitingou *gare* cost CFA1,500 and leave a couple times a day. They are most frequent on Boukoumbé market days, which take place every four days. A *zemidjan* ride costs about CFA2,000, or CFA4,000 including the return trip.

TATA TOURISTIQUE

There is model tata somba just outside of Boukoumbé run solely for tourist visits. Inquire at the Maison des Jeunes or restaurant Chez Pascaline for a guide. One can either take a guided two to three hour hike to the tata somba (CFA5,000), or go by moped (CFA2,000/return). Visitors can spend the night on the roof of the tata somba for CFA3,000. Sleeping mats and mosquito nets are provided, as well as a private pit latrine and shower. Bring drinking water as only well-water is available there. To arrange an overnight stay, call the restaurant Chez Pascaline (*Tel: 23.83.02.02*). Breakfast, lunch, and dinner are available at the tata somba for CFA1,000-3,000.

Tanguiéta

Tanguiéta was the Atakora and Donga deparmental seat under the French, now a charming town with typical colonial style buildings. The population of about 20,000 is comprised of Dendi, Wamma, Nateni, and Biali ethnicities. This town also has the regional hospital, *Hôpital Saint Jean de Dieu de Tanguieta* (*Tel: 23.83.00.11*), which has Italian doctors on staff, and the Pendjari Wildlife National Park headquarter office. There is a CENAGREF office (*Tel: 23.83.00.65*) which can arrange tours through the park and hunting zones toward Tanongou. Internet access is available in town.

GETTING THERE

Tanguiéta is about 50 kilometers north of Natitingou, a CFA1,500 taxi ride.

EATING AND DRINKING

Hotel APP and Hotel Baobab are the best places to eat in Tanguiéta. Otherwise, snacks, bread, and basic local dishes can be found in the market or the kiosks and food stands around town. Tanguiéta's specialty market product is watermelon. Sold in mounds at the town center, they are a deliciously refreshing treat, though highly seasonal depending on the crop and water availability.

Tanguiéta is a good choice to purchase picnic or breakfast food before setting off into the park where food is limited and the few restaurants are pricey.

ACCOMMODATIONS

Hotel Baobab Hotel Baobab has a large, pleasant courtyard with places to sit in the shade, have a cold drink, and recover from a long day of traveling in the north. The rooms are set in bungalows, around a flowery courtyard. The hotel restaurant serves higher-end African meals, complete with salads, a main course of rice, couscous, or fries with chicken, fish, or guinea fowl, and fruit. *Tel: 90.66.56.95; On the north end of town, near the offical Pendjari Park office and along the highway to the Burkina Faso border; CFA8,000-13,000; fan or a/c, private shower and toilet; Extra bed CFA2,000; Meals CFA5,000, drinks begin at CFA500*

APP Hotel-Chez Basile APP stands for 'A Petit Pas' (meaning, In Baby Steps). If looking for a budget backpacker-style room for the night, this is it. The rooms are rudimentary with a common pit latrine in the courtyard. There is a popular nightclub attached, so it can be quite loud on weekends. The restaurant provides hefty and tasty meals of fried guinea fowl and cousous with tomato and onion sauce. The rooftop dining area is a pleasant place to spend evenings or to enjoy bread and coffee at sunrise, before the grueling daytime heat. *Tel: 23.83.01.73; Center of town, off the dirt road to Tanongou; CFA3,000-4,000; some rooms have a fan, mosquito net, shower, shared pit latrine; Meals CFA1,000*

SIGHTS

Tanguiéta is the junction to the **Tanongou Falls** and **Pendjari National Park**. The market is every Monday. The Tata Somba Hotel in Natitingou can provide much of the information necessary for touring Park Pendjari.

Pendjari National Park

Le Parc National de la Pendjari, or Pendjari National Park, is named after the Pendjari River that forms the border with Burkina Faso to the north. This park is a highlight of any visit to Benin. It contains the most important forest and wetland ecosystems in the area. A relatively high annual rainfall of 1,100mm floods many parts of the park and renders access difficult during the wettest times of the year, even though the park now remains open year-round. Pendjari is a UNESCO biosphere reserve and was named a Ramsar Site in February 2007. It belongs to the multi-national W-Arli-Pendjari park complex, a 50,000 square kilometer reserve which stretches across the borders of Burkina Faso, Benin, and Niger, of which 12,000 square kilometers are in Benin. There is an impressive gallery forest at the base of the Atakora mountain range, with savannah and swampy meadows throughout.

The various ecosystems create habitats for many species; the animals are best seen late in the dry season, from February to March, when they concentrate around the few remaining water holes.

Park Entry Fees
CFA10,000 / person
CFA3,000 / Beninese National
CFA3,000 / vehicle

Visitors usually see large mammals—elephants, buffalo, hartebeast, hippopotamuses, and smaller ungulates—harnessed bushbucks, bush duikers, and warthogs. Carnivores include crocodiles, hyenas, lions, and cheetahs. Over 300 different species of birds have been indentified within the park; common large birds are the African open-bill stork, Abdim's stork, saddle-billed stork, and the migratory European white stork.

Three different ethnicities inhabit the zones bordering the park and retain the use of the resources found within. Their main activities are agriculture, animal husbandry, fishing, and hunting. There is a significant source of contention between park authorities and villagers due to the conflict of interests in management of the natural resources.

Park Guides

One must have a guide to enter the park, which can be easily found in Natitingou or Tanguieta. Hotel Baobab in Tanguieta is a launching point for visits to Park Pendjari. A guide named **Razack** organizes tours from there for CFA60,000 per day. This rate includes jeep rental, a *chauffeur* who can also act as a guide, and gas. It is a wise way to go, because the experienced *chauffeur* takes care of all car issues along the way. Razack can be reached through the Hotel Baobab staff or on his cell phone: *Tel: 90.02.92.32 / 97.05.13.70.*

Hotel Tata Somba in Natitingou also has a list of recommended guides. One can set up jeep rental and lodging for the visit from there. Prices are negotiable; guides typically take CFA25,000-50,000 per trip, and vehicles cost CFA30,000-50,000 per day plus gas.

Other recommended guides (most based in Natitingou):

Marce *Tel: +220.97.11.26.84 / 90.98.24.14*

Durand *Tel: 90.91.51.34*

Cherif *Tel: 90.66.21.26*

Joseph *Tel: 97.92.21.95 / 90.02.05.55*

EATING AND DRINKING

The only place to eat and drink in the park is at the Campement de la Pendjari. Because it is so remote, this can be a bit expensive. If desired, bring food to have a picnic at the observation tower at one of the watering holes.

PARK ACCOMMODATION

Le Campement de la Pendjari This hotel is solely run by a generator, and there are no landlines or cell phone reception. Reservations must be made in advance at Hotel Tata Somba (*Tel: 23.82.11.24 / 23.82.20.99 / 97.04.02.83 / 90.04.24.78*) in Natitingou (a list of reservations is sent daily to Campement de la Pendjari by car).

The plush restaurant and lounge has a full bar at its center. Drinks are expensive because products arrive from a long distance, and the camp is run off of generators. Very good main courses cost CFA6,000, and the continental breakfast costs CFA2,500. There is even a swimming pool at the camp in which to refresh after traveling hundreds of kilometers across the parched landscape. *CFA18,000-24,000; Additional mattress CFA3,000, Camping CFA3,000; fan or a/c, private shower and toilet*

Hotel Campement de Porga This is a popular and surprisingly luxurious for a hunter's lodge, though it does not have the same amenities as Le Campement de la Pendjari. There is no pool and the restaurant is not as plush, but the food selection is tasty. Reservations can be made at Hotel Tata Somba in Natitingou. *Tel: 23.82.20.39/ 23.82.11.24 / 23.82.20.99 / 23.82.22.00; CFA 15,000-22,000; fan or a/c; Extra bed CFA3,000; Breakfast CFA2,500; Lunch or dinner CFA6,000*

Camping in the Park
Camping at other allocated sites within the park is available with advance permission from the Tanguiéta park office, or through the Tata Somba Hotel in Natitingou. Campers must be entirely self-sufficient and accompanied by a guide.

Tanongou

Tanongou is a tiny village at the foot of the Atakora range, 30 kilometers northeast of Tanguiéta along the dirt road to Batia in Pendjari National Park. It sits beside the best known waterfalls in the country, *les Chutes de Tanongou*.

GETTING THERE
Tanongou can be reached by *zemidjan* for CFA1,000, though most drivers will require round trip payment, even if you're not returning to Tanguiéta. The road is very dusty in the dry season; a *zem* ride can leave passengers encrusted with red dirt, especially if riding behind another vehicle or motorcycle. The best way to go is in a rented taxi or hired car. This route skirts Pendjari National Park, and wildlife like monkeys and birds are often seen. Eucalyptus, mango, and acacia trees border the cultivated fields, a sign of local agroforestry practices.

ACCOMMODATION

Le Relais de Tanongou Set at the foot of the Tanongou falls, this camp is remote but comfortable. There are six bungalow rooms, and reservations can be made through the Tata Somba Hotel in Natitingou. The center has motor-generated electricity that only runs from nightfall to midnight. The rooms are spacious and tidy. Gravity-plumbing has been installed, involving large containers at the side of each building filled with water from the small stream that runs along the camp. *CFA10,000; Additional mattress CFA2,000; fan with temporary generated electricity, private shower and toilet, some rooms have shared toilet; Continental Breakfast CFA2,000; Full Meal (salad, couscous with guinea fowl, fruit) CFA6,000; Drinks CFA600-1,000*

There are no other dining options in Tanongou. If looking to save money, it is best to bring breakfast items (purchased in Tanguiéta or Natitingou) and kindly ask the kitchen staff for hot water in the morning.

Across the stream lies a more rustic hunters' camp of straw huts and a makeshift kitchen. One might glimpse a vehicle of hunters as they return from a successful trip with an antelope or a buffalo. A portion of this meat will be divided and shared among the villagers of Tanongou.

CHUTES DE TANONGOU

The **Tanongou Falls** are a great place to swim, and those daring enough can leap from a cliff some meters above the pool. Visitors not staying overnight must pay a CFA1,000 entry fee to visit the falls. Young boys and men from the village come to offer their assistance along the slippery rocks to reach the upper part of the falls. If their service is of some use, a tip of a couple hundred francs per guide is expected.

Hiking

The camp staff can arrange a guided hike to the source of the Tanongou Falls. The hike takes about 4 hours. One can also opt to stay overnight in straw huts at the source. The hike costs CFA2,000 per person, and the overnight camping costs CFA3,000 per person plus food costs. The guides will prepare a traditional dinner on site.

Language Charts

FRENCH

English	French
Yes / no	*Oui / non*
Direct pronou 'you'	*tu / vous*
I speak English / French (a little)	*Je parle Anglais/ Français (un peu).*
Good Afternoon	*Bon après-midi*
Good Evening	*Bon soir*
Did you wake up well?	*Tu t'es / vous vous êtes bien re-veillé?*
Yes, I woke up well.	*Oui, (je me suis bien reveillé)*
Welcome!	*Soyez la bienvenue!*
Thank you for yesterday.	*Merci d'hier*
It's been awhile (since we've seen each other!)	*Il y a trois jours!*
Good bye	*Au revoir*
And the family?	*Et la famille?*
And the children?	*Et les enfants?*
And work?	*Et le travail (le boulot, les affaires)?*
Did you do a little?	*Tu as / Vous avez fait un peu?*
Yes, I did a little	*Oui, j'ai fait un peu*
Are you there?	*Tu es / Vous êtes là? / Je suis là.*
Good work.	*Bon travail*
Are you busy? Are you occupied?	*Tu es en train?*
Are you home?	*Tu es à la maison?*
Come eat!	*Viens manger / venez manger!*
It's good, that's good.	*C'est bon*
Hurry up!	*Dépeche-toi! / Dépechez-vous!*
Agreed, okay.	*D'accord.*
I refuse!	*Je refuse!*
Thank you (thanks a lot)	*Merci (beaucoup)*
You're welcome	*Pas de quoi, de rien, etc.*

FON *For more phrases in Fon, see* Fon is Fun *at www.friends-of-benin.org/Fonisfun*

English	Fon
Yes / no	*Enh / é-o*
Direct pronoun 'you'	*ah / mi*
I speak English / French (a little)	*M sé fongbé*
Did you wake up well?	*O / mi fon gonji ah?*
Yes, I woke up well.	*enh, (mm fon gonji).*
Welcome!	*Kwabo! / Mi kwabo!*
Thank you for yesterday.	*Sobedo / doso*

It's been awhile (since we've seen each other!)	*Nisobedo / doyeeso*
Good bye	*Edabo*
And the family?	*Mètowé lè lo*
And the children?	*Vilè lo*
And work?	*azo-o lo*
Did you do a little?	*Ah / mi blo kpédé ah?*
Yes, I did a little.	*enh, mm blo kpédé.*
Are you there?	*Ah do fin eh ah? / mi do fin eh ah?*
Good work.	*Kudazo / mi kudazo*
Are you busy? Are you occupied?	*Ah dé oo wa? / Mi dé oo wa?*
Are you home?	*Ah do hwegbe ah?/ Mi do hwegbe ah?*
Come eat!	*Wa dunu / wa mi dunu*
It's good, that's good.	*Enyo.*
Hurry up!	*Yow-o!*
Agreed, okay.	*Yoh.*
I refuse!	*n'gbê*
Thank you (thanks a lot)	*awanou*
You're welcome	*é yo*

MINA

English	**Mina**
Yes / no	*Enh / ow-o*
Direct pronoun 'you'	*o / mi*
I speak English / French (a little)	*Mm sé guingbé (vide).*
Did you wake up well?	*O / mi fon nwede ah?*
Yes, I woke up well.	*enh, (mm fon nwede).*
Welcome!	*Wheyzon! / Mi wheyzon!*
Thank you for yesterday.	*sobedo / doso*
It's been awhile (since we've seen each other!)	*nisobedo / doyeeso*
Good bye	*Odabo*
And the family?	*Ahometo wo de?*
And the children?	*Deviwo de?*
And work?	*O / mi wo do?*
Did you do a little?	*O / mi wo vidé ah?*
Yes, I did a little.	*enh, mm wo vidé.*
Are you there?	*O / mi lay foonu ah? / enh mm lay fi eh.*
Good work.	*O / mi kudo do.*
Are you busy? Are you occupied?	*O / mi lenti ah?*
Are you home?	*O / mi lay ahome ah?*
Come eat!	*Va dunu / va mi dunu*
It's good, that's good.	*Enyo.*
Hurry up!	*Deblay!*
Agreed, okay.	*Yoh*

I refuse!	*Mm gbé!*
Thank you (thanks a lot)	*Akpe (kaka)*
You're welcome	*dodono.*

ADJA

English	**Adja**
Yes / no	*Enh / oh*
Direct pronoun 'you'	*o / mi*
I speak English / French (a little)	*N'donon adjagbe houedeka*
Did you wake up well?	*o/ mi fon gnuide a?*
Yes, I woke up well.	*enh*
Welcome!	*Ozon/ mi ozon*
Thank you for yesterday.	*Akpéwo éso*
It's been awhile (since we've seen each other!)	*Edjindjin*
Good bye	*Ewa han*
And the family?	*Awohoude?*
And the children?	*Devio fon gnuide a?*
And work?	*O / mi dolo de?*
Did you do a little?	*O / mi wa houedeka a?*
Yes, I did a little.	*Enh, n'houdeke*
Are you there?	*O / mi le ah?*
Good work.	*O / mi koudodo*
Are you busy? Are you occupied?	*O / mi ledji a?*
Are you home?	*O / mi leahoueme a?*
Come eat!	*o / mi va dunu*
It's good, that's good.	*Engnon*
Hurry up!	*Hloindo*
Agreed, okay.	*N'lon*
I refuse!	*N'gbé*
Thank you (thanks a lot)	*Akpenonwo*
You're welcome	*Akpeligo*

IDAATCHA

English	**Idaatcha**
Yes / no	*Enh / non*
Direct pronoun 'you'	*Eh*
I speak English / French (a little)	*Mahn-gbo datcha/ Anglais/Francais*
Did you wake up well?	*Oh soun ré-ré ni?*
Yes, I woke up well.	*enh*
Welcome!	*Ekabo*
Thank you for yesterday.	*Eku-tché onan*
It's been awhile (since we've seen each other!)	*Odi layi-layi*
Good bye	*Odabo*

And the family?	*Irahn-fé?*
And the children?	*Omohn-fé?*
And work?	*Itché-fé?*
Did you do a little?	*Étchédè-ni*
Are you there?	*Ay ah bé ni / o ah bé ni*
Good work.	*Eku-tché / Eku-gbalé*
Are you busy? Are you occupied?	*A bé hou-a*
Are you home?	*N'wa L'illé*
Come eat!	*Wa djé oun*
Hurry up!	*Ay-ah*
Agreed, okay.	*Oh-sahn*
I refuse!	*Mm ô*
Thank you (thanks a lot)	*Eku-tché (ti ti)*
You're welcome	*Ohh*

DENDI

English	**Dendi (Zarma version)**
Yes / no	*O/ m-m or ah-ah*
Direct pronoun 'you'	*Ni*
I speak English / French (a little)	*E ma Anglais-chine/Francais-chine (kena kena).*
Did you wake up well?	*Mate n kani?*
Yes, I woke up well.	*Bani samay! (means 'good' and is a versatile response)*
Welcome!	*Fonda ka.*
Thank you for yesterday.	*Not used in Zarma.*
It's been awhile (since we've seen each other!)	*Fonda jibi hinka!*
Good bye	*Kala ton-ton.*
And the family?	*Mate n cuara?*
And the children?	*Mate ize?*
And work?	*Mate goy?*
Did you do a little?	*Not used in Zarma.*
Are you there?	*N go no?*
Good work.	*Fonda goy.*
Are you home?	*N go fu, walla?*
Come eat!	*Ka wa (nasal wa)*
It's good, that's good.	*A boori.*
Hurry up!	*Zuru!*
Agreed, okay.	*O.*
Thank you (thanks a lot)	*Fonda goy.*
You're welcome	*N-goy-a*

www.otherplacespublishing.com

Log on to find out more about our publications.

CPSIA information can be obtained at www.ICGtesting.com
Printed in the USA
LVOW122008050712

288909LV00022B/47/P